# An Empathy-Building Toolkit for Museums

**American Alliance of Museums**

The American Alliance of Museums has been bringing museums together since 1906, helping to develop standards and best practices, gathering and sharing knowledge, and providing advocacy on issues of concern to the entire museum community. Representing more than 35,000 individual museum professionals and volunteers, institutions, and corporate partners serving the museum field, the Alliance stands for the broad scope of the museum community.

The American Alliance of Museums' mission is to champion museums and nurture excellence in partnership with its members and allies.

Books published by AAM further the Alliance's mission to make standards and best practices for the broad museum community widely available.

American Alliance of Museums

# An Empathy-Building Toolkit for Museums

Edited by
Elif M. Gökçiğdem

BLOOMSBURY ACADEMIC
NEW YORK • LONDON • OXFORD • NEW DELHI • SYDNEY

BLOOMSBURY ACADEMIC
Bloomsbury Publishing Inc, 1359 Broadway, 12th Floor, New York, NY 10018, USA
Bloomsbury Publishing Plc, 50 Bedford Square, London, WC1B 3DP, UK
Bloomsbury Publishing Ireland, 29 Earlsfort Terrace, Dublin 2, D02 AY28, Ireland

BLOOMSBURY, BLOOMSBURY ACADEMIC and the Diana logo are trademarks of Bloomsbury Publishing Plc

First published in the United States of America 2026



Cover image courtesy of Elif M. Gökçiğdem



A catalog record for this book is available from the Library of Congress.

ISBN: PB: 979-8-216-38785-5
HB: 979-8-216-38786-2
ePDF: 979-8-216-38788-6
eBook: 979-8-216-38787-9

Typeset by Deanta Global Publishing Services, Chennai, India
Printed and bound in the United States of America

For product safety related questions contact productsafety@bloomsbury.com.

To find out more about our authors and books visit www.bloomsbury.com and sign up for our newsletters.

*To my late parents, Sevgili Anneciğim ve Babacığım,*
*who nurtured within me the unconditional Love that both bears fruits*
*and continually yields the seeds of possibility.*

# Contents

# Foreword

The English word "empathy" first appeared a little more than a hundred years ago as a translation of the German *Einfühlung*. This original "empathy" surprisingly did not mean a grasp of the experiences of others. Instead, it captured the aesthetic ability to imaginatively project ourselves, with motion and emotion, into the lines and shapes of art and the natural world. While gazing at a mountain in the distance, for instance, we might feel an upward striving in our body that we unconsciously transferred to the mountain, allowing us to sense its majestic height. With aesthetic empathy, we could weave ourselves in and through the worlds of nature and art.

If empathy at its origins was primarily aesthetic, by the early twentieth century philosophers and psychologists expanded its scope to include the capacity to feel another's emotion, grasp another's point of view, or fathom another's facial expression. Empathy was deemed essential to our intersubjective world, as it conveyed the knowledge that others possessed their own experiences and perspectives, both similar to, and different from our own.

Over the course of its history, then, empathy has encompassed the varied and complex ways we connect to others and even to objects. How we do this, however, or what we call empathy's means and mechanisms, have always been contested. In the early twentieth century, empathy was variously defined as projection, transfer, association, animation, vivification, or fusion. Scholars and practitioners today still characterize empathy in different ways: as emotional understanding, cognitive or perspective-taking, emotional contagion, self-projection, and motor imitation, to name the most common. A recent survey of the scholarly literature uncovered forty-three circulating definitions of empathy! That empathy is multifaceted and complex is attributable to the fact that we connect to others in multiple ways; when we empathize, we imagine, feel, think, inquire, imitate, and contemplate others' experiences.

The chapters in this collection, *An Empathy-Building Toolkit for Museums,* skillfully highlight this diversity and complexity.

Educators, museum curators, psychologists, scholars, and experts in an array of fields outline practices for developing empathy with step-by-step instructions that can be carried out in different museum settings. The editor of this volume, Elif M. Gökçiğdem, is an art historian with deep connections to Sufi thought. She tells us that empathy is at its core "relatedness" or "kinship," and reminds us that we need "visceral lived experiences" to fully understand the meaning and reality of our relatedness.

In this collection, empathy as "relatedness" comprises our connection to other people, visual art, treasured objects, images of many kinds, and all types of animals. The reader learns that empathy can be achieved through contemplative practices, thinking strategies, social encounters, and heartfelt conversations. Empathy is built not only through curated encounters, but also by well-structured organizations and partnerships that provide frameworks for empathic interaction.

In this capacious volume, voices from the international community share diverse visions and enactments of empathy. This inclusivity is also central to the seven previously held Designing for Empathy Summits, curated and chaired by Elif. I have been privileged to attend a number of these summits, where in stunning museum spaces, scholars, curators, artists, and practitioners gather to listen, emote, share, and gain experiential practice in the forms of relatedness called empathy. The next best thing to attending one of these summits is to delve into this rich collection, and then to try out these tools in one's community or museum setting.

While some consider empathy to be an inborn trait, empathy as featured in this collection is best described as a "technique of the self." These chapters challenge us to think of empathy as a deliberate practice of finding ways to open, expand and shift our often narrow conceptions of ourselves and of others. We do so by reflecting, fine-tuning our perceptions, thinking, imagining, contemplating, and emoting to learn how to better connect to others and our visual and experiential worlds. Our reward is the discovery of more fruitful, nurturing, and profound ways to connect to our richly veined, interdependent worlds.

*Susan Lanzoni, PhD,*
*Writer and Historian of Science,*
*Author of* Empathy: A History (Yale, 2018)

# Preface

*Elif M. Gökçiğdem, PhD*

*Listen, O drop, give yourself up without regret,*
*and in exchange gain the Ocean.*

–*Rumi*[1]

Experiencing the world from underwater has been a love of mine since I was a little girl spending summers on an island in the Sea of Marmara in Türkiye. After taking a deep breath, I would slowly allow myself to sink to the bottom, where I would often sit cross-legged, using my body as an anchor. I learned how to control and release my breath slowly enough to prolong those moments of total immersion, which felt something like being merged with the sea. From my vantage point, it mesmerized me to see the blurry sun far above, its rays turning to liquid as they entered the water, before cascading downward into the chilly deeper currents. Occasionally, I could hear the muffled pattering sound of a distant motor boat passing through the surface, reminding me that I am from a different reality. I was well aware that my body was not made for that environment, and that I could only ever be a temporary visitor to this underwater wonderland. Yet, for brief moments in time, I found joy in my ability to immerse myself in a different reality, and feel related to something beyond myself—the sea, the sand, the fish, the seaweed, and the clams. I shared space with them as we each—simultaneously in our unique ways—experienced our surroundings. Even back then, I appreciated that while it was impossible to fully understand another's experience of reality, with a little effort, I could place myself in scenarios where I could be proximate enough to witness and imagine—and be awed by—their experience. What felt like mere play to me back then, I now regard as one of my earliest explorations of the human potential for relatedness, which later shaped my understanding of empathy. By playing with my perception, I was able to build relationships and kinship in unconventional contexts. These experimentations in empathy put me in touch with the possibility of developing a deeper intuition about reality through embodied, paradigm-shifting and perception-expanding moments.

Looking back now, it's not surprising that what awakened me to the possibilities of empathy-building in museums, also happened on a seashore, this time in 2006, about three decades after my childhood seaside adventures. By that point, I was probably as far as I could have been from my carefree childhood days. I was a deeply homesick mother of a toddler living in Virginia who, after spending a decade in academic pursuits in art history and museums, was working in a demanding corporate job that had nothing to do with my areas of study. One early Spring morning, I found myself in a rare moment of pause standing on a wooden pier overlooking the Red Sea in Jeddah, a city named "Grandmother" after Eve. I had just returned from an unplanned *umrah* pilgrimage to Mecca with a handful of entrepreneurs and academics who, like me, were on a cultural tour of the country. I was eager to find a window of opportunity to visit Mecca, a place I had heard many stories about from my grandparents and father but never imagined myself going to. The experience unlocked a sense of awe, wonder and sensitivity within me that I wasn't anticipating. Standing on the pier, the feeling of the sun on my shoulders and the warm wood beneath my bare feet took me directly back to my childhood. I was overcome with a sensation of wanting to jump without reserve into this unfamiliar sea, which somehow felt like being called to a reunion with an old friend.

Before even stepping into the water, I imagined the soft sand on the seafloor, the seaweed, the shells, the pebbles, the sharks, the dolphins and barracudas, the colorful corals. I felt subsumed with such love that opened my heart to encompass all that was both within my realm of vision and beyond it. I felt a powerful pull within my heart to dissolve all separation between my being and everything before me. And in that moment, my wish received an instantaneous and unexpected response. It was as though the voice of my deepest authentic self broke through to assure me that the kind of nearness I was longing for, was absolutely natural and, in fact, a truer expression of how reality actually is, and can be experienced. It wasn't as though my rational faculties were absent, on the contrary, I could see my thoughts, doubts, intellectual questions and emotional reactions swirling around with great clarity. Yet it was also clear to me that I could make the choice to not focus on them and instead follow the intuitive guidance emanating from my heart which, for many years, had become almost inaudible. Still standing on the pier, I felt myself give permission to the heart to take control and instantly, I entered into a wider state of consciousness that would be impossible to put into words other than through poetry. It was a taste of what is often called in wisdom traditions; *non-duality, totality, interbeing, wholeness, unity* or *oneness*. In the ecstasy of the insights that had emerged on the seashore that morning, I took an invisible leap and found myself in the drop that is described in Rumi's poem that opens this Preface.

In that moment of clear awareness, I had a deep knowing that my heart would henceforth take the reins and guide my path, although it's taken me twenty years to even attempt to give words to the influence of this single moment. All of my empathy-building efforts are a creative attempt to explore, articulate and share the depths of what I know empathy can be as a result of the gifts that emerged from this experience. It was a turning point because it gave me a deep experiential knowing of the wholeness of Being, a concept that was familiar to me in the Turkish folktales my father told me, which were infused with Sufi wisdom.

> *Come, return to the root of the root of your self.*
>
> –*Rumi*[2]

It feels important to share here the cultural lens that inevitably shapes my understanding of empathy as a deeply rooted human experience of *relatedness* that would be difficult for me to fully convey in English. I believe that language and the narratives we grow up with not only shape our worldview and paradigms, but also allow us to imagine in different ways, reflecting the rich variety of human experience that cannot possibly be captured and expressed through a single language or a particular way of seeing the world. Being Turkish by origin, my native tongue and the Sufi wisdom that is entwined within Turkish culture and language—to such a degree that folktales, folk songs, and even humor, are imbued with an understanding of the oneness of all creation—also has informed the way I experience the world and understand relatedness. There are two Turkish terms that form the core foundation of my understanding: *Kardeş* (pronounced car-desh) meaning "our mother is one" (or, literally: We are siblings, we are from the same umbilical cord) denoting "kinship", and *Özdeş* (pronounced uz-desh) meaning "our essence is one" (or, literally: We are from the same essence), also denoting "kinship". Both of these terms include the suffix *-deş* (-desh), which when added confers a sense of multiples becoming one or being of one origin. *Özdeşleyim* (pronounced uz-desh-layim), a Turkish word for empathy, meaning "becoming of one essence," was introduced into the language in 1983 as a direct translation of the German word for empathy, *Einfühlung* which is also the origin of the English word empathy.[3] In all these Turkish words, there is a strong sense of *multiplicity* becoming *one* (*bir*) through a recognition of a primordial *shared essence*. Since the essence is already one, the default state of all beings is their oneness. The attainment of oneness, or *birlik (pronounced ber-liq)* in Turkish, can be achieved naturally and sometimes through intentional effort, which is the act of empathizing.

These nuances are essential to my understanding of the human experience of the terms empathy, as well as oneness. *Birlik* is at the heart of the Turkish understanding of a fundamental Sufi philosophical concept: *Varlıkta Birlik (Wahdat al-Wujud*, the *Oneness of Being, or Tawhid)*, the idea that all creation emanates from a *Single Source of Life and Being*. I grew up with rich stories that illustrate the wholeness of creation through humor and deep wisdom, and observed my parents and grandparents effortlessly reflect this understanding, simply, the way they were. I remember specifically when I was a child, one morning I was sent to get fresh bread from the village bakery, on the same island where I loved immersing myself in the sea. That morning, as if he just read my mind, my father emphasized that it was important to bring the loaf as a whole, no matter how tempting it might be for me to break its corner for a little snack on the way home. He said:

> *The wheat that bread is made of does not only belong to us; it also belongs to the birds and the ants. They would see you walking home, enjoying a piece of fresh bread, and they might also be hungry and wish to have some of it, but they can't tell you that. They have a right over that morsel you eat. So, out of reverence, it is best to be patient and eat it in the privacy of our home.*

Therefore, I am inclined to introduce the term: *Rooted Empathy*, which gives me a way to convey my understanding of *empathy as rooted in a primordial shared Essence* as in the philosophy of the *Oneness of Being* and coincidentally, allows me to bring my own cultural roots to the conversation on the potential for empathy-building in museums. At best, empathy-building along these lines invites individuals to bring their own wisdom and lived experience to a space that honors and wholly allows the diversity of human experience. Each individual, rooted in their deepest authentic self, flowers in their own self expression and simultaneously marvels at the blossoms stemming from the roots of others, all nourished by and connected to the same Source, the Water of Life.

Since the starting point of worldviews like this lies in the possibility of communion with the Whole, not in separation, empathy isn't naturally a separate concept because it is inseparable from *Love* that is understood as the primary Essence of all creation, as well as the purpose of being and becoming fully human. The heart is the primary spiritual organ of perception capable of experiencing an ever-expanding capaciousness for holding unconditional *Love* (*Agape*, or *Aşk;* pronounced Ashq). This Love with a capital L naturally encompasses empathy. And yet we need a word for empathy because so many of us, especially in the West, have been conditioned by a worldview that prioritizes separation rather than unity and compartmentalizes knowledge. When we are steeped in our duality, empathy is one of the practices we can learn that opens us to the non-dual experience of Love described by ancient wisdom traditions, allowing us to experience our oneness.

From the vantage point of the Oneness of Being, every empathic experience holds the potential of awakening subtle perceptions of unity, and our relatedness to this unity. Empathy leads to Love, and Love itself is what attracts us to feeling empathy for each other. Once an *awareness of unity*, or what I call: *The Oneness Mindset*, develops, and we understand that we are integral to it, we can take steps to harmonize our behaviors and actions accordingly. The absence of this mindset is the cause of much fragmentation and harm in our world today.

Perceiving ourselves as separate, isolated fragments naturally limits our capacity to imagine the possibilities of communion that are at the essence of integrative wisdom traditions, cultures and languages. This is why we need interventions in empathy-building to expose ourselves to experiences of oneness that allude to our *kinship* and *shared essence*, because they allow us to discover innate human capacities that have become dormant, almost forgotten.

Without visceral lived experiences, the interplay between the Ocean and the drop, the Whole and the self, Agape and love, or Oneness and empathy, can remain as abstract metaphors understood only within the realm of the mind. On the other hand, "The heart is that organ of perception which is capable of knowing all levels of reality, and of knowing the Whole as well as the parts. It may be that what the heart can know is the most a human being can know, and that is infinite."[4]

Sometimes these experiences happen naturally and spontaneously in the course of life. Sometimes—as this book will describe—we can intervene to create spaces and design encounters where the conditions for evoking empathy as a path to wholeness are ripe enough that it naturally unfolds. My life's work has been dedicated to discovering how to achieve the latter within the context of museum experiences, as the following pages will go into great detail describing. Such paradigm-shifting experiences are gifts that, while inevitably temporary, can have fundamental and lasting influences on our decisions and behavior, guiding a way of being in the world. We each are designed to be the trustees of this sacred gift, and it is our choice and responsibility to make the most of it.

## Notes

**1** *Mathnawi*, Book IV, 2619–22. Translated by Kabir and Camille Helminski.

**2** *The Pocket Rumi*. Edited by K. Helminski (Shambhala, 2017), 17.

**3** Wilhelm Worringer, *Soyutlama ve Özdeşleyim*. Translated from the German by İsmail Tunalı (Remzi Kitabevi, 1985), 7–16; Worringer, Abstraction and Empathy. Translated from the German by Michael Bullock, first published in English in the USA in 1953 (Elephant Paperbacks, 1997).

**4** K. Helminski, *The Knowing Heart* (Shambhala, 2000), 82.

# Acknowledgments

A wise teacher once said, "What we give our attention to, we energize." In our increasingly distracted and fragmented world, where even human virtues such as empathy, kindness, and compassion are manipulated into human-made, ideological concepts that can be disposed of at whim, it is more important than ever before to nurture relatedness and kinship. These qualities of belonging are intrinsic to human existence, and in disregarding their sacredness, the heart of our humanness is lost, accelerating the descent toward extinction. It is for this reason I am deeply grateful to every contributing author in this book for demonstrating with vivid clarity the role that museums, and other informal learning platforms such as libraries, performing arts centers, and public parks, are actively playing in countering this descent. I have been humbled by the ways you each uniquely expanded our sense of the possibilities for creating transformative experiences that simultaneously deepen self-knowledge while exponentially expanding our sense of relatedness to each other and our world. You have given me hope in the power and potential that is generated when we come together with open hearts to collectively envision a world where the human qualities that evoke empathy are celebrated. Through sharing your lived experiences, you have given the world precious insight into how we can stay rooted in our values and continue the essential work of unity in the face of disintegration.

I am grateful to all those who have been my teachers, care-givers, and companions on this journey. To my late parents, *sevgili anneciğim ve babacığım*, I am unendingly grateful for the unflinching, unconditional love and wisdom I still feel flowing in from your beings. Deep gratitude to my immediate and extended family for being patient companions and supporters. A special thank you to Ela and Ali, my children, whose untainted vision for a just world and love for nature continually inspire and strengthen my resolve to keep doing my part in this awesome universe.

I am thankful to my fellow travelers on the path of empathy-building who inspire me and give me the courage to seek and realize my own meaning in this life through fostering empathy in our world. There are too many of you to mention here by name; may our connection always be felt beyond time and space. Thank you to those who hosted and participated in any Annual Designing for Empathy Summits & Workshops, those who contributed a chapter or more in my previous books, those who collaborated with me on numerous workshops in various conferences, and those who continue to support my efforts and explorations in empathy-building with their friendship, active participation, insights, and expertise.

Special thanks are due to Susan Lanzoni, PhD, who graciously shared her deep insight and understanding of empathy in the Foreword of this volume, setting a strong foundation upon which diverse explorations of empathy and empathy-building could flourish. I am grateful to my dear brother Fatih M. Durmuş, who has been sharing his creative talents with me since the Day 1 of my empathy-building journey twenty years ago. Your illustrations in this volume, the geometric design on the cover, as well as the *drops that contain the Ocean* of the Alchemy of Empathy, which accompany each part and chapter, have meaningfully and visually integrated all the contents in a way that will be a source of inspiration for many. And, my dear friend Daliah Merzaban, a master diver into the infinite Ocean of words and meanings, for helping me to find and bring to surface the most resonant ones for my voice. I'd like to offer my heartfelt thanks to the American Alliance of Museums and Bloomsbury for bringing this empathy-building toolkit to life. May each idea, inspiration, and effort toward empathy-building in our world be drops that merge into an ocean of possibility for nurturing the heart and hope of humanity.

Elif M. Gökçiğdem
April 4, 2025

# Introduction

*Elif M. Gökçiğdem, PhD*

Empathy-building through museums is an emerging field where creative approaches are being explored to foster empathy toward a common goal: to inspire individuals to develop caring relationships with each other, all of humanity, and our natural world. Museums have deep unlocked potential to be incubators of empathy-building. This book offers a collection of chapters containing tangible examples for designing intentional experiences that more fully realize this potential. The contents of this book present a spectrum of approaches that provide the reader with a variety of tangible ideas and examples that can be either directly implemented or further customized to create institutionally relevant practices in empathy-building.

Readers are given a peek into the creative processes of multiple experts who are pioneering ways of approaching everything from policy and public programming to designing museum experiences that transform how people relate to themselves, others, and the wider world. Specialists from a variety of institutions, from aquariums and zoos to museums dedicated to art and children, as well as creatives, social entrepreneurs, and experts from academia, healthcare, and design, offer guidelines that can be adapted by museum professionals seeking to incorporate empathy-building into their work with greater intention. As our world becomes increasingly more fragmented, it is urgent to develop ways of reminding humanity of interconnectedness and our responsibility to the well-being of the whole. To this end, museums are paramount.

The interdisciplinary approach I've taken in my two previous books has been replicated here as I have witnessed the transformative power of bringing experts from across disciplines, sectors, and cultures who would not normally find themselves in the same room discussing a subject like empathy that concerns them all. *An Empathy-Building Toolkit for Museums* takes this further because the majority of contributing authors have met each other and collaborated at the Annual Designing for Empathy Summit and Workshops, the first of which was hosted in Dharamshala in 2018 by the Office of His

Holiness The Fourteenth Dalai Lama. In a true spirit of connecting humanity, our growing community of empathy-builders have discovered the wellspring of inspiration that unfolds through being together in a space of openness where, through conversation and the exchange of ideas, true creativity and innovation are able to emerge. Attendees from sectors as varied as healthcare and technology have consistently brought their enthusiasm, ideas, and curiosity—and many have spoken of walking away with a sense of feeling nourished, an understanding of tangible new ideas of what empathy can look like in their respective contexts, and with new —and often unexpected— friendships and creative partnerships. By bringing greater intentionality to discussions of empathy, we are developing a way of understanding how its potential can be unlocked through museums.

It's phenomenal to me how quickly these new ideas are taking hold through creative collaborations. Therefore, it is worth taking a brief look at the two preceding edited volumes that helped shape this book. When I published my first book ten years ago, *Fostering Empathy Through Museums* (Rowman and Littlefield, 2016), one of the biggest takeaways for me was realizing that only a few museums were exploring empathy as a human phenomenon that could be an intentional subject and an outcome of a museum experience. While empathy was often an unnamed byproduct of museum experiences, it wasn't explicitly articulated as a core purpose of exhibitions, educational public programs, and institutional mission and policies. For that book, I asked contributors to answer four questions to determine if and how museums relate to empathy, namely: *In your day-to-day work, do you take empathy into consideration? If yes, how do you define empathy and its impact within your context? Do you consider empathy as an intentional outcome of a museum experience? If yes, what are some of the ways you foster empathy?* The responses seemed to prove what I had been intuiting up to that point: Much of the potential for museums to act as incubators for empathy-building lies dormant. And yet, the potential is enormous because museums are readily available platforms with five qualities that are conducive to fostering empathy: They are storytellers and sites of storytelling, they offer experiences of awe and wonder, they are platforms for dialogue, they are places of experiential learning, and they hold space for contemplation.

With this knowledge, I became curious about what it would take to utilize museums more fully as empathy-building incubators, which is the question that inspired my second book in 2019, *Designing for Empathy: Perspectives on the Museum Experience* (American Alliance of Museums). I wanted to distill a framework for initiating conversations on this theme that could enable a variety of actors to be able to visualize how they could actively contribute to empathy-building in our communities while using museums as a platform. The framework that resulted had three defining qualities, each of which became a section of the book, and collectively, they demonstrated how museums could be positioned in our communities as incubators for empathy-building. These three components formed the basis of what has become the *Designing for Empathy®* framework (the subject of Chapter 1 in this book). Each one was a conversation starter that sought to add texture to our understanding of empathy. The first question: "*What is the 'object' of your empathy?*" sought to draw out how empathy is perceived by individuals who, by virtue of their area of expertise, applied radically different filters through which they defined what *the other* meant to them. An artist gave voice to the heart, a neuroscientist to the brain, a philosopher to the mind, a social psychologist to the worldview, and an augmented reality expert to the artificial layers of perception. The second question: "*What are the ingredients of the Alchemy of Empathy?*," was posed to thirteen creatives, most affiliated with museums, who each described an intangible quality that was conducive for empathy to naturally unfold: Intentionality, Intersectionality, Curiosity, Play, Vulnerability, Contemplation and Nuance, Proximity, Storytelling, Synchronicity, Awe and Wonder, Collective Journeying, Breaking Bread, Optimism, and Hope. By bringing the properties of each of these qualities into conscious expression, the goal was to explore how they could inform our design efforts with greater intentionality. The third question: "*What is the Scope & the Spectrum of Empathy?*," sought to imagine how the positioning of museums as incubators of empathy-building could reverberate beyond the walls of the museum. Experts were invited to reflect on the broader potential of such an approach on ethics and values, the environment, education and entrepreneurship, innovation and design, and societal progress.

> *Wherever a difficult question is,*
> *that's where the answer goes.*
>
> –*Rumi*[1]

There is something so meaningful for me about asking questions. Through the act of formulating a question, we build a relationship with our own intention and learn to trust the source of inspiration behind that intention.

We show our commitment by returning continually to these questions, even when the lack of immediate answers can tug at our vulnerability. What I have found is that the answers emerge always through a collective effort of churning our raw ideas, intuitions, and concepts until the ingredients solidify into new wisdom that can nourish the next stage of innovation. In the case of this book, innovation looks like museums taking more steps toward realizing their own power to become incubators of empathy. The churning that has happened since my second book raised questions about empathy-building that have resulted in a hands-on, hearts-on experimental effort to show how this is both entirely practical and possible.

Authors contributing to *An Empathy-Building Toolkit for Museums* were invited to describe concrete examples and applicable tools that can make the concept of empathy-building tangible in the museum context. It is important to emphasize that this book is rooted in actual experimentation with ways of Designing for Empathy to naturally unfold. It intentionally approaches the human phenomenon of empathy as it is *lived* rather than *intellectualized* into categories such as emotional, cognitive, compassionate, or kinesthetic. These categorizations are useful in scientific and academic contexts, but can silo our thinking in empathy-building experience design, as often one category already includes many elements from the others within. Empathy exists on a spectrum that cannot be confined to a single description. Empathy is porous and the experience of it naturally moves between and beyond our human attempts to define it. While the design process can create the conditions for nurturing its growth, what blooms in the space that is shared depends on the qualities that are present in the space and on what people bring into the space. The degree of receptivity and perception will determine the spectrum of empathy that is inherently experienced by the participants, even though some aspects of it can go unarticulated. In keeping with this fluidity, what can really help us to fertilize the ground for empathy-building is to cultivate the presence of the *Alchemy of Empathy* ingredients in the spaces that we create. These ingredients, which I define in Chapter 1, include such qualities as intellectual humility and reverence, expressed by an institution through its prioritizing of emotional and physical comfort, safety, and openness in ways both subtle and explicit. Over time, the presence of the ingredients creates a fertile ground for empathy. As visitors enter and interact with the energy of the space, bringing their own sensibilities and receptivity, an alchemy occurs within them and is simultaneously transmuted from them into the space.

Empathy is contagious. Its potential is infinite and, while we can till the ground to nurture it, what unfolds cannot be fully intellectualized in our minds. Yet it isn't merely an ethereal, disappearing force either. On the contrary, the empathy that is built cross-pollinates and permeates into all aspects of our lives, finding expression and manifestation in the world through acts of love, justice, and service. Understanding the importance of the ingredients in this way, authors were invited to offer three ingredients to the mix that best describe the essence of the empathy-building approaches presented in their chapters. Like a single drop of the Ocean containing all the qualities of the Ocean, each ingredient of the *Alchemy of Empathy* holds the potential of supporting empathy-building across the spectrum. By describing the ingredients explicitly, the authors offer museums a way forward in intentionally reflecting on how they can apply these ingredients toward empathy-building. Many of the ingredients, such as storytelling, are already present in most museums, although they aren't harnessed specifically for empathy.

In reading the chapters as they arrived, I was struck by how the same ingredients for empathy were mentioned in many different, seemingly unrelated contexts. Shared qualities appeared over and over again in chapters written by representatives from museums, education, art, science, design, and entrepreneurship. What became clear to me is that, in having each contributor articulate the ingredients that lie at the heart of their individual approach, a common ground emerged among them. While the ingredients were used in different ways, the ultimate outcome was the same: They all led somewhere along the spectrum of empathy. The defining feature in all cases was an *intentional approach* to include these ingredients within the design of their individual experiences.

Each author in this book is an expert in their field. What we all share is a common goal to be of service to humanity and our world by utilizing our expertise to foster empathy through unique approaches. And through this uniqueness and intentionality, we can identify principles that can be broadly applied within museums. In particular, the variety of experiences expressed in this volume leads us to the following *five pathways* that museums can take to cultivate empathy-building, each of which will be explored in a dedicated part in this book:

1) ***Holding space for experiential, holistic learning of relatedness and kinship through contemplative practices.*** Part I offers creative approaches that evoke the universality of human experience using

ancient wisdom as inspiration, including expanding the experience of self, other, and oneness through mindful, contemplative encounters and experiences designed around Sufi (1–3), Vedanta (4), and Tibetan Buddhist (5) teachings; tapping into the intangible power objects have to hold a mirror to shared humanness (6, 7), and connecting with nature through Shinto and Zen Buddhist practices (8).

2) ***Promoting understanding through perspective-taking and thinking strategies.*** Authors in Part II offer strategies that encourage an intentional approach to effortful thinking and perspective-taking, including a chapter on the power of imaginative empathy and wonder (9); another looking at how to build new understandings by connecting viewers to the creative process of art (10); explorations of the power of using Visual Thinking Strategies to try on others' feelings and emotions (11) and shift perspectives through a slow-looking approach (12); and a look at how objects can be portals connecting past and present (13).

3) ***Creating space for perspective-expanding social encounters through creative, unconventional approaches.*** In Part III, social entrepreneurs stretch the imagination of the potential for dialogue in museum settings through chapters that describe an immersive experience designed around Sign Language (14); another that gives participants a taste of nonjudgmental listening and sharing (15); as well as chapters that explore how art can be used as a backdrop for difficult civic conversations (16) and as a contemplative tool to answer personal questions (17).

4) ***Practicing and sharing empathetic organizational policies and methodologies.*** Part IV reveals tangible ways for museums to approach empathy as an organizational value shaping culture, mission, ethics, policy, and practices, including a national perspective on museums as centers of curiosity (18); a case study on the culture of care at the Museum of Us in San Diego (19); a look at the Mississippi Museum of Art's efforts in meaningful community engagement (20); a chapter endorsing the role of apprenticeship in organizational value-building (21); and a toolkit for crafting an emotional culture in the workplace (22).

5) ***Positioning empathy-building as a shared value in multi-sector partnerships.*** Authors in Part V offer multiple strategies for building

bridges between museums and other industries where museums are positioned as incubators of empathy, including two chapters exploring different approaches to using art to teach medical students how to empathize (23 and 24); and another about how play can be used widely, beyond the walls of museums, as a tool for serious learning as practiced by the Children's Museum of Pittsburgh and inspired by the philosophy of Fred Rogers (25).

The tools that we choose to use determine who we become. Empathy-building is a powerful tool that can transform individuals, institutions, and communities alike. By utilizing the tools; the ideas, insights, concepts, examples, terminologies, ethical considerations, and step-by-step guidelines presented in this book, museums can incorporate empathy more deeply into their practices and become platforms for experiential learning of empathy while utilizing their existing context and content. By becoming platforms for empathy-building, museums can play an active role in the health and well-being of our world by intentionally helping humanity develop a strong sense of relatedness to each other, our kin that we share our world with, and our planet.

Empathy permeates all aspects of our lives. It is intended that this book will spark creative partnerships across disciplines, institutions, and sectors to co-create new, context relevant solutions that foster a culture of empathy in our world, while utilizing museums as incubators of empathy-building. It is our collective hope, as contributing authors to this book, that more museums will be inspired to develop their own unique empathy-building approaches. I am humbled by the rich and varied content of this volume, which has shown me that this book can be seen as a literary version of the empathy-building circle I describe in Chapter 1. The circle is an archetypal symbol of potential and unity, and the chapters in this book animate the vibrant diversity of vantage points required to realize this potential and unity. It is my hope that the circle of generative and creative applications described here will reverberate beyond the confines of these pages.

## Note

1 *Mathnawi.* Book III, 3204; 3208–13. Translated by Kabir and Camille Helminski.

# Part I

# Holding Space for Experiential Learning of Relatedness and Kinship Through Contemplative Practices

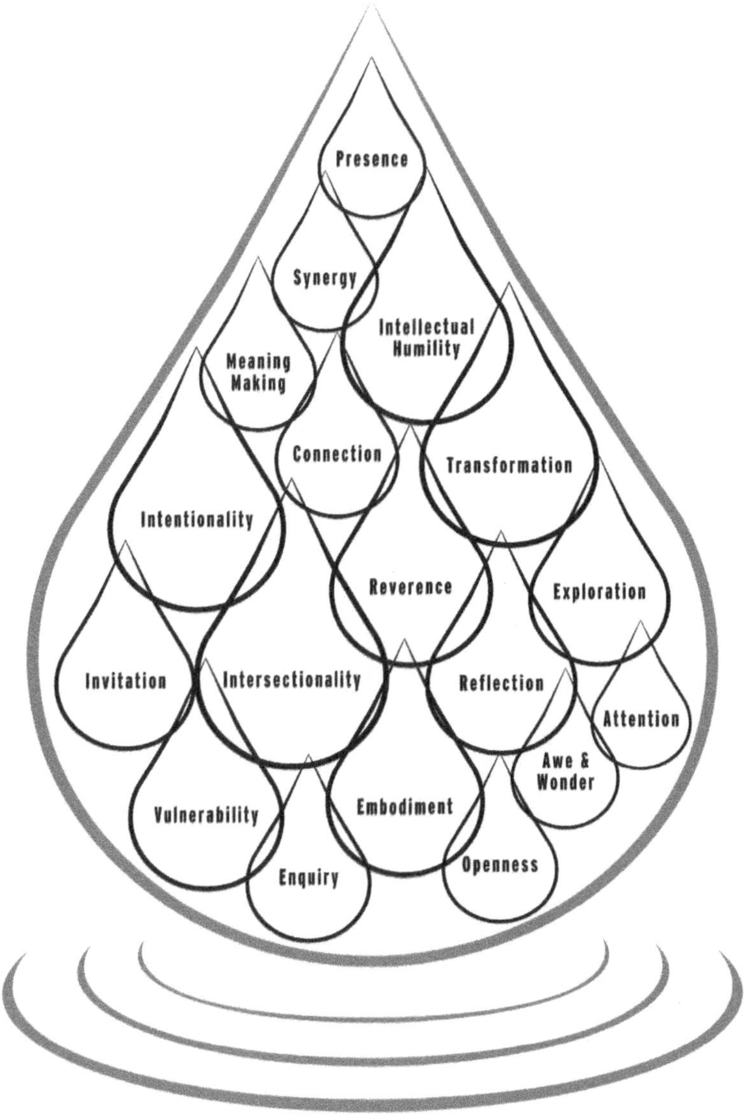

# 1 What Is Empathy-Building Through Museums?

*Elif M. Gökçiğdem*

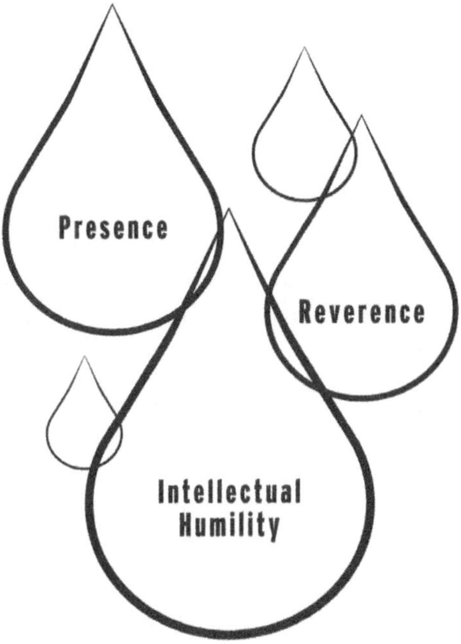


Imagining a *circle* is a helpful way to conceptualize empathy-building in a museum. The outline of the circle is drawn by those who intend to create and hold a container in which empathy-building can unfold. In this circle, there is a center (the shared experience being offered), and a multitude of vantage points on the periphery forming a circumference (the participants). The combination of these elements creates the Whole. Each vantage point, like a dot on the circumference, has a position unique and sovereign to that vantage point. Each is equidistant to the center, facing, perceiving, and experiencing the center from slightly varying angles. There is no hierarchy of vantage points in the collective experiencing of the Whole. Each vantage point simultaneously perceives only a certain slice of the greater reality, and what is experienced is real and true to the knowledge, the capacity of understanding, and the comprehension of that perspective holder. In a successful empathy-building experience, every participant contributes to the creation of the Whole. They are simultaneously witnesses of unity and diversity, understanding that there are multitudes of perspectives and modes of perception simultaneously occurring. Each experiences the Whole from their respective vantage point, in their own unique way, and their perception of the Whole is what is real and true to each. Empathy-building is a dynamic unfolding which, at its best, leads to a kind of presence that enables the expansion of perception to encompass ***Triple Awareness***, which includes the following *three realizations attained through lived experience*:

**1)** A realization of the ***diversity of perception and perspectives*** that are simultaneously occurring within the Whole, around an intentionally designed shared experience.

**2)** A realization that this diversity stems from each vantage point's unique positioning, which prompts curiosity and self-inquiry into one's own vantage point and perception, as well as those of others around, who together form the Whole. A capacity to zoom out to a higher vantage point is unlocked within, which allows the habitual layers that inform one's vantage point to be perceived. From this higher vantage point, one gains a capacity to objectively witness the complex array of thoughts, emotions, and voices within. This individual self-witnessing takes place in a social setting, and within the context of a shared experience. The witnessing-self is simultaneously aware of what is happening inside and around it. It realizes that others are going through a similar process, that it is witnessing as well as being witnessed. The ego, the lower self, normally fixated on its narrow self-serving vantage point, suddenly becomes disoriented. Feeling vulnerable and in survival mode, the ego is compelled to adapt to this new reality. Its aperture of awareness is widened, becoming more refined and expansive, and able to consider other vantage points. This signifies the move from the lower self to the ***expanded self***. This newfound perspective is similar to the *overview effect* that astronauts report when seeing our planet from outer space for the first time. The experience fills them with awe and a newfound sense of scale within the vastness of the universe, where existing paradigms for all kinds of borders and limitations dissolve, including those between the self and the other. It is as though once the astronauts have taken off from the surface of the earth and ascended into the cosmos, the ego follows a similar journey. Whereas on familiar ground it followed its whims and desires and thrived in fragmentation at the expense of the Whole, as it transitions into the reality of the vast unknown, its entire worldview is shattered. From afar, the self forms a new empathic relationship to the earth, seeing how vulnerable and small the globe looks in the context of the universe, and yet how magnificent. The earth becomes a mirror in which the self simultaneously reflects on its own insignificance and preciousness. Emancipated from its own constriction, it experiences the true sovereignty that is reached only through profound humility.

**3)** Having tasted the capaciousness of the *expanded self*, a realization of the self's bandwidth to view the greater reality through a multitude of vantage points emerges. The self becomes more free and confident of its capability to try on others' meanings without losing its own identity. It becomes curious to truly make space for and hold another's lived experience without judgment, and with a deep sense of reverence and appreciation for their dignity. Practicing this in the context of the empathy-building experience provides a tangible reference point that can be taken into scenarios of everyday life. An understanding that our perceptions of the Whole lie on a spectrum, gives each participant a choice—and a responsibility—to tap into the capaciousness they now know is inherent to their humanness. The effort and the will that is dedicated to consciously practicing empathy in this way is rewarding as the self realizes more and more that through curiosity and openness, the creative imagination flows. Therein lies a wellspring of meaning and purpose which the *expanded self* can draw upon for nourishment of its unique creative expression and manifestation within the ***wider belonging***, always in service of the Whole.

Through practice, the *expanded self* carries with it a deep realization that at any given moment, our perception, our meaning-making, and our actions are related to something greater than ourselves. Through *Triple Awareness*, the self realizes that, along with others, it is integral to the Whole, and nothing is disconnected, isolated, disposable, or separate in this existence.

The *Triple Awareness* cultivated through the empathy-building journey is not a linear unfolding. While it is offered as a shared journey, the comprehension and insights that each individual takes with them will be in alignment with the degree of openness, intellectual humility, and reverence they bring to the overall experience. For the participants' experience of the circle to be complete, it is essential that the facilitator draw attention to each *Triple Awareness* realization, which up to that point could only have been subjectively experienced rather than explicitly articulated.

Giving language to the lived experience in this way is empowering. It allows each participant to understand how *Triple Awareness* unfolded in their own experience, which enables them to transfer these learnings to their lives. Empathy can be learned and can be cultivated through practice over time. Empathy-building through museums therefore offers a variety of choices, contexts, and platforms through which individuals of all ages and backgrounds can exercise and practice their empathy. What is learned through continuous practice, when reflected upon, and translated through each participant's embodied expression, matures into deep, meaningful, and guiding wisdom.

Having conceptualized the *Designing for Empathy® Framework*'s metaphorical circular container within which empathy-building can unfold, what comes next is an exploration of what this can look like in a museum. At the end of this chapter, I offer a glossary of terminology that may be useful in providing precise explanations for the recurring concepts that come up in my empathy-building work (Box 1.3).[1] But first, I will walk you through the five stages of designing an empathy-building experience (see below and Box 1.1), followed by considerations for ethics and best practices (Box 1.2):

1) **Inner Well-being**

   As designers and holders of space for empathy-building, our preparations begin with our own inner world. Holding space for empathy-building requires intellectual humility, reverence to human dignity, equanimity, presence, and a sense of service to humanity. Presence, the state of being consciously and simultaneously aware of all our faculties (physical, mental, emotional, spiritual), is a prerequisite to equanimity. And equanimity, our capacity for calmness and composure even in the face of difficult situations and opposing viewpoints, is essential to cultivating a space where vulnerability can be expressed and lived experiences can be witnessed, held, and received without judgment. In this way, the facilitator bears the responsibility of modeling presence and equanimity, qualities whose energy naturally leads to participants bringing down their barriers and opening the ground for mutual trust. The ultimate goal for the facilitator is to nurture a space where participants move out of their thinking-minds and into a *heartful* space of intimacy. This is not something that can be learned overnight. The most skillful facilitators will likely have meditative practices of their own choosing in their daily lives to help stay grounded and nurture self-awareness and presence.

2) **Preparation**

It is important to remember that empathy is not something we create. It is also not an *object* that is outside of us, waiting for us to reach out and grasp it for immediate *possession*. Empathy is already available within each of us, yet our intention is to be able to design an environment where hearts can be softened and empathy can naturally unfold gradually through continuous practice. Keeping this in mind, the facilitator should identify a physical space that is spacious enough for everyone to have enough personal space, while also being able to see and hear each other, as well as to move around. Beginning and ending with everyone in a circle can be useful, depending on the nature of the exercise. Empathy-building experiences can involve groups or can be designed as self-guided experiences that are spread out around a museum's galleries and public spaces, which could be experienced by groups as well as individuals. For group experiences, the space should be intimate enough for everyone to co-create a shared experience around whatever object or theme the museum is offering as a focal point for the empathy-building event. Ideally, the space should be reserved exclusively for the experience to avoid distraction and encourage focus. Depending on the nature of the exercise, arranging for comfortable seating will be an important element. The space should be physically and emotionally safe, inclusive, and accessible. Two decades of collaborative empathy-building efforts have shown me that people who are drawn to this work tend to share some common demeanors, such as openness, kindness, a collaborative outlook, and an aspiration to be in service to the Whole. Even so, it can be important to offer attendees guidelines before the day of the experience that set the tone and intention of the gathering and advise them of the expectations and manners that are conducive for empathy to occur. On the day of the experience, it can be helpful for the facilitator to arrive at the space early enough to set an intention and perform grounding exercises of their choice before participants arrive. Through such self-anchoring, the facilitator will be more able to welcome everyone into the space from a place of calm centeredness.

**3) The Opening**

After introductions and a welcome that includes going over the guidelines, participants can be invited to reflect on what brought them to the space and to articulate for themselves an intention that may or may not be shared with the group. This period of silence is a gentle way to turn down the volume of noise in the thinking-mind and encourage participants to tune inward with presence and attention. This is a prerequisite for the possibility of empathy-building because it compels the person to leave behind the preoccupations of their day and acknowledge their inner world. This is the beginning of a self-inquiry that will gradually deepen as the experience unfolds. Setting an intention can offer a reference point for each individual to track how the experience is unfolding for them in relation to their intention. Any learnings they derive from the experience can become more personal and applicable in everyday life. From the opening, the facilitator is taking small steps to encourage everyone to subtly ease into their own bodies and bring down their barriers for the softening of the heart. Empathy-building places an emphasis on the sharing of lived experiences, which can open hearts to each other on the basis of shared humanity. It is an *integrative* practice, unlike the sharing of opinions, which are restricted to the conditioning of the thinking-mind and are more *separative*.

**4) The Experience**

Empathy-building experiences are curated encounters that prompt participants to make real-time choices and act on these while simultaneously being witnessed by others. The purpose is to create moments of vulnerability that are objectively witnessed by each participants' own self and every other participant. In noticing their responses to momentarily being in the spotlight, each individual gets a window into the unique, individual lens through which they view the world and is confronted with the habits and conditions that have informed the aperture of their perception. Through a number of such curated encounters, each self faces the inner struggle of coming to terms with the differences in vantage points, while also finding common ground in vulnerability, realizing that every other is on a similar journey. The desired outcome of this approach is that the fear of differences gradually melts into mutual reverence of the shared humanness that weaves through each individual expression. This experience is disarming and unifying and tends to invite greater courage in sharing vulnerably, as well as openness in holding others' lived experiences without judgment. The climax of the experience is therefore a tuning into the *expanded self* that can see itself in others and others in itself. Designing a simple structure for an empathy-building experience in a museum requires the following six building blocks that are listed in Box 1.1:

## Box 1.1 The Building Blocks of an Empathy-Building Experience

(1) ***A social setting* that is nonjudgmental, emotionally and physically safe, and inclusive for each participant.** The ingredients of the *Alchemy of Empathy* (further described in Box 1.3), those intangible qualities that are conducive to bringing about empathy, such as storytelling, awe and wonder, proximity, dialogue, play, or breaking bread, among many others, can be useful design factors to determine the relevancy of the experience to be designed, as well as its intended learning outcomes.

(2) **An intentionally designed encounter that positions the self (each participant) as both its *object* and its *subject*.** This stands in distinct contrast to most other encounters one would have in a museum, which focus on learning about what is on display. The display piece is positioned as the object and the

subject of the visit. The knowledge the visitor takes away is generally intended to be *about* the object, which again is strikingly different from the intention of an empathy-building experience, whose focus is on the visitor gaining self-knowledge through an engagement *with* the object.

(3) **An encounter crafted with the intention of presenting *a dilemma* that each participant unavoidably interfaces with and is asked to make a quick choice in reaction to the dilemma and act on this choice.** This action may come in the form of a verbal response, a bodily motion, or through an intervention with props that leads to a physical change in the environment that is visible to everyone.

(4) **The inclusion of a mode of response or acknowledgment to each individual's choice that has a sensory element to it, which may be embodied, tactile, visual, auditory, or olfactory in nature.** This moment of witnessing completes the cycle of the encounter. It is designed so that each individual becomes conscious both of their power to cause change and, with vulnerability and humility, of how their choice fits within the collective in relation to others' choices.

(5) **The incorporation of *moments of pause* where the facilitator intervenes to give language to an experience that up to that point had been subjective, individual, and unarticulated.** This is an opportunity to highlight the elements of *Triple Awareness* that may have manifested for each individual, bringing home the sense of each human experience being universal and unique at the same time.

(6) **A *time for group sharing* where participants are voluntarily invited to share their insights and reflections.**

## 5) The Conscious Closing

This is also a good time for the facilitator to invite individuals in the group to revisit their initial intentions and reflect on how the experience may have informed those intentions. Based on what they discover from this inquiry, the facilitator can invite everyone to commit to bringing their most poignant learning from the experience into their daily lives so empathy becomes a tangible habit. Parting thoughts from the facilitator might include recommending people to take some time off right after the experience to sit with what was experienced, and reflect before going back into what might be routine for them. I have noticed that some participants prefer solitude, while others enjoy a deep dialogue after the experience. It might be useful to have some suggestions ready to provide the participants with a few options on certain locations where they might find solitude or continue their conversations in and around the museum. In my experience, empathy-building workshops leave participants with the following:

- A more nuanced understanding of empathy.
- A deepening in their capacity to notice entrenched perspectives and habits.
- A greater openness to vantage points, perceptions, and lived experiences different from their own.
- A sense of agency in exploring creative ways to apply empathy in their personal and professional lives.
- A deeper commitment to community-building with other empathy-builders.
- An appreciation for the intrinsic ways museums can be incubators of empathy.

### Box 1.2 Ethical Considerations for Empathy-Building through Museums

Creating emotionally and physically safe, inclusive spaces and experiences for empathy-building requires a consideration of the following six ethical responsibilities, where each experience is designed to be:

**(1) Invitational:** Empathy-building engagements should honor each individual's sovereignty, dignity, freedom of choice to participate, and freedom of expression throughout.

**(2) Humanitarian:** Empathy-building should not be utilized to manipulate others' perceptions, thoughts, emotions, and perspectives with the goal of gaining power, status, or profit. Manipulating the outcomes of empathy toward such transactional gains would be harmful to the Whole, short-changing our unique human capacity to become a force for good in the world. The self-knowledge attained through empathy-building is not intended for helping only the self, but on the contrary, is intended for applicable outcomes and expressions of empathy that find their living manifestations in our world.

**(3) Nonhierarchical:** While as facilitators of empathy-building experiences practitioners and the institutions they represent might have the authority to set narratives and certain rules, it is important to acknowledge that we are not there as teachers, but as *keepers of space* for the humanness within each other to emerge and be objectively witnessed and held through empathy and mutual trust. Empathy-building is not about participants agreeing with each point of view they encounter, nor is it for the entire group to agree on a single point of view. On the contrary, empathy-building leads to self-knowledge, a humbling realization of the limited perspective of each self within the wholeness of reality, and that there is no hierarchy in a whole. And the wholeness of reality, as perceived and experienced from each vantage point, is considered as real and true to the holder of that vantage point, in alignment with the capacity of their understanding.

**(4) Physically and Emotionally Safe:** The empathy-building journey is intended to honor the unique vantage points of each self while simultaneously reaching to that which connects us beyond differences. Empathy-building does not require one to be in complete agreement with another or to let go of existing boundaries. It does not assume that one can thoroughly understand or feel another's lived experience. Each participant is invited to speak from lived experience and insight, and not to react with an opinion statement to another's sharing. Building empathy enables us to learn through practice that we each have the capability to create a nonjudgmental space for each other, where mutual trust and understanding can develop.

**(5) Grounded in Reverence and Intellectual Humility:** In an empathy-building experience, regardless of the artwork, the artifacts, or other props that might be used to create a shared journey, the *subject*, the *object*, and the *container* of the experience is always the *human being*. Cultivating intellectual humility, as well as a reverence toward the dignity of humanity in each other no matter how different a vantage point may be, is essential. The same principles apply when relating to our *nonhuman kin* in the natural world around us.

**(6) Intentionally Co-Created by Honoring Diverse Cultures, Wisdom, and Languages:** It is essential to develop processes that intentionally integrate into the design and practice of empathy-building the spirit and knowledge of diverse cultures, languages, and traditions. Indigenous cultures and wisdom traditions that might not have a word for empathy because it is integral to their way of life are particularly vital. Coming in touch with the rich depths of universal human experience requires a sincere reckoning with the entrenched ways of doing things that may serve dominance rather than diversity.

As I hope the *Designing for Empathy® Framework* illustrates, empathy is inherent to our humanness, is a remedy for fragmentation, and is a pathway to experiencing the wholeness of Being. Through its gates, our separate selves can again and again return to the sea of wholeness. Empathy-building suggests that intentionally designed experiences can bring about pragmatic perspective shifts that have the potential to alter one's perception to first create, and then deepen an appreciation of the Whole. What I have witnessed time and again in individuals who participate in empathy-building experiences is the gradual emergence of an *expanded self.* This self that is aware of its capaciousness; can see *itself* in *everything*, and *everything* in *itself.* The ultimate result is a compassionate sensitivity, and dedication to altruistic action to serve the greater good, in recognition that, in the truest experience of the *Oneness Mindset*, there is no *other.*

## Box 1.3 An Evolving Terminology for Empathy-Building Through Museums

To capture the process of unfolding empathy, as I understand and use it in my *Designing for Empathy® Framework*, I have compiled the following glossary of terms based on my insights and reflections over two decades of research and explorations into empathy-building:

**The Oneness of Being (The Whole):** The wholeness of Existence to which the self and the other are innately integral, regardless of their capacity of perception of their integral-ness. Not to be confused with "sameness," the Oneness of existence is the primordial state of the Universe and is comprised of infinite Diversity. Revered by many Indigenous cultures and traditions of wisdom, this concept can also be referred to as: *Unity, Interconnectedness, Oneness, Non-duality, Interbeing, Ubuntu, Tikkun Olam, Hishuk Ish Tsawalk, Yin and Yang, Totality, Advaita Vedanta, Varlıkta Birlik*, and *Wahdat al-Wujud*. For example, the Sufi philosophy of *Wahdat al-Wujud* explains this concept as follows: "Traditional wisdom conceives of the Whole in terms of a single Creative Power acting on different levels through different means, or reflectors, to produce an infinite variety of creative results. In other words, everything that exists is the manifestation of a single Source of Life and Being."[2]

**The Self:** Our embodied identity which has various degrees of capacity to perceive and relate to the Whole. Innate within it is the capacity to expand its perception and relatedness. The *lower self* considers itself as a separate entity and feels safe and secure in its own vantage point. It is not yet aware of the nature of the Whole. The *expanded self* can objectively witness the lower self's actions while also witnessing the Whole, and itself, as part of the Whole. This *Triple Awareness* enables the self to take responsibility and to regulate its behavior within the Whole.

**The Other:** All things that exist beyond the embodied self, tangible or intangible. Within the context of this book, this can include artworks, the natural world, and museum objects, as well as what is unknown, strange, or unfamiliar to the self, such as new and different concepts, ideas, perspectives, and worldviews.

**Triple Awareness:** An experiential realization that expands perception to include the self's inner world, those around it, and the greater Whole, to which the self and others are integral.

**Self-Knowledge:** The self's capacity to witness its inner world in all its complexity, which can include *the thinking-self* (the mind), *the feeling-self* (the heart), and *the willful-self* (the faculty of conscious choice, the will). Noticing entrenched biases, worldviews, and paradigms, and developing a sense of accountability and self-regulation.

**The Oneness Mindset:** A worldview that seeks to apply an awareness of the Oneness of Being into everyday choices, behaviors, ethics, and values, with the intention of developing harmonious relations with the Whole. Through this mindset, even when we aren't experiencing ourselves in the transcendent state of Oneness, we strive to consciously align our actions and calibrate our behaviors as though we are.

**Oneness:** The self's embodied experience of itself as integral to the Whole. Like sugar dissolving in water, the self merges with the Whole and becomes transparent, experiencing unity with the Whole. There is no longer the self, the other, or even a Whole that is separate from Itself.

**Empathy:** The self's innate ability to *relate* to the other. It is a form of perception that allows the self to connect with its inner world such that it is possible to connect with the perspectives and lived experiences of the other and, eventually, the Whole Itself. The term *Rooted Empathy*, is suggested to qualify *empathy, as rooted in a primordial shared Essence,* as in the philosophy of the Oneness of Being.

**Empathy-Building:** The design and use of holistic experiences involving the self and the other, whose goal is to progressively bring about shifts in perspectives and perception among participants that expand their sense of self. At best, the self experiences a gradual expansion of its relatedness, starting with its inner world and widening to encompass others and the Whole.

**Designing for Empathy®:** An intellectual framework and an international platform led by ONE—Organization of Networks for Empathy (ONE Empathy Network), for cross-disciplinary, cross-cultural, and cross-sectoral collaborative explorations that deepen our understanding of our humanness through the lens of empathy, utilizing the Oneness Mindset as a master perspective.

**The Ingredients of The Alchemy of Empathy:** The transformative qualities that naturally occur between the self and the other which act as catalysts for empathy. Included among these are: Reverence, Intellectual Humility, Presence, Intentionality, Intersectionality, Curiosity, Play, Vulnerability, Contemplation and Nuance, Proximity, Storytelling, Synchronicity, Awe and Wonder, Collective Journeying, Breaking Bread, Optimism, and Hope. Designers of empathy-building can intentionally seek ways to create experiences that manifest these qualities, and identify new ones.

# Notes

**1** This evolving terminology is the result of two decades of research and explorations in empathy, where the primary sources of information and inspiration include the following resources, listed in the order of my encounter with them as they shaped my approach: Kabir Helminski, *Living Presence: The Sufi Path to Mindfulness and the Essential Self* (TarcherPerigee, 2017); K. Helminski, *The*

*Knowing Heart* (Shambhala, 2000); Wilhelm Worringer, *Abstraction and Empathy* (Elephant Paperback, 1997); Peter Senge and C. Otto Scharmer, *Presence: Human Purpose and the Field of the Future* (Doubleday, 2004); Daniel Goleman and P. Senge, *The Triple Focus: A New Approach to Education* (More Than Sound, 2014); Jack Mezirow & Associates, *Learning as Transformation* (Jossey-Bass, 2000); Abraham H. Maslow, *Toward a Psychology of Being* (Sublime Books, 2014); Susan Lanzoni, *Empathy: A History* (Yale University Press, 2018); Helminski, *The Mysterion: Rumi and the Secret of Becoming Fully Human* (Shambhala, 2023); Arthur Zajonc, *Meditation as Contemplative Inquiry: When Knowing Becomes Love* (Lindisfarne Books, 2009); Greta Gerard and Bengü Ergüner-Tekinalp, *Contemplative Practices and Anti-Oppressive Pedagogies for Higher Education* (Routledge, 2022); Stephen Murphy-Shigematsu, *From Mindfulness to Heartfulness* (Berrettt-Koehler Publishers, 2018); Daniel J. Siegel, MD, *IntraConnected* (Norton, 2023).

**2** Helminski, *Living Presence*, 23.

# 2 Empathy-Building with Rumi's MAP

## Meaning, Awareness, Potential

*Elif M. Gökçiğdem*

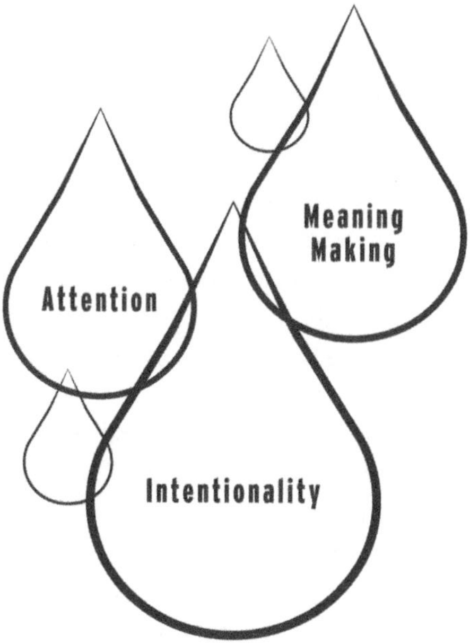


*We are the mirror as well as the face in it.*
*We are both pain and its cure.*

—*Rumi*[1]

On the final day of our seventh-annual Designing for Empathy Summit and Workshops at the Glencairn Museum in October 2024, I had participants try out a new experience that I had designed based on a mysterious geometric pattern encountered on the marbled main entrance to Rumi's tomb, which today is the Mevlana Museum in Konya, Turkiye (Figure 2.1). The design features a black dot enclosed in a pink square in the center, surrounded by four concentric rhombus-shaped black lines alternating with four white ones, radiating outward. During a visit in 2023, I was so mesmerized by the pattern that I spent the following year researching its origins in art and architectural history, and came up with nothing, even though my graduate studies focused on Islamic geometric patterns. It turned out to be a contemporary addition during a recent renovation, and its designer remains unknown. This felt like an urgent sublime invitation to go on a journey of meaning-making for myself, and articulate in words what each component of the design could be seeking to convey. The result of this effort was the creation of an experiential platform for empathy-building I have named MAP, which stands for Meaning, Awareness, and Potential, and which felt like a gift from Rumi. Nearly forty participants consisting of museum professionals and creatives from different disciplines and institutions took part in MAP's first prototyping, which is the subject of this chapter.

Divided into pairs, the participants sat across from each other (Figure 2.2). A replica of the geometric design printed on a thick paper mat was placed between them. Situated on the circle in the center was a single small cubicle glass tessera, left over from the construction of the Glencairn Museum's interior mosaic ceilings and walls. The points of the rhombus were positioned intentionally to face each person, as if to invite them to go together on a journey of meaning-making toward the central dot. At every black line, each representing a threshold, the participants were given incrementally more information about the object, and prompted to pay attention and briefly articulate in writing what was taking place in their thinking-mind and feeling-heart at each stage. The outermost black line represented the initial encounter, asking them to reflect on their first impressions of the tessera, without knowing any information about it. With the second black line, the "what" of the object was shared, as in its physical properties, such as size, weight, color, and shape. At the third and fourth lines, the "how" and the "why" of the object were shared, each point incorporating a human story to deepen the understanding of the object's context. They were also allowed to touch the object at that point. Once the participants arrived at the pink square, they were invited to share with each other their experience of witnessing their thinking-mind and feeling-heart as they crossed each

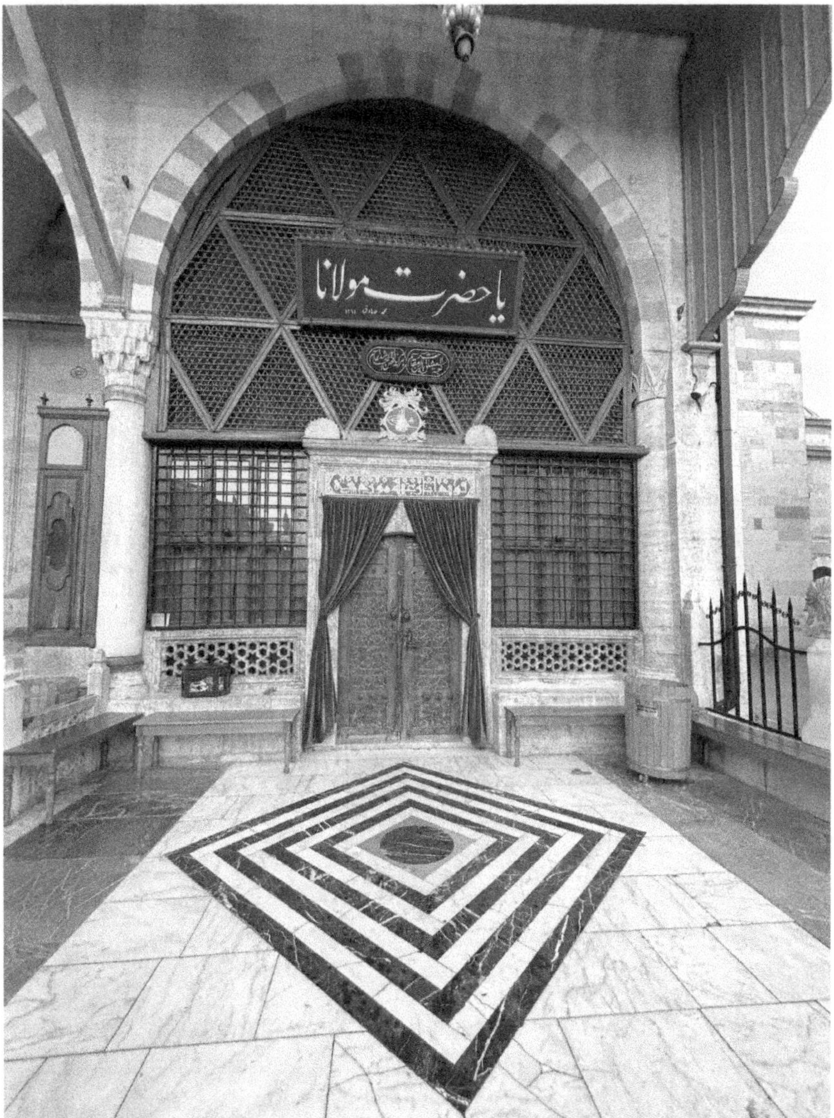


**Figure 2.1** Mevlana Museum, Konya, Türkiye. Main entrance through the *Dervishes* Gate. Credit: Photography by Elif M. Gokcigdem. Courtesy of Designing for Empathy® by ONE.

threshold. As a final step, when they arrived at the central black dot with the object, the object between them was removed entirely, and they were asked to reflect on a deeply personal question inspired by the stories shared about the object.

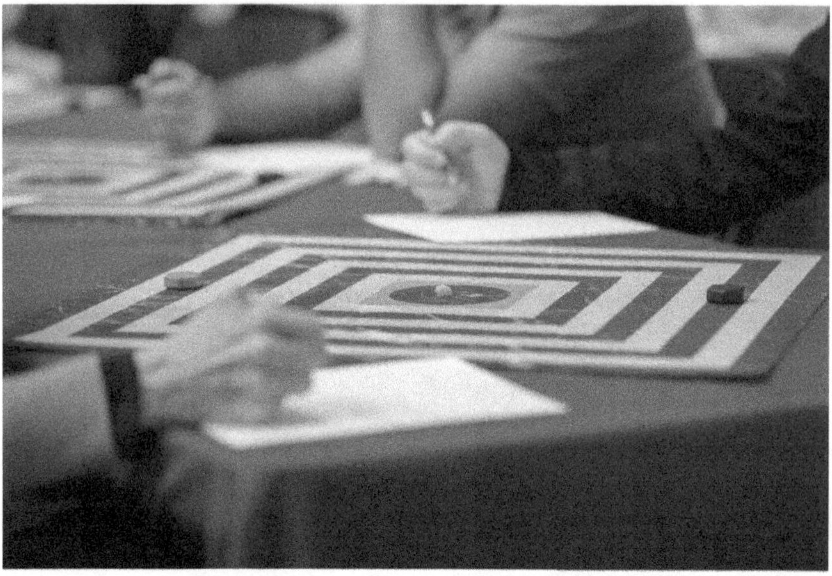

**Figure 2.2** The MAP experience prototyping at the seventh Annual Designing for Empathy Summit & Workshops, Glencairn Museum (October 23–25, 2024). Credit: Photography by Leah Fisher Photography. Courtesy of Glencairn Museum.

The sharings that unfolded were truly spontaneous, deeply intimate, and unexpectedly rich for all of the participants, most of whom did not know each other beforehand. The emotional responses by several participants spoke to me of the depths of shared humanness the MAP experience was able to elicit and hold a mirror to. The encounter was, in the end, not about the object at all—but rather, the object was a way of arriving at a different kind of integrative knowing experienced through the heart.

Just as Rumi describes in the opening poem, this mirroring between hearts has a healing quality to it. Arriving through the thresholds of separation that each black line represented, the participants found themselves face to face, mirror to mirror, able to move beyond their respective habitual library of narratives to a place of deep, nonjudgmental communion. Their very embodied selves were, in a sense, the final threshold they needed to cross to experience oneness.

This was an embodiment of the kind of empathy-building I imagined could be possible, and my ongoing work is for the sake of exploring how this possibility can become manifest in museums.

## Meaning-Making

Because my personal journey in meaning-making was very much at the heart of the design and the prototyping of this experience, I feel drawn to sharing its layers, through which the Glencairn prototype came into being.

My first encounter with this mysterious geometric design took place during a somewhat rushed late-afternoon visit. The main entrance to the Mevlana Museum, where this design is on the floor, was already closed to visitors. As the last few guests were moving in and out through what is normally the exit door adjacent to the entrance, this striking pattern caught my eye. Later, on my return visits, I realized that I might not even have seen it if our visit was earlier in the day, as this surface is often concealed beneath the clamor of feet queuing to enter the space. But on this occasion, I felt a magnetic pull to leave my group and walk toward it. I stood above the design, awed by its shape and the scale of it, which I longed to imprint in my memory. I stepped onto the design's outermost black line and looked up toward the breathtaking ancient wooden double door adorned by green velvet curtains on either side, and calligraphy above it. In a way, the entrance is so unassuming in its appearance, yet it carries an unspoken grandeur, evoking a reverence within the visitor even before they step over the threshold. The subtle and refined qualities of the space emanate through the materials; the building has an anchoring quality to its character that almost makes it feel like the materials, from wood to marble, are alive and trying to communicate with those who take a moment to listen. I felt an animate invitation to meaning-making and quickly took a few photos (Figure 2.1), hoping to be able to revisit these moments later on.

Little did I know that the same evening, after museum hours, our group of travelers would be invited back into the mausoleum for a very special visit led by Nadir Karnıbüyükler, a master Sufi teacher (*Dede*), and the head of the Konya chapter of the International Mevlana Foundation. As we gathered in front of the open entrance door, the *Dervishes* Gate, Nadir Dede stood there for a moment as if to invite us all to presence, and through a translator, shared a few words about the significance of the space we were about to enter, reminding us the importance of realizing the meaning of this special moment. My jaw dropped when I saw what happened next. Nadir Dede looked down at the design and casually placed his feet on each black line step-by-step, while pointing to and naming each one: "This is the exterior, this is *sharia*, this is *tariqah*, this is *marifat*," he said, naming the stages of arrival through different forms of knowledge toward Truth. Drawing the shape of a square with his pointer fingers in the air, he said: "This pink square here, is the *heart*." Then, he slowly entered the black dot inside the pink square and stood there for a moment to explain further: "This is *nur-u süveyda*, the black dot inside each human heart. This black dot represents *haqiqa*, the Truth." He then looked up toward the entrance and continued to explain: "You see two doors ahead. The first one is *zahiri* (the exterior; the visible outer form, what is apparent from outside), and the other one inside is *batını* (the interior; what is hidden, the meaning that lies beyond appearance). So, we will go in as *zahiri* (in our physical form), and leave as *batını* (as having found our essence and meaning), if God wills."

Nadir Dede's interpretation of the design was through the Sufi lens, a contemplative approach to understanding the religion of Islam for its nuanced meanings, where the progressive stages of attaining knowledge of the Truth requires one to pass through four thresholds that gradually deepen one's understanding: First, through a distant awareness of the knowledge of the Truth as something that is available out there (such as seeing a building from a distance and having a vague idea of what that building is for, without ever having walked into it). Then, the first step is an intentional quest for knowledge that begins with a literal, word-by-word memorization and understanding of the rules (*sharia*). Those with a yearning to know more, can take a few more steps toward the attainment of a qualitative understanding, which is possible with the help of a trusted teacher and community of practitioners, as in an apprenticeship (*tariqah*). Through practice, there is a possibility of opening into a deep experiential realization about the nature of the Object of all knowledge (*marifah*). Once the experiential learning is under the guidance of a teacher and within a community, the concepts and manners are internalized; they become real for the person who experiences them firsthand. This subjective deepening in knowledge through self-realization leads one to develop a personal understanding, and a personally meaningful knowledge of the Truth (*haqiqah*). The Absolute Truth is believed to be held *only* by the human heart, and is considered as a trust of the Divine to humans. The pink square represents this realm of *the heart* (*qalb*) where it is believed that a non-dimensional black speck (*süveyda*) is the point of connection between the visible (*zahiri*) and the invisible (*batını*) realms, where each human heart has a natural and primordial direct access to

## Box 2.1 MAP Experience Set-up

This prototype is illustrative of the possibilities for a MAP experience and can be modified based on the shared-narrative objects at hand at any given museum, which will determine the number of participants who can be accommodated. *Duration:* Minimum 50 minutes to 1 hour. *Participants:* 40.

Requirements for a *set-up for 20 pairs*:

- Large, unobstructed space where the entire group can see and hear each other.
- Pre-arranged seating, including chairs and tables, for 20 pairs.
- 20 similar/identical objects that share the same narrative. (1 object per MAP, to be placed in the central black circle)
- 20 printed MAP placemats. (1 per pair)
- 40 simple wooden tokens. (1 per person)
- 40 pencils. (1 per person)
- 40 sheets of paper with two separate columns to write on. (1 per person)

Single MAP set-up per pair:

- 1 MAP placed on the table between each pair, ensuring that the pointed corners of the rhombus are situated facing the direction of each participant, seated across from each other, as shown in *Figure 2.2*.
- 1 object to be placed atop the central black circle. (1 per MAP)
- 2 simple wooden tokens. (1 per person)
- 2 blank pages, with 2 columns in each for writing. (1 per person)
- 2 small pencils. (1 per person)

The MAP experience comprises multiple stages, each of which is outlined below, along with examples and suggestions for prompts and transitions that facilitators can reference for inspiration, based on the Glencairn Museum experience (Box 2.2).

## Box 2.2 The MAP Experience Step-by-Step Flow

**The Opening** (5 minutes)

**Snapshot:** Welcome, Introduction of the MAP concept, Placement of the object(s). Welcome the group, place a tessera on each MAP, introduce the MAP concept, and request that participants not touch the object.

**Contemplative prompt:** "On this journey, as we progress through each of the thresholds towards the center, I will reveal new information about the object in the middle. As you progress, you will be invited to pay attention to what might be taking place in your mind (thoughts, questions) and your heart (feelings, emotions) at each stage. Like the wings of a bird, the voices of the thinking-mind and the feeling-heart always accompany us on each journey and each encounter. On this journey, you will be invited to take brief notes about what you are witnessing in your thinking mind and feeling heart by using the blank sheets available to you. You will use these impressions later on, when sharing and exchanging notes with your partner."

**Transition prompt:** "Now, let's begin!"

**The Seven Thresholds of the Experience** *(45–50 minutes)*

**Snapshot:** Guide participants through the seven steps of the experience as follows.

**(1) *"The First Impression"*** (1 minute)

Ask participants to place their wooden tokens on the outermost black line.

**Contemplative prompt:** "Consider this as your first impression of the other, in this case, the object in the middle. Please take a moment to look at the object and notice what is emerging in you at this moment? Please note (on the right column): What does the object make you think? (. . .) Now, gently bring your thinking-mind into your feeling-heart, and write (on the left column): What does your heart tell you? Is there anything that you might have noticed about yourself in this encounter?"

**Transition prompt:** "Thank you. Moving on . . . Please move your token to the next threshold (black band) to continue our journey.

**(2) *"The What?"* of the object** (2 minutes)

**Factual prompt:** Offer simple facts about the object's physical properties. "This is a cubical piece of glass mosaic, also called a tessera. Glass is made of sand, soda ash, lime, lead, sodium nitrate, arsenic, feldspar, and borax."

**Contemplative prompt:** Same as in 1.

**Transition prompt:** Same as in 1.

**(3) *"The How?"* of the object** (5 minutes)

Invite participants to take turns to touch and hold the object as you continue to share facts about a human story behind how the object was made.

**Factual Prompt:** "Bryn Athyn glassworks created hundreds of formulas for stained glass windows, but when it was time to start producing opaque glass for mosaics, lead artisan Ariel Gunther asked himself, 'How do we do that?'. The know-how had been lost over time. Eventually, during his research on medieval glass, he unexpectedly stumbled on the answer in an old German manuscript that had a section on stained glass-making —it said: 'In the case of making stained-glass windows, it is best not to heat the furnaces too hot, or the glass turns opaque and looks like stone.' This was the key to solving the mosaic glass formula puzzle. Instead of heating the furnaces to 2000°, as they did for producing translucent window glass, they heated the glass to over 3000° to get the results they were looking for."

**Contemplative prompt:** Same as in 1.

**Transition prompt:** Same as in 1.

**(4) *"The Why?"* of the object** (7 minutes)

As participants continue their tactile encounter with the object, you may choose to draw their attention to an element of the physical surroundings that helps to place the object in a wider context, thereby expanding their consciousness. For example, in the Glencairn Museum, participants were asked to look up at the ornate ceiling designed with thousands of tiny tessera that was originally home to the Pitcairn Family. You will next share facts about the meaning of the object.

**Factual prompt:** "The intricate mosaic designs for the ceiling in the Great Hall were inspired by the *Book of Kells*, a medieval Celtic manuscript produced around 800 CE containing the four New Testament Gospels. The precise reason for Raymond Pitcairn's decision to decorate the ceiling of his home with stars is not known. Pitcairn had admired the famous mosaics of the 5th and 6th century Christian monuments of Ravenna, Italy, and he would have been aware of the mosaic decorations in Sainte-Chapelle, a 13th century royal chapel in Paris, France. He set out to decorate his home with mosaics of similar quality, embedding artistic reflections of his spiritual beliefs and values into the fabric of the building. Pitcairn was pleased with the result. When he specifically referred to the star mosaics on the ceiling, he said: 'The effect of this rich blue ground with the gold stars set off, or framed, by mosaic-covered beams done in rich color is really thrilling.'"

**Contemplative prompt:** Same as in 1.

**Transition prompt:** "Thank you. It's now time to move your token to the Pink Square."

**(5) *"Pause & Share"*** (7 minutes)

In this stage, you invite participants to reflect on the journey thus far, and it is recommended to offer a short-lived experience as an example of a time when your own first impression about an "other" changed over time as you gained more facts and understanding. This will set the stage for participants to share reflections on the MAP experience and prepare the ground for a deeper sharing at the final threshold.

**Contemplative Prompt:** "Please take a moment to pause and reflect on the MAP journey so far, and when you are ready, share with your partner any insights and observations about yourself."

**Transition Prompt:** Before asking participants to move their tokens to the black circle, offer a couple of questions that encapsulate how our experience of "the other" is always subjective. "What was similar and/or different about your individual journeys with the MAP? Have you noticed that even though we are all under the same roof, and all looking at similar objects, prompted by the same facts and questions, yet our individual experiences can be very different?"

**(6) *"The Conscious Removal of the Object"*** (5 minutes)

At this stage, you will draw awareness to the objects being collected from each table and placed in a safe space.

**Transition prompt:** As the objects are collected one by one, you will share a personal story related to the narrative of the central object to prepare ground for the final threshold. For instance, I shared the story of my own meaning-making journey with the MAP symbol, which began as an intellectual curiosity about the design (the object), and then of its historic origins and meaning, and "*now, I find myself here with all of you co-creating a space for deep empathy-building and meaning-making, which to me, transcends any object.*"

7) ***"The Intimate Dialogue"*** (20 minutes)
Ask participants to move their own tokens into the black circle. Pose a question related to the MAP experience that invites deep and vulnerable introspection and aims to bring to the surface the essence of the MAP encounter, which is the realization of our relatedness and shared humanness.
**Contemplative prompt:** "Have you ever been on a journey that seemed to be all about the other (an object, a goal, or another person) in the beginning, but turned out to be a journey into a deeper knowing of yourself and what holds meaning for you?"

**The Conscious Closing** (5 minutes)

**Snapshot:** Invite participants to share with the entire group on a voluntary basis. Conclude with a thoughtful intention for how the experience can be carried forward into everyday life, as well as suggestions for post-experience self-care, as some participants may wish to continue their contemplation quietly while others will want connection.

## Important Considerations

Every step of the MAP experience is deeply intentional. In order to capture and recreate its richness and spirit, I recommend adhering to the integrity of its contemplative aspects, the time allotted regardless of the size of the group, and using objects and a physical space that support reverence, contemplation, and connection.

## Acknowledgments

The author would like to acknowledge that this exercise has been developed within the knowledge and permission of Sufi masters of *Mevlevilik*, a tradition known for its encouragement of artistic expression and creativity. Any shortcomings belong solely to the author.

## Note

**1** K. Helminski, *The Knowing Heart* (Shambhala, 2000), 13.

# 3 Empathy Through Contemplative Practices

## Transcending Self and Other

*Bengü Ergüner-Tekinalp*

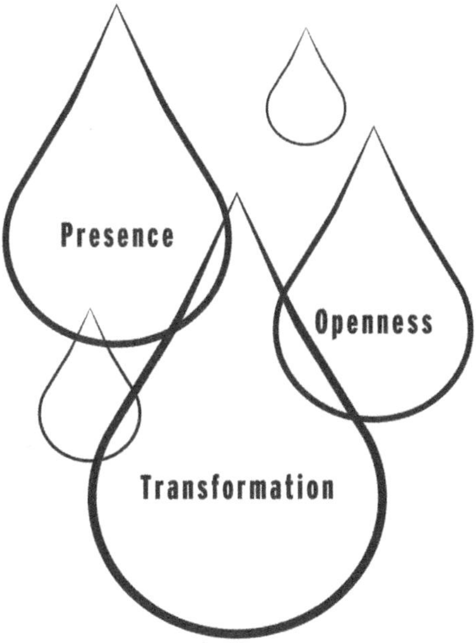


Contemplative practices are awareness-cultivating activities and experiences that integrate reflection, mindfulness, and holistic and embodied self-awareness. Generally, these practices ask people to connect with their thoughts, sensations, body, emotions, and values, fostering immersive, introspective, and personally significant experiences. They emphasize cognitive, emotional, and somatic integration while deepening connections with subjects and others.[1] Although reflective and contemplative learning are used interchangeably, reflection is more of a cognitive process, whereas contemplation is an invitation to contact different parts of the self, including the body, emotions, and soul.[2]

Contemplative practices are used in various fields and are increasingly applied in higher education. As learning spaces, contemplative practices can be a significant part of the museum experience with the goal of a deeper understanding of the self in addition to understanding a work of art. In fact, "in 21st-century museums, a self-directed education is clearly necessary; in order to successfully facilitate one's own museum experience, one must develop a contemplative practice."[3] Contemplative practices are most effective when they integrate the following qualities:

## *Presence*

Contemplation is a process of reflection to focus using various capacities of the mind. It is both a cognitive and spiritual activity; it is a way to connect to our souls, others, the earth, and the cosmos in an embodied way.[4] The context of contemplation is presence, a state of being consciously aware and thus being in alignment with our most profound and highest capacities, a quality of consciously *being here*.[5]

The goal of contemplative practices is to increase one's capacity to focus, develop a more open awareness, and develop inner peace, mindfulness, compassion, empathy, and a deeper connection with self, others, and the world. Through continued contemplative practice, an attitude and responses that are more encompassing, free, and holistic develops.[6] Practices bring wakefulness with a steady mind, open heart, and deep calmness.[7] Contemplative practices involve meditation, mindfulness, journaling, and body-based approaches like yoga, breath-work, contemplative reading, listening, mindful walking, and the like.[8] Contemplation is a meditative state where awareness and listening within are cultivated, and the superficial layers of thought and emotion are subdued with an emerging continuous awareness, which requires a still body and relaxed attention.[9] Contemplation is usually understood in a religious or spiritual context, and therefore, using contemplative practices in secular settings poses the challenge of adapting practices. However, it is essential to note that not all contemplative practices have religious or spiritual roots.[10]

## *Embodied Open Awareness*

Modern times encourage us to interact with the world through analysis and intellectual reasoning, causing us to disconnect from our deeper human experiences. We are conditioned to live as if we are *brains on sticks*, disconnected from the body, unaware of emotions, and having no contact with a deeper part of ourselves one might call a soul. When we participate in contemplative practices that are centered on our interactions, a quieter, more stable mind, embodied awareness, and deeper contact with feelings emerge, and as a result, a more empathic connection may arise. Integration of contemplative practices in higher education demonstrates that contemplative teaching practices enhance deeper social justice awareness, encouraging critical inquiry and social action, awakening to the suffering of not only one's own but of their communities.[11] As learning spaces, a similar justice oriented and empathic awareness can be cultivated in museums.

## *Non-Judgmental Reflection*

Contemplative practices help uncover mental conditioning and ingrained beliefs, allowing one to observe one's inner world without judgment simultaneously experience the outer and the inner.[12] Such nonjudgmental emotional and cognitive space allows compassion and empathy, bringing social justice awareness and exploring differences with curiosity.[13] Human beings are constantly distracted by internal and external stimuli. An example of an internal distraction is mental chatter, which is a persistent inner dialogue and flux of thoughts. Similarly, there exists a "systemic chatter," which refers to broader social narratives that impact attitudes and behaviors unconsciously.[14] Systemic chatter emanates from subtle and widespread societal beliefs, including biases that pose a distraction and a barrier to respond with empathy.[15] Contemplative practices actively foster deep self-reflection, enabling individuals to identify and confront the various influences and become more aware of personal and systemic chatter. Individuals then can engage more authentically with the world leading to significant mental and emotional clarity, which is crucial for empathy. As the mental and systemic chatter becomes clearer and loosens its grip over the mind, there is more room for connection with others empathically and compassionately. Empathy is our ability to imagine what it might feel like to be the other.[16] In contemplative practices, the "other" includes not only humans but also nonhuman species and anything that exists in the world. The true goal of contemplative practice is just like life, joining with insight, compassion, wisdom, and love.[17]

## *Mindful Awareness*

When the learning process allows deep engagement with the material, knowledge is co-created with bodies, minds, and emotions, and curiosity and connection to intuition open, guiding us to uncover and question assumptions that can create distance between ourselves and others.[18] Contemplative practices facilitate developing empathy, which involves suspending immediate judgment, emotional reactivity, and approach with curiosity and willingness to change perspective. Contemplative practices awaken the emotions, and we become more sensitive to our feelings.[19] When individuals are touched by the emotional experience of the other through empathy, grief and anxiety may emerge, and one might want to avoid or start intellectualizing to manage these feelings. Instead, contemplative practices invite individuals to stay with their feelings.[20] Contemplative practices should not be used for numbing our feelings; instead, they can create an opening and opportunity to see the challenges and injustices and engage with difficult experiences deeply and consciously.[21] The outcome of contemplation is not adjusting to stress and injustice but rather is a practice in which people can analyze, resist, and challenge sources of injustice.[22]

## *Purposeful Action*

Contemplation should open the possibility of the next right action, not an avoidance of the pain. Therefore, contemplation is more than being aware and mindful; it is a more profound experience of *heartfulness*, a way of being mindful, compassionate, and responsible with a purpose through connecting to something larger than the individual self, which allows the natural ability to connect deeply through empathy and kindness.[23]

## *Transformation, Interbeing, and Oneness*

When we think of empathy-generating situations, we may immediately create an illusion of us versus the other. The engagement with the *other* can be from (a) for the other (improving the experience of the othered), (b) about the othered, (c) critical of privileging and othering, and (d) changing ourselves and the society that maintains oppression.[24] Although empathy can stem from all of these perspectives, contemplative practices allow a different state, replacing the mindset of "knowing best," "knowing for," and rescuing the other.[25] Instead, through contemplation empathy, shared experiences, vulnerabilities, and wounding can be recognized.[26] With an increased capacity to stay with the difficult, the gap between the self and the other may lessen.

Contemplative practices emphasize "I feel, therefore I can be free."[27] The focus of the experience is invited to the emotional space rather than overemphasizing the intellect. Connecting with our emotions enhances our capacity to empathize and understand others, ultimately leading to action. Empathetic action is crucial and requires full engagement, objectivity, clarity, and active participation. The experience may not be from a state of right or wrong, as Rumi says: "Out beyond right doing and wrongdoing," but a state of compassionate, empathetic awareness of shared human experience.[28]

Empathy requires a sense of intimacy and interconnection with self, others, life, and the world. *Interbeing* is a term popularized by Buddhist Monk Thich Nhat Hanh to express that all things are interconnected, exist in relation to everything else, and nothing is isolated.[29] There is a sense of responsibility toward all existence. This idea is closely related to the Islamic concept of *Tawhid*, The Oneness of All Beings; everything in existence is a manifestation of the Divine. Both *Interbeing* and *Tawhid* emphasize that separateness is an illusion and encourage seeing oneself as part of a larger reality. Contemplative practices bring out engagement from this level of deeper consciousness where "subject-object consciousness disappears and a non-dual form of awareness takes place."[30] Cultural and personal conditioning, reactionary responses, and underlying assumptions can be questioned from which the separation between the self and the other—human, nonhuman, and material—diminishes. A consciousness of experiencing the other as an "other me" or a reflection of me transpires. An example of contemplation bringing a profound attentiveness and a sense of interconnectedness, including with nonhuman beings, was provided by Parker Palmer:

> *Through contemplative practices, we can dissolve the boundaries that separate ourselves from others—be they human, nonhuman, or even the materials around us, such as the one demonstrated by Nobel Prize-winning geneticist Barbara McClintock, who studied genetic transposition and gained valuable knowledge by empathizing with her corn plants, submerging herself in their world and dissolving the boundary between object and observer.*[31]

Through contemplation, one can empathize with the human and all existing phenomena.

## Guidelines for Designing Contemplative Experiences

The term contemplative practice can be misleading as this is more than a series of practices or techniques; contemplative *processes* might be a better term. Contemplation is not a new idea; it is our natural state. When invited, we can "fall into awareness" naturally. When we are aware, a natural state of openness and interconnectedness emerges. It is not something we learn anew but a process we remember. Recommendations listed below can be useful to consider when designing contemplative experiences in museums:

1. Acknowledge the complexity and tension with secularizing some practices and ourselves.
2. Contemplative practices must be presented as invitations with the option to opt-out. A choice among multiple practices should be provided. Be aware of the power dynamics and clearly express voluntary participation.
3. Provide the culture, history, and the context of specific practices to avoid cultural appropriation.
4. Invite setting intentions.
5. Bring embodied awareness, invite attention to the body.
6. Invite holistic awareness, including body, breath, emotions, sensations, and mental and systematic chatter. Carefully consider what is centered in the experience (e.g., thinking or emotions).
7. Remember these practices are connecting with oneself to connect with the "other."
8. Invite a connection to the place one is practicing at the moment.
9. Invite slowing down.
10. Honor silence, meet the externally silent space with an internal silence.
11. Consider reducing the number of experiences/works of art and focus on the depth.

## Facilitating a Contemplative Seeing/Beholding Practice

This practice awakens different ways of seeing: seeing far, seeing close, internal and external, peripheral seeing, seeing differently, imagining, and seeing with the heart.[32] The steps provided below do not have to be done all at once. The facilitator can choose different steps and determine the length of the practice. Make sure the steps you choose bring awareness, holistic experience including the body and emotions, presence, and a sense of interconnection. The concepts related to "Contemplative Seeing/Beholding" can be brought to life by the guidelines presented in (Box 3.1).[33]

### Box 3.1 Guidelines for "Contemplative Seeing/Beholding"

**Presence and Embodied Awareness**

1. Take mindful breaths of which you are fully aware.
2. Leave the day and what came before behind and let go of the preoccupations with what is coming up.
3. Enter with the intention, which is a "clearly formulated aim or wish in words that activate the energy to attain that aim." Set your aim and gather your energy around it.
4. Be fully aware of your body, notice your bodily sensations and tension, and slowly let them go.

**Non-Judgmental Reflection**

1. Choose two works of art, one that you "like" and one that you do not "like" much. Spend at least five minutes on each work. If you choose to spend time only with one work of art, that is okay, too. Try different distances: Getting close, very close, or stepping back and looking from greater distance.
2. Even with the same art, you may have conflicting or ambivalent responses, a part of you might like the art, and a part may dislike. You can invite these conflicting parts into a conversation?

3. Stand in front of the work of art you chose. Spend a moment bringing yourself here and now. Notice your body as you stand. Feel how your legs carry you, how your feet push against the floor, and how you find your balance. Relax all the muscles you do not need to use, such as your facial muscles, your shoulders, or your arms.
4. As you stand before the chosen work, try to spend at least 5 minutes on it. You may be surprised by how long it feels. We usually quickly look at things and move on.
5. Practice being fully aware and fully present in the moment.

## Mindful Awareness

1. As you do the seeing practice, your mind may wander to different places. When you notice this, gently bring your attention back to the work of art. Be present with what you are seeing. Try to avoid judging, analyzing, or labeling what you see. Open your mind to curiosity; you may discover something new.
2. Notice if your patience wanders. If this happens, look at a different part of the work. Try to notice something you have not noticed before. See how light impacts what you see.
3. When images, thoughts, and inner chatter emerge, let go and remind yourself: "I will come back to you later, not now."

## Transformed Relationship

1. Bypass the commenting mind, get outside of yourself and your immediate experience, and bring an observing and witnessing self. What is happening within you? Rather than an awareness that is captured by the chatter, allow a more intentional, comprehensive awareness of the full seeing experience.
2. Can you bring your experience of the object as not a thing to see but from a more relational or deeply touched space? "How is this work of art like me?"
3. Your analytical thinking-mind or reactionary emotions, likes or dislikes, and boredom may kick in. Don't get tangled up by these reactions, let them go. Stay connected to what you are seeing and experiencing.

4. Bring wonder, connect with a sense of "wow," and engage with curiosity. "I wonder . . . " "Wonder can change to reverence when we ponder the force or agency that lies behind the phenomenon beheld. As in the work of art, we recognize the wisdom and beauty . . . "
5. Do not worry about how much or what you should "see." Just see . . . do not look, do not glance but see.
6. Something dies within us every time we change. Sometimes, something must be gone for something new to emerge. Can you make room for a new experience? What needs to die for that to happen?
7. Close your eyes if you feel comfortable and see the image in your mind's eye. Then try with your heart's eye. We experience life through our heads: our head-eyes, head-ears, and head-mouths. Can you rest your head and bring your sensory organs to your heart-space? What would it be like if you saw the work with your *heart-eyes*?
8. Connect with the artist and ask what might have been happening with them while creating the artwork. See the work of art not as a technical analysis but more of a human expression. Can you connect to the artist as a fellow human? Can you relate to the artwork from oneness, dissolving the separateness between you and the work?

**Connecting with Empathy**

When you are done, find a quiet space and reflect. Remember, not all experiences should be expressed with words; silence is an expression too. You may want to write about your experience, or you can express it with your body movement, or you can have clay to shape the experience. As Rumi says: "*However much we describe and explain love, when we fall in love, we are ashamed of our words. Explanation by the tongue makes most things clear but love unexplained is clearer.*" Translated by Nicholson, Rumi, *Mathnawi*, Book I:112.

**Reflection Questions**

What was your initial reaction to the work of art? What did you notice as you kept your focus on the work? What feelings emerge? What did you do about those feelings? Has your relationship with this work changed as you continued the practice? What became clear for you? What shifted, if anything?

In my experience with a similar process of contemplative seeing, both with colleagues in the contemplative learning community I led at my university and with students in my courses, I observed that individuals often spend more time engaging with artworks they initially disliked. Most of the time, through this reflection, they ultimately begin to enjoy the art they initially found unappealing. Contemplation, like empathy-building, is a process that emerges through intentionality, presence, awareness, and practice. When practiced in a museum setting, contemplation can lead individuals to expand their sense of self and their capacity for relatedness to others, including human and nonhuman life, as well as the material world we live in.

## Notes

**1** Greta Gaard and Bengü Ergüner-Tekinalp, *Contemplative Practices and Anti-Oppressive Pedagogies for Higher Education: Bridging the Disciplines* (Routledge, 2022), 3–16.

**2** Beth Berila, *Integrating Mindfulness into Anti-Oppression Pedagogy: Social Justice in Higher Education* (Routledge, 2016), 44; Marie Eaton, Kate Davies, Sarah Williams, and Jean MacGregor, "Why Sustainability Education Needs Pedagogies of Reflection and Contemplation," in *Contemplative Approaches to Sustainability in Higher Education: Theory and Practice*, ed. Marie Eaton, Holly J. Hughes, and Jean MacGregor (Routledge, 2017), 3–15.

**3** Meghan S. Estep, "Contemplative Practices in the Museum Setting" (Master's thesis, Corcoran College of Art and Design, 2012), 10.

**4** Kabir Helminski, *The Book of Language: Exploring the Spiritual Vocabulary of Islam* (The Book Foundation, 2006), 126; John P. Miller, *The Contemplative Practitioner: Meditation in Education and the Workplace*, 2nd ed. (University of Toronto Press, 2014), 3.

**5** Helminski, *The Book of Language*, 139.

**6** Rhonda V. Magee, *The Inner Work of Racial Justice: Healing Ourselves and Transforming Our Communities through Mindfulness* (TarcherPerigee, 2019), 17.

**7** Arthur Zajonc, *Meditation as Contemplative Inquiry: When Knowing Becomes Love* (Lindisfarne Books, 2009), 10.

**8** Daniel P. Barbezat and Mirabai Bush, *Contemplative Practices in Higher Education: Powerful Methods to Transform Teaching and Learning* (Jossey-Bass, 2014), 5; Gaard and Ergüner-Tekinalp, *Contemplative Practices and Anti-Oppressive Pedagogies*, 3.

**9** Helminski, *The Book of Language*, 126.

**10** Gaard and Ergüner-Tekinalp, *Contemplative Practices and Anti-Oppressive Pedagogies*, 7.

**11** Barbezat and Bush, *Contemplative Practices in Higher Education*, 5; Zajonc, *Meditation as Contemplative Inquiry*, 11.

**12** Gaard and Ergüner-Tekinalp, *Contemplative Practices and Anti-Oppressive Pedagogies*, 9; Zajonc, *Meditation as Contemplative Inquiry*, 109.

**13** Berila, *Integrating Mindfulness into Anti-Oppression Pedagogy*, 19; David Forbes, *Mindfulness and Its Discontents: Education, Self, and Social Transformation* (Fernwood Publishing, 2019), 180; Ruth King, *Mindful of Race: Transforming Racism from the Inside Out* (Sounds True, 2018); Magee, *The Inner Work of Racial Justice*, 17.

**14** Berila, *Integrating Mindfulness into Anti-Oppression Pedagogy*, 20; Diane Prevatt-Hyles, "LPI's Life Source Mapping: 7 'E's of Liberation and Spirituality" (conference presentation, First North American Conference on Spirituality and Social Work, Renison College, University of Waterloo, Ontario, May 25, 2006), https://www.spiritualityandsocialwork.ca/2006.html.

**15** Janelle Adsit, "Pursuing Antiracist and Anticolonial Approaches to Contemplative Practices," in *Contemplative Practices and Anti-Oppressive Pedagogies for Higher Education: Bridging the Disciplines*, ed. Greta Gaard and Bengü Ergüner-Tekinalp (Routledge, 2022), 17–32.

**16** Elif Gökçiğdem, *An Empathy-Building Toolkit for Museums* (American Alliance of Museums and Bloomsbury, in press).

**17** Zajonc, *Meditation as Contemplative Inquiry*, 13.

**18** Adsit, "Pursuing Antiracist and Anticolonial Approaches to Contemplative Practices," in *Contemplative Practices and Anti-Oppressive Pedagogies*, 26.

**19** Zajonc, *Meditation as Contemplative Inquiry*, 74.

**20** Jennifer Atkinson, "Eco-Grief and Climate Anxiety in the Classroom," in *Contemplative Practices and Anti-Oppressive Pedagogies for Higher Education: Bridging the Disciplines*, ed. Greta Gaard and Bengü Ergüner-Tekinalp (Routledge, 2022), 35–51.

**21** Gaard and Ergüner-Tekinalp, *Contemplative Practices and Anti-Oppressive Pedagogies*, 9.

**22** Forbes, *Mindfulness and Its Discontents*, 180.

**23** Stephen Murphy-Shigematsu, *From Mindfulness to Heartfulness: Transforming Self and Society with Compassion* (Berrett-Koehler Publishers, 2018), 14; David J. Voelker, "Inner Tracking: A Reflective Practice for Transformative Learning," in *Contemplative Practices and Anti-Oppressive Pedagogies for Higher Education:*

*Bridging the Disciplines,* ed. Greta Gaard and Bengü Ergüner-Tekinalp (Routledge, 2022), 115–30.

**24** Kevin K. Kumashiro, "Toward a Theory of Anti-Oppressive Education," *Review of Educational Research* 70, no. 1 (2000): 25–53.

**25** Adsit, "Pursuing Antiracist and Anticolonial Approaches to Contemplative Practices," in *Contemplative Practices and Anti-Oppressive Pedagogies,* 24.

**26** Gaard and Ergüner-Tekinalp, *Contemplative Practices and Anti-Oppressive Pedagogies*, 9.

**27** Audre Lorde, *Sister Outsider: Essays and Speeches* (Crossing Press, 1984), 38.

**28** Zajonc, *Meditation as Contemplative Inquiry*, 38.

**29** Thich Nhat Hanh, *Interbeing, 4th Edition: The 14 Mindfulness Trainings of Engaged Buddhism* (Parallax Press, 2020), 3–4.

**30** Zajonc, *Meditation as Contemplative Inquiry*, 57.

**31** Parker J. Palmer, *The Courage to Teach*, 20th ed. (Jossey-Bass, 2017), 46.

**32** David Barry and Simon Meisiek, "Seeing More and Seeing Differently: Sensemaking, Mindfulness, and the Workarts," *Organization Studies* 31, no. 11 (2010): 1505–30, https://doi.org/10.1177/0170840610380802.

**33** Helminski, *The Mysterion: Rumi and the Secret of Becoming Fully Human* (Shambhala, 2023), 238; Zajonc, *Meditation as Contemplative Inquiry*, 10, 39, 57.

# 4 Building Empathy Through Art-Inspired Meditation

*Aparna Sadananda*

*Donna Jonte*

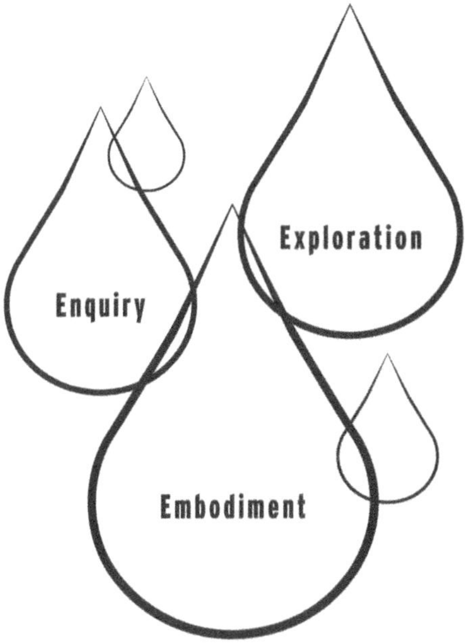


Guided meditation at The Phillips Collection is a virtual program integrating visual art and meditation. Designed by Aparna Sadananda, a yoga teacher, and Donna Jonte, a museum educator, meditating is informed by art, and responding to art is informed by meditation. Following a 30-minute guided meditation, the online community reflects on the practice and poses questions about the artwork that were sparked by the meditation. The museum educator then presents a spotlight talk on the artwork, using some of the techniques practiced during meditation: looking closely and posing questions, as well as weaving in contextual information, thereby inviting participants to wonder, connect, and find complexity.

These guided meditations promote mindfulness skills through engagement with the formal and thematic qualities of art, helping participants see self and others from a place of presence, embodiment, and empathy. Additionally, practitioners may take the meditation outside the Zoom room, finding a way to perceive everyday objects as prompts for bringing nonjudgmental awareness to complex as well as quotidian moments. In this chapter, we will describe the origins of this program and introduce yoga-based practices such as Square Breathing and Panchakosha meditation in response to *Spandana* (Figure 4.1), an artwork created by Aparna Sadananda. These examples enumerate the typical ingredients of the weekly meditation and its scope as a tool for building empathy in museum spaces and beyond.

The Phillips Collection in Washington, DC is uniquely positioned to present art-based meditation as one of its signature public programs. The weekly, guided meditation reflects Duncan Phillips' belief in the profound connections between art and wellness. In 1921, he opened his home as a museum in direct response to another pandemic. He lost his brother James to influenza in 1918. The brothers had lost their father unexpectedly the year before to a heart ailment. In his sorrow, Duncan Phillips said that he turned to his love of art for the will to live. In opening his Dupont Circle home as The Phillips Memorial Gallery, he found "a constructive social purpose," intending art to bring solace to others as it had to him. He described his vision: "And I saw a chance to create a beneficent force in the community where I live—a joy-giving, life-enhancing influence, assisting people to see beautifully as true artists see." He wanted the museum to be a contemplative space, an intimate space where visitors would feel welcome and at home. Today the mission statement emphasizes the power of art and its connection to empathy:

> *The Phillips Collection is America's first home for modern and contemporary art, where the intimate and experimental meet. Through art, every visitor can explore the most pressing ideas of our time via dynamic collaborations, innovative inquiry, empathetic forms of public participation, and diverse voices.*[1]

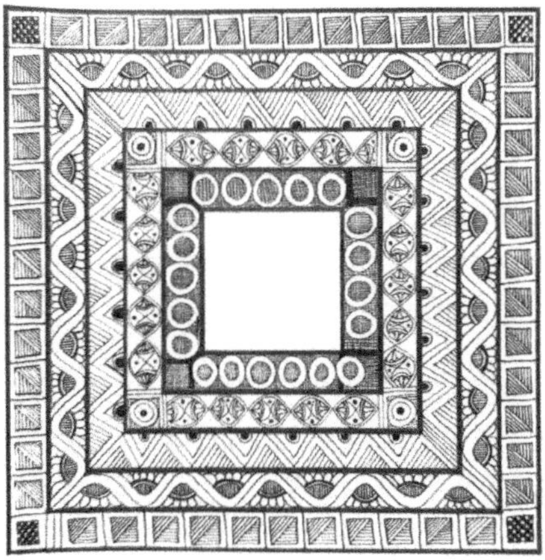

**Figure 4.1** *Spandana.* Artwork by Aparna Sadananda. Credit: Courtesy of Dr. Aparna Sadananda.

Duncan Phillips' empathetic mission shapes our meditation program: It is designed to be joy-giving, life enhancing, and empathy-building. Through guided meditation and facilitated conversation, participants can build and belong to a community, engaging cognitively and emotionally with the meditation prompts, and connecting to the stories in the artwork, in the lives of the artists, in their own lives and those of their peers. Duncan Phillips believed that "Artists speak not only for themselves but for those of us who are intensely interested in other ways of seeing than our own."[2] Meditation offers a way to assume different perspectives, to "see differently."

## Square Breathing and *Spandana*

Our first example focuses on square breathing in response to *Spandana*, a Madhubani-inspired artwork composed of intricately detailed concentric squares created by Aparna Sadananda (Figure 4.1). In the virtual meditation program, we have used artworks that rely on a similar design of concentric squares for their compositional unity, like Joseph Albers' *Homage to the Square* or a Gee's Bend quilt like Malissia Pettway's *Housetop.*

As we prepare for square breathing, we will first find a posture of stillness and take a few deep breaths. Visualize that you are breathing in energy and breathing out peace. When your attention feels centered, open your eyes to gaze at *Spandana*.

Fix your gaze at the central empty square and then try to see the concentric square patterns. What did you notice? Does the artwork remain two-dimensional, or do you see it assuming a three-dimensional shape, funneling your gaze in toward the paper? Focusing the gaze is a *hatha yoga* practice called *trataka*, generally practiced by gazing at the flame of a candle or lamp. It can help to cultivate mental clarity and alleviate eye strain by cleansing the tear glands and strengthening the eye muscles.

Next, let's focus on the innermost blank square. Inhale as your eyes trace one edge of the square and exhale as you trace through the adjacent edge. Then, visually trace the third edge on the next inhale and the fourth on the subsequent exhale, thereby tracing the square's perimeter on every pair of breaths. In Sanskrit, this practice of square breathing is called *Samavritti*, where the inhales and exhales are equalized. It is said to be centering and calming. When you feel that you can breathe more deeply, move your attention to the next larger square, repeating this exploration until you identify the square whose side length aligns with the depth of your breath. Spend some time practicing *Samavritti* in response to this square. When your breath expands, you can shift your attention to the next square, repeating the practice until you reach the outermost square.

Now let's breathe starting from the largest to the smallest square and then square breathing from inside out, as if you are weaving a quilt with your breaths. Imagine this quilt of breaths wrapping around your body. How does it feel to be draped in the warmth and life-giving energy of your own breath? Now, completely let go of all these efforts and visualizations. What bodily sensations do you notice? How does this practice shift your awareness of your presence? How does it feel to interact with art in this way?

Next, let's focus on the designs in each square of *Spandana*, beginning with the largest square filled with the repeating square-shaped motif. The square shape represents the element of earth across many cultures as it is one of the most stable structures. In your present mind-body, how do you relate to the various aspects of stability such as structure, rootedness, support, belonging? Then shift your attention to the next inner square filled with wave-like floral patterns, representing the element of water. What are some of the fluidic aspects of your being that facilitate creativity? Where could you bring more ease into your body and life today? What is the nature of your breath?

Moving inwards, we notice triangular motifs representing the element of fire. Let's observe one major emotion that dominates our present state of mind. Can we identify this with a specific word? Where in the body do we feel the impressions of this emotion? Let's observe this space in the context of the whole body to recognize that there is much more to us than this one impression. Stay with this awareness for a few minutes. How did the emotion transform, if it did, and what new emotions reside in its place?

The next inner square is filled with leaf-shaped designs denoting the element of air. The outlines of these motifs are formed by wavy lines, like sound waves that need air to travel. Placing a hand on your heart, notice the wave-like movement in response to the breath. What sounds do you hear? And, what is the feeling hidden within the sound of your breath?

Shift your attention to the next inner square filled with circular motifs. Across many cultures, the circle represents the element of sky/ether/heaven. Visually, observe the empty space in your immediate surroundings and then close your eyes, sensing this spaciousness. Notice the small space of silence between successive breaths.

## *Panchakosha* Meditation and *Spandana*

This practice of guiding our attention through the details of the *Spandana* squares facilitates an awareness of the *Panchakoshas*; hence we call it the *Panchakosha Meditation*. In Sanskrit, the word *Pancha* means five and *kosha* means sheaths. *Panchakosha* translates to the five sheaths. In fact, the design of the artwork *Spandana* is inspired by the *Panchakosha* model of health (Figure 4.2) that informs the healing modalities of yoga therapy. The five sheaths, from the most tangible to the most subtle, are described below:

*Annamaya kosha*: The physical body, made from the food it consumes, has solidity, which makes it comparable to the element of earth.

*Pranamaya kosha*: The energy body, primarily composed of the breath, has energy's fluidic quality, and is likened to the element of water.

*Manomaya kosha*: The psycho-emotional body, with emotions, like fire, can transform our perception of reality.

*Vignyanamaya kosha*: The wisdom body, referring to reasoning and discernment, can help us transcend emotions and see things as they

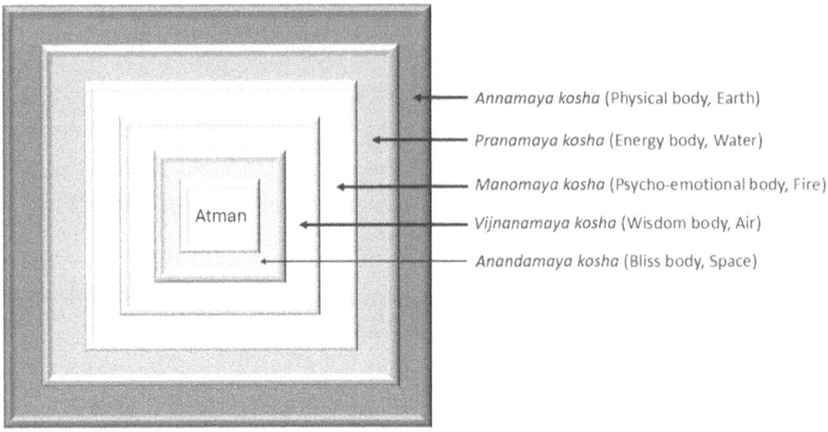


**Figure 4.2** The *Panchakosha* (five sheaths) model. Illustrated by Aparna Sadananda. Credit: Courtesy of Dr. Aparna Sadananda.

are. Since air and vibration are considered to be the earlier stages of manifestation, the element of air is attributed to this *kosha*.

*Anandamaya kosha*: The blissful body that refers to a state of being and witnessing, is like a drop of water on a lotus leaf. The ease and spaciousness of such an existential state is symbolic of space/ether. After all, to manifest anything, we must first create space. Hidden behind these layers is the *Atman*, the soul or consciousness.

The *Panchakosha* model reflects the cosmological view of manifestation of the individuated consciousness, as prescribed in Vedanta, gnostic texts called *Upanishads*. As we meditate from the *Atman* to the *Annamaya kosha*, we are essentially meditating on the process of manifestation. And, when we proceed in the reverse order, it is a contemplation on dissolution. Since all of creation is in this pulsation between manifestation and dissolution, it is called *Spandana* (pulsation). The artwork we have chosen for the guided meditation in this chapter thus offers a visual map to contemplate this pulsation and hence is named *Spandana*.

## Empathy Leading to Oneness within the Context of Yoga

The practice of meditation is prescribed as one of the eight limbs of yoga by the sage Patanjali in the Yoga Sutras. It is called *dhyana* and refers to a seamless flow of cognition between the meditator and the subject of their meditation with the eventual goal of *samadhi* or "the union of the two." Empathy is defined as the ability to assume another's perspective, to understand, feel, and possibly share or respond to their experience. In these definitions, we can see how the practice of meditation and empathy is rooted in the same foundational idea of yoking the self to the other. In fact, it is interesting to note that many of the yoga poses (*asanas*) such as *kakasana* (crow pose), *adho mukha shvanasana* (downward-facing dog), and so on are named after and mimic the body shapes of different animals. This inspires a yogi to wonder if the postural practice of yoga could actually be an invitation to cultivate somatic empathy.

The Yoga Sutras of Patanjali describe *Atman* as *Purusha*, the seer who cannot be seen but without whom seeing cannot happen. The practice of yoga's eight limbs, including meditation, is essentially to know and therefore be in the awareness of the *Atman* experiencing its infinite dimensions through the finite phenomenological experiences, interactions, and responses of the *Panchakoshas*. When this perspective is acknowledged through practices such as this guided, art-inspired *Panchakosha Meditation*, it has the potential to help us realize the *oneness in all creation* that may not necessarily be the sameness. That is, despite the external (physical, mental, and emotional) diversity, all creation is centered in the *Atman*. This idea of *unity* being the *Absolute Truth* and all separation being an illusion is further supported by some of the *mahavakyas* or great sayings of the Vedantic philosophy, from which the concept of *Panchakosha* is derived. For example, the *Brihadaranyaka Upanishad* states: "*Aham Brahmasmi*" "I am *Brahman*"; and, the *Mandukya Upanishad* states: "*Ayam Atma Brahma*" "This self is *Brahman.*" Here, the word *Brahman* refers to the *cosmic consciousness*. These sayings further support the notion of mapping the *Atman* to the *Brahman*. Conversely, that which is out there is also within. By urging us to see the other within the self, these perspectives could help release our attachments and aversions, fostering equanimity. They also elucidate the scope of meditations that are themed on yoga philosophy and inspired by art in facilitating compassionate, cognitive, and communal empathy.

In the square-breathing meditations, we have found that a Gee's Bend quilt with a housetop pattern encourages an empathetic response. The artwork is familiar; we recognize it as a handmade, functional quilt that offers comfort and warmth and as an object with a specific history, a story. By spending time with the quilt, noticing the stitching, worn fabric, stains, and innovative composition, we can enter imaginatively and empathically into the world of the artist and the object. With this empathy, we can honor the resilience, resourcefulness, and creativity of the Gee's Bend quilters, whose work was created in hardship and poverty. Mary Lee Bendolph's *Housetop Variation* is among the five Gee's Bend quilts in the Phillips Collection. Bendolph describes the story embodied in her quilts: "Old clothes have a spirit in them. They also have love. When I make a quilt, that's what I want it to have too, the love and the spirit of the clothes and the people who wore it."[3]

We often follow the square-breathing meditation with one centered on *Panchakosha*. To make this abstract idea concrete, we have selected Leo Villareal's *Scramble* (2011) as inspiration. Villareal's light sculpture mirrors the layered complexity of *Panchakosha* and the metaphor of unity in diversity. Each five-foot square of colorful concentric squares is composed of LEDs that, controlled by custom software, move fluidly, non-repeating, fusing into another display of concentric squares.

Villareal welcomes challenge and complexity through technological innovation. His artwork illuminates our physical worlds, both interior and exterior, as well as providing metaphors for our emotional landscapes. Inside museums, he creates site-specific installations that respond to the building's architecture. For instance, The National Gallery of Art's *Multiverse* (2008) connects the East and West Buildings. Other works converse with the natural world, embracing surprise, like the reflections on moving water, as in *The Bay Lights* (2013) on the San Francisco Bay Bridge and *Illuminated River* (2019) on the London bridges. *Scramble* at the Phillips winks at past experiments in the art world, as we see in its referential title, naming Merce Cunningham and Frank Stella's 1967 avant-garde collaboration, which embodied color, shape, movement, and music. Stella designed the set for Cunningham's dance *Scramble*, stretching brightly colored cloth over lightweight rectangular, wheeled frames. Dancers moved the frames across the stage in a blur of color—purple, blue, red, green, yellow, and orange. Stella later created his self-referential *Scramble* paintings and prints based on these set designs. And, Villareal conceived of his LED-based, computer-generated *Scramble* after a 2011 symposium at the Phillips during which he conversed with Stella.[4]

Collaborating with a mindfulness teacher has benefited the museum, expanding its audience and bringing rigor to the museum's art and wellness programming. For instance, the Phillips now pairs meditation with art in teacher workshops, school tours, after-school activities, and public programs. In the weekly meditation series, we have partnered with the Curatorial Department during special exhibitions, inviting curators or artists to present the spotlight talks, highlighting the meditative process of art-making. Here are just a few of the programs that include guided, art-based meditation:

- *Nature, Spirit, Art* investigated art from the lens of eco-consciousness. This six-week, onsite course was developed by a university art-history professor and a Unitarian minister in partnership with a mindfulness teacher and a museum educator.
- *Reframing Care,* a series of workshops for care partners and their loved ones living with memory loss, which combines gallery experiences, meditation, and art-making.
- *Meditation + Art:* Workshops for survivors of domestic abuse during Marta Perez Garcia's Intersections exhibition, *Restos/Traces.*
- *Mindful Vibes,* weekly yoga and art for middle-school girls.
- Weekly yoga for the museum staff.

We have found the "alchemy of empathy" in art-based meditation: It can ground us in the present moment through contemplation and attention to the breath.[5] The Phillips' weekly meditation began in early March 2019 as an onsite program with eight attendees. It pivoted to an online platform a few months later, during the Covid pandemic. Now averaging sixty participants each week, most of whom have been attending steadily for at least one year, the program helps participants discover and practice techniques for mindful looking, thinking, and being that we can carry with us wherever we are. These techniques—mindful breathing, slowing down, feeling connected to the natural world and to each other—may help us empathetically identify with the other as well as recognize *"the interconnectedness and the oneness of being."*[6]

## Notes

**1** The Phillips Collection's mission statement: https://www.phillipscollection.org/about.

**2** Duncan Phillips, *A Collection in the Making* (1926). Reprinted in *A Collection in the Making: The Eye of Duncan Phillips,* edited by Erika D. Passantino, in connection with *Renoir to Rothko: The Eye of Duncan Phillips* (September 25, 1999–January 23, 2000).

**3** For more information on Gee's Bend quilts, visit: https://www.soulsgrowndeep.org/artist/malissia-pettway/work/housetop; and, https://vasari21.com/ripe-for-rediscovery-mary-lee-bendolph/.

**4** For more information on *Scramble*, 1967, and Villareal's light sculptures visit: https://www.mercecunningham.org/the-work/choreography/scramble/; and, https://www.phillipscollection.org/collection/scramble.

**5** Elif M. Gökçiğdem, *Designing for Empathy: Perspectives on the Museum Experience* (American Alliance of Museums, 2019), xviii.

**6** E. Gökçiğdem, *Designing for Empathy*, xv–xx; Gökçiğdem, *Fostering Empathy Through Museums* (Rowman and Littlefield, 2016), xix–xxx.

# 5 Designing for Emotions

## The Mandala Lab at The Rubin Museum

*Jamie Lawyer*

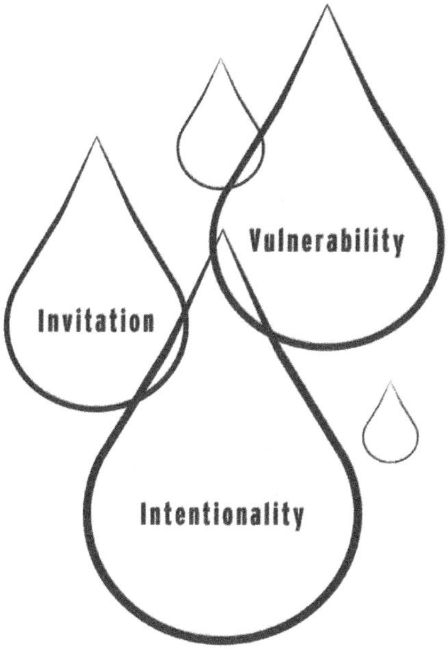


Every museum experience, regardless of subject matter, should care for the emotional dimensions of audiences. As museum workers, we should ask not only what we want audiences to understand but how we want them to feel. Building more empathetic museums means using emotional intelligence in the design process to facilitate emotional responses in audiences. If we design for these emotional needs, we can create more integrated exhibitions and museums where audiences can both learn and feel.

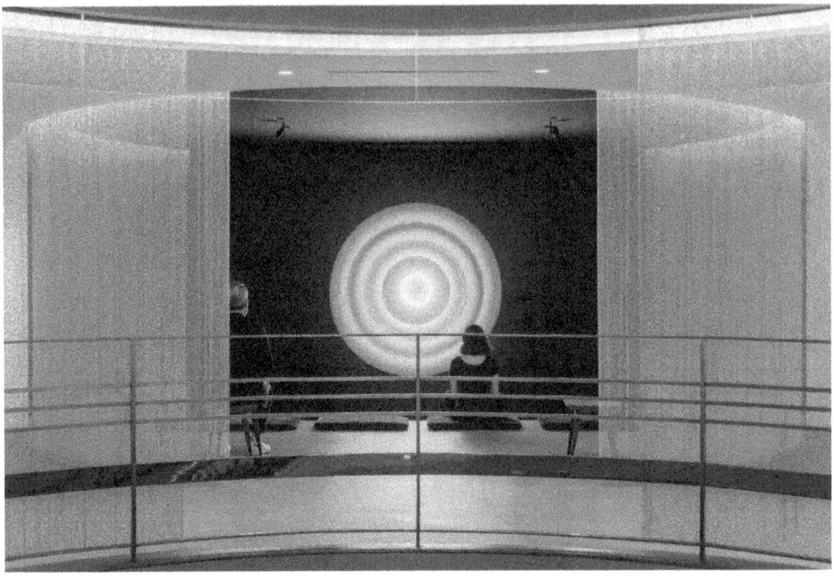

**Figure 5.1** The Rubin Museum of Himalayan Art's Mandala Lab installation features a breathing alcove where visitors are invited to breathe in and out to the rise and fall of light radiating from a sculpture by artist Palden Weinreb. Credit: Photo by Rafael Gamo. Courtesy of the Rubin Museum of Himalayan Art/Peterson Rich Office.

This chapter will discuss the Rubin Museum of Himalayan Art and its participatory exhibition *The Mandala Lab,* created for its New York City presentation as a case study (Figure 5.1). It will describe the exhibition development process and present key learnings on designing for emotions. In this project, I served as co-creator and led interpretive strategies and content development, facilitated experimental workshops, and trained staff. The learnings from this project have broader applications for museum professionals and leaders who aspire to create museum environments with emotionally driven outcomes.

## About The Mandala Lab

*The Mandala Lab,* which opened in October 2021, was inspired by a seventeenth-century painting of a Tibetan Buddhist mandala from the Rubin Museum's collection. Mandalas are diagrammatic representations of deities' abodes and are used as aids in religious practices. This particular mandala depicts a central figure, Buddha Vairochana, who is surrounded by four other deities. Symbolism associated with each deity influenced the exhibition design and content.

While mandalas have many purposes, one such use centers on navigating afflictive emotions that impede the path to enlightenment. These afflictive emotions—represented by inner sections of the mandala—are pride, attachment, envy, anger, and ignorance. Each of these emotions has an accompanying wisdom to be learned, necessary to reach the ultimate goal of Buddhist practice: Enlightenment.

We designed *The Mandala Lab* to mirror these five aspects of the mandala. Each section is organized around an individual emotion and its accompanying piece of wisdom, and audiences are provided with interactive exercises to deepen their understanding of these feelings in their own lives. To bring the space to life, our museum staff collaborated with artists to devise a mix of analog and digital experiences.

The five experiences of *The Mandala Lab* are:

*Pride*: Audiences drop tokens in tubes while looking at themselves in a mirror. They are asked to contemplate which type(s) of pride shows up in their lives. Short statements appear above the tubes highlighting themes of arrogance, entitlement, low self-esteem, and gloating, which are inspired by the Buddhist understanding of pride as an overly self-centered view of the world that should be called into balance and seen free of judgment.

*Attachment*: Six touch-screen interactives appear, and audiences can smell scents, identify the emotions they attach to those scents, see how others respond to the same stimuli, and watch videos created by the contemporary artists who selected the scents. As the artists tell stories associated with scents, audiences are invited to contribute their own scent stories.

*Envy*: Audiences sit before a circular sculptural work pulsing with an 11-second light cycle and are asked to synchronize their breathing with the light and with one another while contemplating envy and its accompanying wisdom.

*Anger*: In one of the most popular experiences, eight gongs selected by musicians hang over a 20-foot aquarium filled with water. Visitors ring the gongs using a mallet and lower the gong into the water to hear the sound fade, imagining anger transforming and exercising patience as the water returns to stillness once the gong is submerged.

*Ignorance*: In the final experience, audiences contemplate ignorance by continuing to learn. They read a synthesized version of the material presented and are given a personal quote on screen. Quotes include wisdom shared by Buddhist teachers, musicians, famous luminaries, movie quotes, and other visitors. Inspired by the teacher-student relationship that is a part of the mandala practice, visitors can also submit a teaching about an emotion to be featured; in this way, a community of teachers and learners is formed.

## Designing for Emotions

*The Mandala Lab* is the result of a meaningful design process that can be replicated by other organizations interested in serving both the hearts *and* the minds of their public. The project team's process included some of the steps below that may be useful to your process:

- *Define the function of your space*: At the end of 2019, the Rubin Museum set out to create a multipurpose space on its third floor that would house educational programming during select times and serve audiences when programs were not on view. This type of multifunctional space presented a specific design challenge that *The Mandala Lab* addressed.
- *Clarify the project team*: The Museum didn't follow its usual curatorial-led process to design this installation. Project leads emerged from the Programming and Partnership Department and the newly formed Visitor Experience & Interpretation Department (established in January 2020). This new team structure was specifically designed to fit the project and was accompanied by a range of individuals including designers, marketing and communication teams, operations, collections management, and more.
- *Bring in outside voices*: When designing *The Mandala Lab*, we brought together experts from different disciplines to shape the installation. Olfaction experts, neuroscientists, psychologists, artists, musicians, and Buddhist practitioners, scholars, and teachers were consulted.

- *Empathize with your audience*: The *Mandala Lab* team adopted the design thinking tool of empathy mapping to imagine visitors' experiences of the exhibit. We considered what a visitor might see, do, hear, think, feel, gain, and fear—before, during, and after their visit. The results of this exercise influenced color choices, wayfinding, language, programming, and even staff training. This process also created a safe space for team members to ask questions and share their perspectives. If you aim to create an emotionally fulfilling experience for your audience, your design process should allow staff members to engage emotionally with the subject matter, too.
- *Let duration factor into decisions*: *The Mandala Lab* was a long-term investment and needed to serve audiences for five years minimum. This necessitated sustainability in materials, design, and maintenance. Given the timeframe for this project, we also considered that audiences might revisit the space with new life experiences or different emotional states. Would the content and experience design adapt to them?
- *Align with broader museum offerings*: This installation needed to complement other permanent and rotating exhibition galleries, as well as the Education Department's new pedagogical approach focused on Social, Emotional, and Ethical Learning.
- *Gather audience feedback*: It can be easy to overlook the importance of one-off comments shared from audiences, but over time, we noticed patterns. Visitors repeatedly shared statements such as, "I felt my blood pressure lower" and, "I needed to come in today to sit in the Shrine room (after a tragic global event)." Rubin audiences were providing feedback that pointed to how the Museum and its offerings impacted their well-being. Additionally, they indicated that they used the space for reflection, awareness, and increased self-understanding. These anecdotal trends were later affirmed through formal audience research on psychographic motivations of audiences. We used these outcomes to inform the exhibition content and design.
- *Let the past inform the future:* Unexpected audience behavior from past exhibitions informed how we conceptualized *The Mandala Lab*. For example, after the Rubin expanded its installation of its *Tibetan Buddhist Shrine Room* in 2016, visitors began to repeatedly visit the exhibition, making it a regular habit. We asked ourselves how

*The Mandala Lab* could similarly become a habit. By continuously observing audience behavior, you can identify positive outcomes—even those that are not intentional—and find ways to design for those same outcomes in the future.

- *Operationalize informal learning opportunities*: With my oversight of Visitor experience roles and interpretation, I created standard operating processes that allowed this valuable feedback to be shared more broadly across the institution and archived for the future. This meant feedback from the points above could more easily be referenced and later applied.
- *Ask the question: How can you be of service to your audiences?* Do you know your visitors? What are their expectations? As the Rubin was deciding what the topic and focus for the new installation should be, the Covid-19 pandemic struck and the world changed. New research from La Placa Cohen's *Culture Track* study in 2020 titled *Communities in Times of Crisis* revealed new audience needs and expectations from cultural institutions. Connection, safety, and decompression were top of mind. *The Mandala Lab* chose to respond to these undeniable audience needs. Service was top of mind for all of the Rubin's offerings.
- *Design for skeptics*: Let's face it: The world is filled with skeptics, and not everyone wants to talk about emotions. If we spend all of our time designing for one specific outcome, we can forget to serve skeptics and take their needs into account. Knowing this, it was important that *The Mandala Lab* be able to support a visitor who might be skeptical or even apprehensive about experiencing it. Designing for emotional outcomes should allow for the full spectrum of engagement with the subject. It is important that exhibition creators respect the variety of responses from audiences and challenge ourselves to consider if it might be possible to move a skeptic along the spectrum of awareness and participation.
- *Know your limits*: Designing for emotional awareness starts with recognizing your limits as a cultural institution. The Museum could not promise emotional transformation, but it could support audiences in becoming more aware of their emotions. Every design element was

meant to facilitate emotional awareness: text, interactivity, graphics, participatory moments, wayfinding, seating, and more.

- *Understand what it takes to be vulnerable*: Museum creators and professionals cannot assume audiences are comfortable, ready, willing, or able to share or partake in the experiences we design. At its core, *The Mandala Lab* asked audiences to be vulnerable. Brene Brown's book *Daring Greatly*, which explores the power of vulnerability and the courage that is required to be vulnerable, informed text design, language, and interactive design. The end result created designed elements that functioned as *invitations* for our audiences to engage in the subject matter at a level that felt appropriate to them (Figure 5.2). This ensured visitors could be their own guides by building choice into each moment on the floor. The Mandala Lab invites visitors to imagine their anger, gently strike a gong, and lower it into the water. As the sound fades and the water stills, visitors listen to their anger transform.

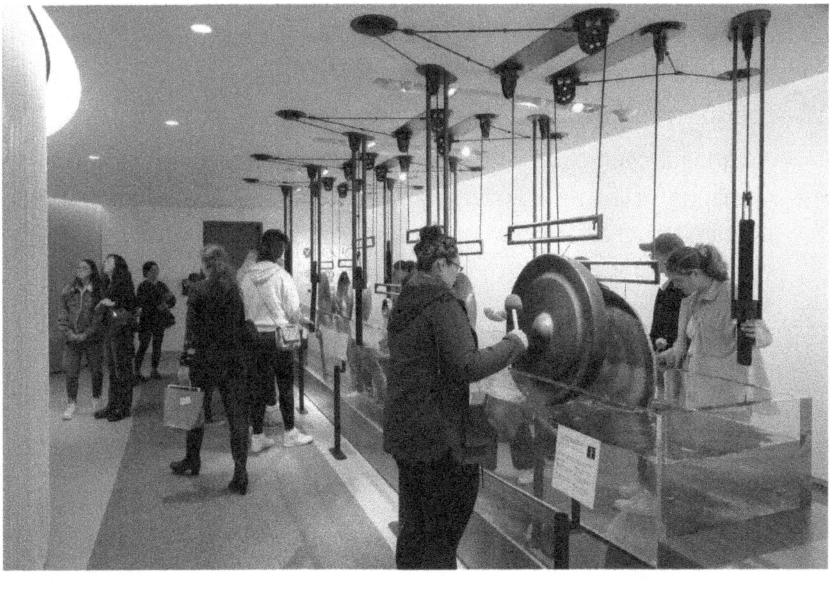

**Figure 5.2** Photography by Filip Wolak. Courtesy of the Rubin Museum of Himalayan Art.

## Lessons Learned

- *Give your planning phase more time*: Designing for emotions takes time. For *The Mandala* Lab, we spent almost a year in the concept development phase before anything was built. This process allowed for flexibility, consulting with others, testing ideas, internal alignment, and finding new ways of working with one another.
- *Design for emotion-based outcomes*: Regardless of the exhibition topic or theme, include an emotional outcome as one of your goals. This influences content development, exhibition design, and can complement other intellectual outcomes for the experience.
- *Consider points of view from different disciplines and experts*: With each project, what expertise would be beneficial to complement understanding of the subject matter? Are there out-of-the-box thinkers who might help your museum staff reconsider old stories or break open new angles?
- *Be willing to work in new ways*: If we want different outcomes for our projects, we need to be willing to try to approach our work in new ways. What experiments can you conduct with your teams? Are there low-stakes activities that might bring new ideas, approaches, or perspectives to the work?
- *Define your anti-goals*: As part of the process of reaching clarity on exhibition purpose, key messages, and outcomes, we take time as a team to get clear on what we *don't* want. This exercise can help you understand the position of each member of your team as well as see where you may not be aligned. Often, individuals know what they *don't* want before they know what they *do* want, so doing this exercise at the beginning of your process can help ensure that the later conversations go smoothly.
- *Be realistic about what role you can play*: Avoid having a savior complex with your audiences and be pragmatic about what you and your exhibition can actually achieve. Aim high, hold onto a vision, but also be realistic about the demands you're placing on audiences and teams. If you're asking audiences to confront uncomfortable emotions, how are you allowing them to lean into that work or lean back from it as appropriate? Are there moments throughout the experience or work that allow them to opt out, decompress, or reflect?

- *Sum of the parts*: When it comes to the exhibition design process, each area of your work is essential in supporting the whole. Whether it is installation, design work, interactive development, furniture, lighting, language, narrative, or staff training, all elements are interlinked and can support, challenge, and complement one another. Take the time to make sure that each area is supporting the same outcomes. Care for audiences must be applied to every level of this work.
- *Invest in the entire staff*: Asking audiences to become aware of their emotions requires staff to do the same work. I am a believer that we should not ask our public to go through experiences that we would not feel safe enough to go through ourselves. The entire staff, from the finance department to the front line, had the opportunity to experience *The Mandala Lab* ahead of its launch. They also underwent training to not only understand the subject matter but to allow them to better understand what was being asked of audiences. This practice promotes empathy for audiences and made staff members better ambassadors for the institution and its projects.
- *Let the content inform the process*: The content of *The Mandala Lab* informed the entire exhibition design process. To create an exhibition that supported emotional awareness and understanding in relation to art, team members needed to go through that same process as well. Which training, processes, and adjustments to the exhibition design process may need to happen in order to best serve the material and subject matter? If the project team harbors any biases, fears, or discomfort around the subject matter, this will manifest in the exhibition in subtle or overt ways. Listen for discomfort, consider how you and your teams can find empathetic ways of understanding the material, and make sure this work is reflected in conversations with your team. Give your teams space to discover and reflect on their relationship to the subject matter so they can approach the material and project from a place of awareness.

## *If You Want to Inspire Empathy, Design with Empathy, Yourself*

Designing for emotions requires project processes and exhibitions that allow for emotional awareness and emotional intelligence. This takes time, discipline, honesty, and understanding of the ways you can collaborate with both your staff and your audience. If museums are to be spaces where audiences can emotionally engage, we need emotionally aware design processes that create space for trust-building, agency, and empowerment. In this way, audiences can be supported to interact in ways that feel comfortable and appropriate to them. Museums are powerful conveners and spaces that facilitate intellectual and emotional engagement with some of the most difficult issues facing our world today. They can also be change agents that establish the building blocks for empathy, resilience, and hope needed to address those issues.

# 6 The Eyes of the Heart

## Nurturing Deep Empathic Connection Through Beauty

*Mary Hall Surface*

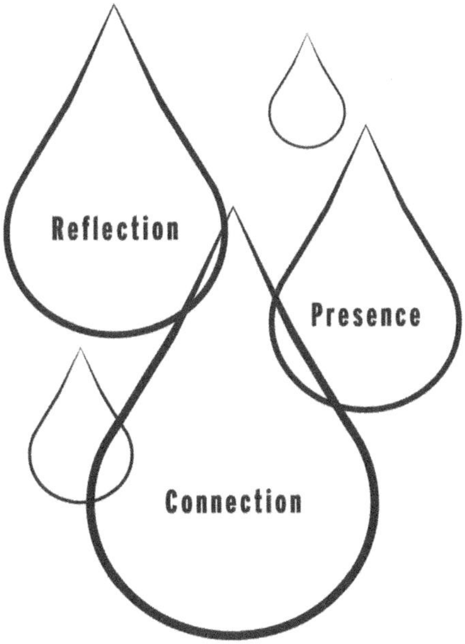


My art form would not exist without empathy. Theater demands empathy. Actors must literally embody another person's emotions, thoughts, and behaviors. Playwrights must imaginatively step into the inner and outer lives of their characters. Audiences must enter the pretend world of the play, then laugh and cry in response to the imagined lives on stage. Theater is the world's best gym. It strengthens our empathetic muscles while it transforms our perspectives and opens our hearts.

I bring the power of theater into museums. I step inside of paintings to imagine plays that I write and produce. I invite museum visitors to improvise and move as a new way to explore art. I lead creative writers to find inspiration in the characters, settings, and stories within museums' collections. Then the world changed in 2020. In the fractured, fearful new landscape, I wanted to craft experiences that could support well-being and offer healing and connection. I moved online and presented art-inspired reflective writing through the National Gallery of Art, the Smithsonian American Art Museum, and the Smithsonian Associates. These workshops were my answer to what the world now seemed to be asking of me.

Then, a 2022 conversation with Elif Gökçiğdem, author and founder of ONE, the Organization of Networks for Empathy, encouraged me to take my new calling a step further. Together, we pondered how empathy might also contribute to well-being, since empathy involves essential intra- and interpersonal capacities—self-knowing *and* a desire to understand one another. We wondered how an encounter with Beauty might invite this kind of inward-outward knowing. While my first thought was to delve into Beauty philosophically, Elif urged me to think less and feel more. She suggested I embrace the heart, our spiritual center in Islam, as a way to see and know. Her generous, generative prompt opened me to creating the tool outlined in this chapter. I first presented "The Eyes of the Heart" at the Smithsonian's Freer Gallery of Art for ONE's 2022 Designing for Empathy Summit and Workshops, a multidisciplinary gathering of empathy-builders. Since its premiere, this five-step practice has anchored my work with museums.

"To see with the eyes of the heart" is my metaphor for entering an experience through emotion-centered perception rather than brain-based cognition. A heart-led experience honors the seat of mind, emotion, and spirit that the heart symbolizes across cultures and faith traditions. Our life-animating organ is poetically revered as a third eye of wisdom, the center of our being, the source of love and compassion. To see with our heart implies a deeper knowing, a chance to express what can feel beyond our words. In my workshops, I playfully say that our hearts help us "ef" the ineffable of Beauty in art.

Of course, "Beauty" is a word that comes with freight. Even if we dismiss its association with fashion and bodies, we can still hear it as a standard, imposed, dictated, divisive. But I use the word to describe the transformative power of an intentional encounter with art. This tool approaches Beauty not as a *quality* that *art has,* but rather as an *experience* that *art offers*. Specifically, participants are guided to experience Beauty as a reaching inwardly to discover self-knowledge and an opening outwardly toward connections beyond the self. Participants have shared that this outward opening attunes them to their family, culture, history, even to the whole of humanity, or to creativity, life-affirming energy, or a sense of the sacred and Divine. This beyond-self transcendence can also spark awareness of our interconnected existence. So Beauty, as experienced in this approach, not only supports healing and wholeness; it strengthens our capacity for empathy in each of the five steps. Participants engage with an unknown, deepen self-knowledge, and then connect beyond themselves to another person and to larger interconnections.

The structure of this tool is inspired by my work with Project Zero, a research group at the Harvard Graduate School of Education dedicated to understanding and enhancing how we think and learn. I owe a special debt to Project Zero researcher Ron Ritchhart's Thinking Routines, which are a short series of moves that guide and support your thinking.[1] I also want to acknowledge my colleague and friend Nathalie Ryan at the National Gallery of Art, who was an essential thought and feeling partner during the pandemic realignment of my work. And thank you to my participants for their willingness to share their words from our Eyes of the Heart workshops.

## The Eyes of the Heart: Outline of Steps

### *Introduction*

Invite participants to "see with the eyes of the heart." Frame Beauty as an experience that art offers, rather than a quality that art has—one that draws us into a deeper knowing of self and that opens us into connection to what transcends the self.

### *Step 1*

Warm-up of the Heart. Recall an experience of Beauty using scaffolded moves to "See, Feel, Reach In, Open Out." Collect single word reflections.

### *Step 2*

Participants engage individually with an unknown work of art. They "See, Feel, Reach In, Open Out." They then write about their experience using Handout One. Collect single word reflections from the full group (20+ minutes).

### *Step 3*

Participants create a short, found poem from their words on Handout One to express an aspect of their Step 2 experience (5+ minutes writing time). Collect single word reflections. Then pair-share about the process of crafting the poem. Do *not* share the poem.

### *Step 4*

Participants use their poem to introduce their chosen work of art to their pair-share partner. Use Handout Two to guide partners to "See, Feel, Reach In, Open Out" in response to the new work of art. Reflect on dual perspectives (15+ minutes).

### *Step 5*

Facilitate final reflection on process: Surprise, Value, What's Next?

## Keys to Facilitating the Tool

An ideal number of participants is 15—20, but that can vary depending on program goals and available space. I have had groups of 8 and a group of 80. Select a gallery or adjacent galleries that will allow adequate but not overwhelming choice. Provide stools or other places to sit, two handouts (described below), and clipboards with a sheet of paper if participants do not have journals. Best length is 75—90 minutes.

### *Introduction*

Set a tone of welcome and warmth. Arrange stools for proximity and connection. Thank your participants for being curious, creative, and open by coming. Assure them that the process honors their personal aesthetics while opening them to Beauty as an inward-outward experience that centers the heart.

## Step 1

The contemplative series of moves of "See, Feel, Reach In, Open Out" is repeated three times during the workshop. The warm-up is crucial as it allows participants to experience the moves with something familiar before approaching an unknown. The language I use for the warm-up articulates the specifics of these contemplative moves:

> *Let's taste the inward-outward notion and flow of Beauty by warming up our hearts. Let's each recall an experience from your own life that* to you *was beautiful. Our focus today is on art, but experiences of Beauty can be found in music, in nature, in community, in the eyes of a newborn, so you choose what you would like to recall. Place one or both hands on your heart. Lower your eyes to a soft point in front of you on the floor or close your eyes if you wish. Now picture in your mind and most especially in your heart an experience of Beauty from your life. Whatever that may be for you. Let your breath slow down and deepen as you bring the experience to life. As you remember, notice the sensations in your body. Notice the emotions rising in you. Try to connect the emotions to specifics in what you are recalling. To a color, a sound, a sensation, an image. Notice how this Beauty draws you inwardly –to reach and connect with something deep within you. Now, notice how the Beauty opens your heart outwardly– connecting you to that which is beyond you. Whatever that phrase means to you in this moment. As you breath, hold and treasure this inward-outward gift of Beauty. Now bring your attention back to our gathering. Welcome back.*

At the conclusion of the warm-up, I collect single words from participants to describe the experience they just had. Responses have included "comforting, warm, nostalgic, loving, awe."

Inviting just single words or short phrases encourages participants to crystallize their sensations or impressions, a move they will use throughout the workshop.

## *Step 2*

Tell participants that they will soon move through this gallery (or galleries). Invite them to open their hearts to the works of art and choose one that is unknown to them, one with which they would not normally engage in a museum. Encourage them to avoid signage to let go of a brain-based approach to the art. Ask them to move in silence to keep in the contemplative tone established in the warm-up. I do say: "Let your heart move you to a work with a certain speed so we will have ample time for all the steps of our process." More than one person may choose the same work of art, but participants should work individually without talking.

Then share Handout One (Box 6.1), which serves as both a guide through this step and as a place to write. Encourage participants to take time to see and feel before they write, and then use single words, phrases, and sentences to respond to the prompts in italics. Invite them to trust their responses. Just get words on the page.

### Box 6.1 Handout One

**See**

Place your hand or your hands on your heart. Breathe. Look closely at your work of art.
Experience its Beauty.

**Feel**

Notice what emotions and sensations arise in your body and heart. Name them.
Write: *I feel . . . [what?]*

Stay in touch with your breath. Notice what within the artwork seems to evoke the emotions and sensations. Is it your aesthetic response to color, line, shape, texture, or energy? A link to a memory? Or association? A visceral connection to something present on your mind and heart?

Write: *I feel . . . [what?] . . . in / through/ because of . . . [what?] . . .*

**Reach In**

Notice how the Beauty draws you inwardly.
Connects you with something deep within you.
Write: *The Beauty draws my heart toward . . . [what?] . . . within me.*

**Open Out**

Notice how the Beauty draws you outwardly.
Connects you with something which is beyond you.
Write: *The Beauty opens my heart to . . . [what?] . . . beyond me.*

In seeking to experience beauty in Robert Delaunay's *Political Drama* (Figure 6.1), whose title I do not share, one might be drawn by the progressive rings of color to reflect on what is most centering in one's life or what spirals or pulls one away from that center. The position of the figures could suggest separation, leading to feelings of family or societal alienation. Or their position might suggest flow or movement across obstacles, inspiring feelings of personal potential or belief in the possibility for change in the larger world. During this step, if a participant seems challenged to connect beyond the self, I coach them to seek it in what they feel within. One responded:

> *At first, I did not feel a connection beyond me, but then I realized that the longing I feel from the painting is like the longing other people feel in their lives. This connected me to others, to a more universal longing, something I had never considered.*

After fifteen to twenty minutes, reconvene the group. Collect single words or short phrases that describe their experience. Words have included "enlightening, surprising, sense of wholeness, discovery." The contrasts and commonalities among the words quickly expand perspectives on the experience of Beauty.

## *Step 3*

I intentionally do not tell the participants that they will write a poem until this point in the workshop. This allows them to write freely during Step 2 without anticipating an outcome. To counter any jitters from those who might not consider themselves poets, I say:

> *As a way to capture what your heart is perceiving and discovering, let's each create a found poem. Know that when I use the word "poem," I am embracing the most ancient meaning of the word which comes from a Greek verb that just means* to make. *So, we are just going to make some patterns of words that express some aspect of your experience of Beauty with your chosen work of art. Choose maybe 8 – 15 words from anywhere in your writing and arrange them into lines of any length, however many lines you'd like. Nothing needs to rhyme. Just craft the words together. Find a poem in the words you've already written that captures a part of your seeing this unknown with the eyes of your heart.*

A participant created this poem in response to the Beauty she experienced in Robert Delaunay's painting (Figure 6.1):

> *Rings like a target.*
> *I aim for the center.*
> *But I rush away like the woman*
> *on broken circles of color.*
> *Why do I rush away*
> *From meaning waiting for me?*

After five to six minutes, reconvene the group. Again, collect single words or short phrases that describe their writing experience. Then invite participants to pair-share about the poem-creation *process*. Do *not* share the poem itself. Some participants will want to jump to that step, so make the instruction very clear. Suggest they partner with someone they do not know. Ask: "How did crafting this poem help me capture the Beauty I experienced? The inward-outward knowing?" The maker of the poem above said writing it helped her distill how her small daily tasks distract her from exploring a more meaningful world beyond the everyday. This opportunity to share process is usually met with enthusiasm and builds good rapport between partners for the next step.

## Step 4

Now that participants have tasted how the experience of Beauty deepens understanding of the self, they are primed to discover how Beauty can

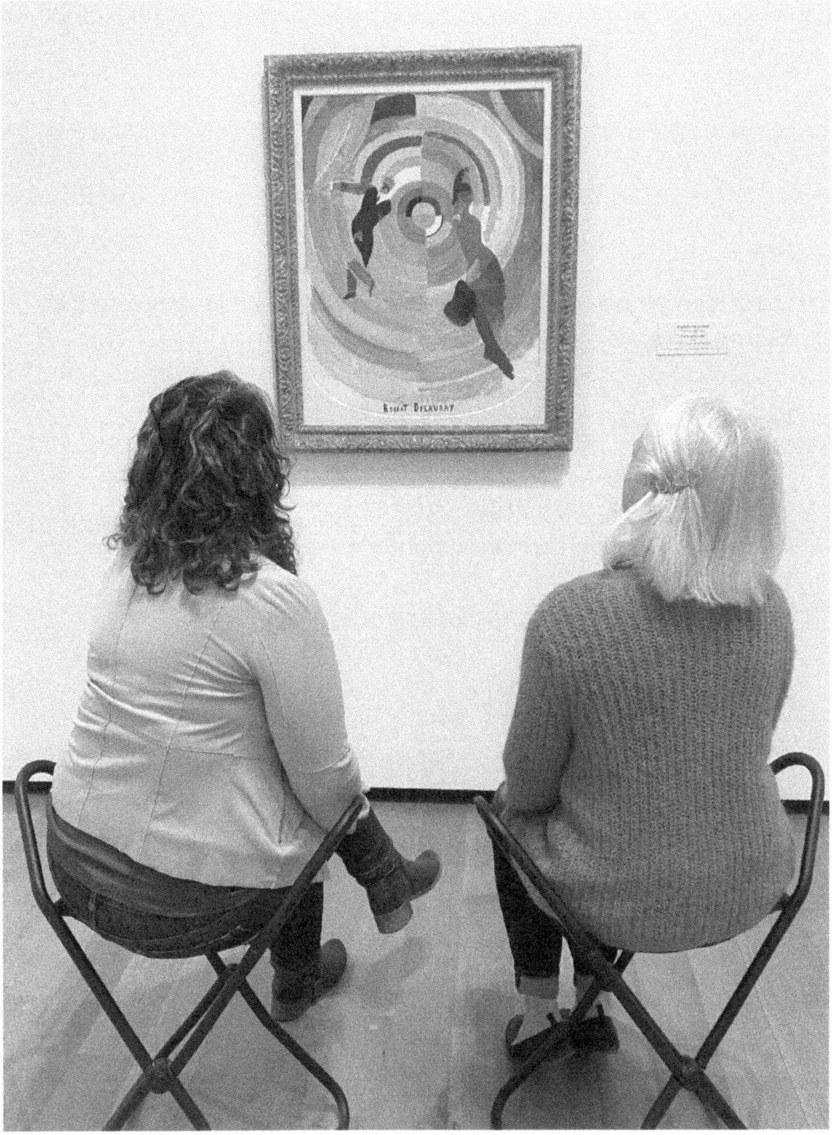

**Figure 6.1** Workshop participants with Robert Delaunay's *Political Drama.* Courtesy National Gallery of Art, Washington, DC.

deepen understanding of "the other." In this step, the participants' poems now become the window through which their partner meets both the new work of art and their partner's perspective. Distribute Handout Two (Box 6.2) so participants can follow along as you talk through each move. While participants do not write in this step, ask participants to use the prompts in italics when together in front of their works of art.

### Box 6.2 Handout Two

**See**

Stand together before Partner #1's chosen work of art in silence, so that Partner #2 may take a close look at the work of art.

**Feel**

Partner #1: Share your poem inspired by the work of art with Partner #2, who listens deeply. Say nothing else.
Partner #2 responds, naming emotions in the heart, sensations in the body.
*Through the eyes of your heart, your poem, I feel . . .*

**Reach In**

Then, about the poem and its inspiration, the work of art, Partner #2 responds:
*The Beauty draws my heart toward . . . [what?] . . . within me.*

**Open Out**

*The Beauty opens my heart to . . . [what?] . . . beyond me.*
Then, together ask:
*What else would our hearts like to know about the work of art? About each other?*
Repeat the above steps with Partner #2's work of art and poem.

The power of this rich, expansive step grows from witnessing another person's creativity and vulnerability as you share your own. One pair who encountered Delaunay's *Political Drama* found that they flipped perspectives on the inner lives of the two figures in the painting after "seeing with the eyes of the heart" of the other. Another pair had opposite responses to the energy of the painting but were able to hold and explore that tension as a source of deeper understanding of the art and of one another.

## Step 5

After fifteen to twenty minutes, reconvene the group for a final reflection. Ask: "What *surprised* you about seeing through the eyes of your partner's heart and what do you *value* about this step?" I begin with surprise to celebrate the delight that can grow from unexpected discoveries. This welcomes ambiguity and complexity, states which are often seen as unsettling rather than generative. Naming the value of the process most often leads participants to reflect on how their perspectives shifted and expanded. Participants who engaged with abstract, non-figurative sculptures said:

> *I was surprised by how differently our hearts see while looking at the same object. Yet, both are so valid.*
>
> *I valued standing in silence in response to my partner's poem. That pause opened up a deep flow of connection between two people who had never met before.*
>
> *I valued being allowed into the space of another person's seeing and having to articulate my own seeing. It felt like a duet, not a solo.*

If reflection is done in pairs, follow with collecting from the full group short insights that participants gained from their partners. Inviting them to honor what they discover from one another strengthens their empathetic connection.

Conclude by considering "what's next"—a key to this experience becoming transformative. As a whole group, consider:

1. What might you now do differently in your life or in the world?
2. How might you think, feel, or act in a new way when encountering an unknown?
3. Where else might you seek and share experiences of Beauty?

The goal is to name small, tangible steps. I encourage participants to craft their response into an *"I will . . . "* statement to carry with them from the workshop—an affirmation of action. Participants have said that they will be "more curious, more intentional in close looking, more open to new perspectives, and less fearful of the unknown."

## Possibilities Moving Forward

"The Eyes of the Heart" was born out of my desire to support individual well-being and to help rebuild connection and care in our communities and society. Like the plays I write for the theater, the workshop was designed to take people on a journey to new places within and beyond themselves. I invite you to join me in exploring and expanding this new tool's implementation. How might we use this 5-step process to engage with other art forms, or nature, or built environments, or community rituals? How might we intentionally gather participants around objects, ideas, or events from the past and present that provoke strong and varied responses so we might discover their Beauty and interconnection? How might we give words to difficult emotions and find new poems that are tangible expressions of both our whole selves and our shared humanity? How else might Beauty-inspired experiences interrupt othering? As a theater artist, my world is imagination and collaboration. So, I welcome your thoughts, insights, and possibilities for seeing further with the eyes of our hearts. Please reach out through my website: maryhallsurface.com.

## Note

**1** Ron Ritchhart, Mark Church, and Karin Morrison, *Making Thinking Visible: How to Promote Engagement, Understanding, and Independence for All Learners* (Jossey-Bass, 2011), 43–9.

# 7 Agents of Empathy

## Objects, Health and Healing in Exhibitions and the Everyday

*Brenda Cowan*

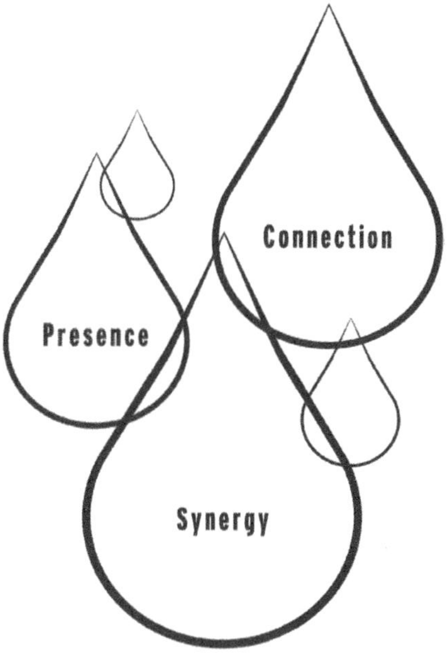


*These are the keys to my house, my love, my memories, my everything. They open all of this, they open my house. When you move from your home you are like a plant in a changed environment. You need time and hard work when you change your home. It's very hard. I have keys but no home.*

*—Syrian Refugee in Sweden, 2019*

## Objects and Oneness

On a hot summer evening in Sweden, the warm yellow glow from a table lamp moved over the bearded face of my napping translator, his profile deepening into sleep-softened shadow. That day I was a researcher learning about the meaning of personal objects from people whose lives were vastly different than my own. Objects that had witnessed a family's flight from their home in Syria, their slow acclimation into a new life on the outskirts of Stockholm, and their objects' participation in a museum exhibition about their experience. And, as the sun slowly faded and my translator reclined on the sofa after a full day of relaying conversations in English, Swedish, and Arabic, an awakening occurred among the women in the room, and objects became our translators, our guides, and our unifiers. We sat on the living room floor and circulated hand to hand, first a pair of earrings, then a set of house keys, and several small gifts I brought for their children. Each object was held, touched, and wordlessly shared among us women as if in a ritual, a moment that went from a pragmatic scholarly exploration into a moment of unity among mothers, sisters, and daughters. Then a beautifully decorated hairbrush emerged, and together we brushed the children's hair and continued our silent conversation through the objects that had given us permission to share. A connection through a shared moment among people who didn't speak the same language, yet one rich with meaning. We were brought together through the language of these objects and their stories: The earrings had been secreted away in a baby's diaper when leaving Syria; the house key was for a home that didn't exist anymore; the hairbrush brought comfort and normalcy when the world outside was anything but. These were objects recently returned from an exhibition telling the life stories of Syrian refugees and immigrants at a museum in Sweden. Objects that were, through being on display and then through their return, helping their owners cope through upheaval and transition into an unfamiliar new home. The objects were the theme of the familiar in a world that was not, and on the floor cushions where I sat as a researcher, a woman, a mother, the objects connected strangers without a shared language in a moment of oneness.

In studies investigating the role of objects in museums and everyday life with health and healing, I have been fortunate to collect many stories and moments of beauty just like these. Over and again, in museums and homes in Sweden, England, Bosnia-Herzegovina, and the United States, with people from all over the world, I have heard time and again how objects were active participants in lives in myriad ways. Object stories that, across the span of geography, culture, and time conveyed unifying themes in surprising and profound ways:

> **Familiarity**, as with a pair of earrings, a set of house keys and a hairbrush, is a connecting theme, just like a moment when an American visitor called out in surprise at seeing a childhood toy on display in Sarajevo at the War Childhood Museum. It was the same toy they had had in their own youth, only the one on display belonged to someone whose childhood was spent in the Bosnian War. Familiarity brought first the joy of nostalgia and then, an appreciation for the fragility and innocence of another's childhood. The two people were different, and they were the same.
>
> **Family** is a theme that you will hear about often: A Korean student living in New York talked lovingly about a pair of jeans as being his spouse; a Caribbean grandmother living in England referred to each of the many bracelets she wore every day as being her grandchildren; a police officer and a September 11 first-responder referred to his ash covered boots as his twin boys.
>
> **Loss** is another unifying theme. A woman of privilege from New York spoke to me with regret about having thrown away her grandmother's kitchen utensils. She shared her feelings of loss, guilt and ingratitude. Years later, a Syrian immigrant spoke with me with regret about her grandmother's kitchen utensils, and how she chose not to take them with her as she left her home. She too felt feelings of loss, guilt and ingratitude. These two women could not have been more different yet their connections to objects made meaningful through loss were profound, and their stories were universal.

We are connected with each other through experiences with objects, in a moment, and across time and place. Our experiences are unifying and illustrate, make tangible, how it is that we are more alike than different. My object research studies identify the ways in which objects in our lives and in the museums we participate with impact our well-being and our healing, and through this work, I have come to know them as portents, messengers, conduits for love, hope, and forces of reality when the world can seem anything but real. I have come to know objects as agents of empathy in a world where humans can feel lost or alone, and where they can feel unification and togetherness. Through the object stories I've collected, I have imagined the lives of others and experienced empathy; through active listening, I experienced empathy; through the giving of gifts, I've experienced empathy; through the sharing of my own stories, I experienced empathy. Through object experiences where I've felt awe, wonder, spirituality, and compassion I experienced empathy; through holding others' objects with reverence, I experienced empathy; through writing this story, I experience empathy.

## A Primal Dialogue: Phenomenology and the World of the Evocative Object

When listening to stories and encountering meaningful objects in people's lives—in the moments spent wordlessly communicating with those who welcomed me into their homes, museums, and into their lives, I am awakened to an unseen yet deeply felt world where cognition, perception, identity, communication, and socialization catalyze in moments spent sensing, sharing, considering, and activating objects. People connect with and through objects in inherent and associative ways, whether they be the objects in our daily lives, in the museums we visit, or in the exhibitions we create. With objects, we can experience and understand ourselves as physical things, because we live in relationship to them. Without objects, we would be in a void, both literally and psychologically. According to philosopher Hannah Arendt, objects ground us and stabilize our consciousness through their tangible reliability.[1] With objects, people make meaning through their perceptual relationships with them, going beyond the action of recognition alone and into an interaction that is cognitive, physical, and emotional. In this powerful mechanism between objects, personhood, and emotion, we have what John Dewey called *Unified Experience*:

> *Perception replaces bare recognition. There is an act of reconstructive doing, and consciousness becomes fresh and alive . . . an act of perception proceeds by waves that extend serially throughout the entire organism . . . The perceived object or scene is emotionally pervaded throughout.*[2]

In our encounters, we experience an object with our senses, we recognize it for its socially ascribed value, and then the magic happens: We attribute personal meaning to it. It takes on subjective characteristics, we give it perceived and personal value. It is a silent, primal dialogue that we move into and through like a life breath that sustains us—a breath we share with objects and the universe. With objects, we experience a deep and primary oneness with our way of being. With them, we are alive, we are seen, we are shaped, and shown who we are.

> *In the act of perception . . . I enter into a sympathetic relation with the perceived, which is possible only because neither my body nor the sensible exists outside the flux of time, and so each has its own dynamism, it's own pulsation and style. Perception, in this sense, is an attunement or synchronization between my own rhythms of the things themselves, their own tones and textures . . . In this ceaseless dance between the carnal subject and its world, at one moment the body leads, at another the things.*[3]

Objects and their phenomenological factors become even richer when we look at them for their evocative characteristics; objects through which we embrace our memories or imagine our futures. They are objects we think of as companions to our emotional lives, or as silent life partners. Evocative objects are witnesses to life's events and experiences, they are provocateurs, prompts, and inspirations.

> *Objects that are evocative are things we feel at one with. Evocative objects lead us into and through the mystery of things.*[4]

When we have an evocative object encounter, our emotions awaken and we are called to action. We can mark moments in time and connect with others in ways that transcend time, space, and words. At times, the mechanism of perception, identity, and the evocative denote reality in explicit ways, as with a Syrian refugee who talked about seeing his personal objects in an exhibition: "*The objects were not art they were reality. They are social, cultural reality*." In this manner, objects co-create the changing life narratives through which we construct our own truths.[5] They embody events, places, and moments in time, bearing witness, serving as markers along the way. They are autobiographical metaphors that can prompt deep self-awareness and personal narratives. Evocative objects can also be numinous, imbued with transcendent, spiritual, and transformative life.[6]

A visitor to the Museum of Mediterranean and Near Eastern Antiquities in Stockholm, Sweden, when walking through a hall of ancient oil lamps, described how "*The lamps illuminate me . . . my mind, heart, creativity. I feel passion, spirit, past lives, mission, ambition. It [the object] takes you back to the ancient times—a transportation.*"

The evocative object experience bears strong relationship to awe, wonder, and empathy, as in moments where a person encounters a piece of art, an object from nature, or a personal item imbued with meaning. Awe and wonder come with feelings of elevation, amazement, and a loss of ego, and are associated with prosocial, humanitarian, and spiritual activity.[7] It is here in the realm of the evocative object moment that we connect with empathy; in here, we lose ourselves in the moment and experience feelings of openness, gratefulness, hope, and connection with ourselves and others. The link between awe and empathy is powerful in object encounters in museums:

> *They indicated a feeling of smallness or a sudden understanding of the grandeur of the world around them and their place in it. This element of the numinous experience...speaks to the basics of what it means to be human.*[8]

In my research, the words of a staff member at the War Childhood Museum in Sarajevo stand out: remarking on seeing objects donated by victims of war, she described feeling grateful, filled with awe and admiration for the people who did this; "who shared their irreplaceable precious things."

## Psychotherapeutic Object Dynamics

> *These objects are about my healing journey. I've become acutely aware of my gratefulness. Things that were once negative can now be positive. These things help me build myself up through a bad time. Each item represents a part in my healing journey.*
>
> —*Anonymous Object Donor, National September 11th Memorial and Museum.*

I am a professor of exhibitions and experiences, and museums are my world. To me, the objects that reside within them are alive, potent, and powerful, and as I entered into many years of research into their mysteries, I came to understand them as agents of empathy, health, and healing. With objects, we experience the fundamental psychological stability that comes with recognition and the perceptual associative ability to make meaning through them individually and sociologically. Further, the wonder-filled, evocative object encounter brings us into worlds of deep insight, connectivity, and the spiritual. When objects with all of these potencies are activated through certain interactions, they aid our well-being and even help us when we are in times of healing. In essence, sometimes intentionally and sometimes subconsciously, we use everyday objects—and objects in museums—in ways that are therapeutic in form and function. This is the *Psychotherapeutic Object Dynamics* (Figure 7.1). It is a framework that articulates the healthy psychological impacts inherent to the human-object relationship and consists of a convergence of three factors:

- An individual's subjective associations with an object.
- The object's unique evocative characteristics.
- The catalytic dynamic activity between the object and the person.

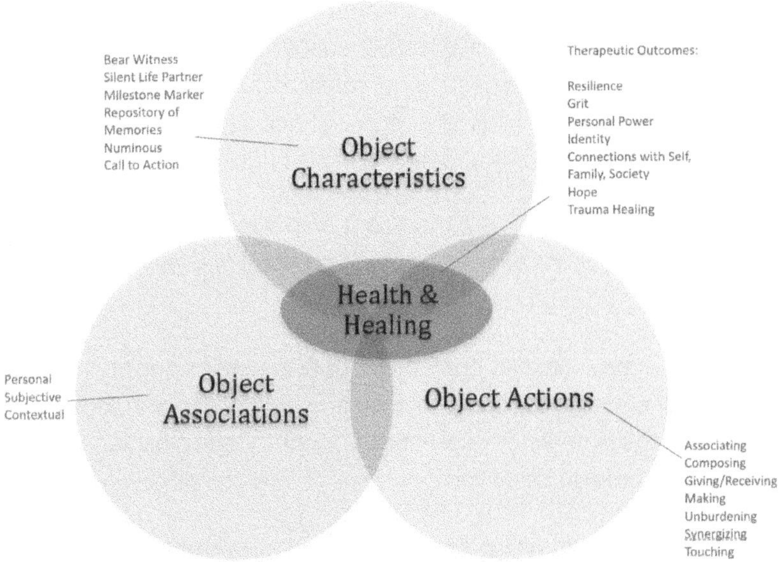


**Figure 7.1** The Psychotherapeutic Object Dynamics are part of the human-object psychological mechanism that underpin healthful and healing object encounters. Credit: Brenda Cowan.

Altogether, these factors activate and produce outcomes that are healthful and even therapeutic, such as feelings of resilience, grit, personal power, and hope. They reinforce self-identity and connections with others. The dynamics include seven distinct actions, each of which is automatic, therapeutic in nature, and can be directly linked to well-being and healing:

- Associating (the action of keeping an object near).
- Composing (the action of grouping multiple objects).
- Giving and Receiving (exchanging objects with reverence).
- Making (the act of creation).
- Releasing/Unburdening (the action of permanently removing an object).
- Synergizing (the action of contributing to a collective of objects).
- Touching (with any skin receptor).

I developed the Psychotherapeutic Object Dynamics framework for identifying and understanding the psychological underpinnings of people's inherent relationship with objects, and the healthful and healing impacts of museum and exhibition encounters. As a theory, it is at once simple and complex. It is an organism with distinct parts that enables us to see the dynamic experience in every object encounter. It is a window into the powerful human ability to heal. In my research, I heard about the healing power of objects in hundreds of interviews, including one with a museum visitor to the Derby Museum and Art Gallery in England:

> *The biscuit tin had a lot of buttons in it and when I was extremely ill as a child I would touch the buttons and imagine where they were from and that's what healed me. I associate it with getting well.*

I learned how museums can open their doors to help us nurture the health, healing, and empathy-building that our hearts, minds, and bodies seek, such as with the experience of an object donor to the collection of the War Childhood Museum in Sarajevo:

> *I feel more relaxed in a way. Sharing the objects . . . makes me feel relaxed. It's important to hear stories; it helps us forgive . . . we can heal ourselves.*

And with the experience of an object donor to the Museum of Mediterranean and Near Eastern Antiquities in Stockholm:

*After visitors learned [the objects] were mine they cried and hugged me. I felt so proud that I shared. I could show and help create our humanity together.*

## Utilizing the Psychotherapeutic Object Dynamics as Tools for Health and Healing

Experiencing object-rich museum spaces, engaging in touching, smelling, or object-making experiences, contributing a personal object to an exhibition—even digitally—and co-authoring themes and curatorial content are all tools for activating the Psychotherapeutic Object Dynamics and their well-being and healing outcomes. For example, at the Derby Museum and Art Gallery in England, the public co-develop exhibitions and programs, donate images of personal objects to digital exhibits, and restore and make objects in the galleries. In studies, visitors, staff, and volunteers were experiencing all seven of the Psychotherapeutic Object Dynamics through these specific types of engagement. The Dynamics of Releasing/Unburdening, Synergizing, Giving and Receiving, and Associating were prevalent in studies at the 9/11 Memorial and Museum in New York and the War Childhood Museum in Sarajevo, where staff, visitors, and the public donated their personal objects related to the stories the institutions tell. All seven of the Dynamics were also observed at the Museum of Mediterranean and Near Eastern Antiquities in Stockholm, where refugees and immigrants participated in donating personal objects and co-authored an exhibition that told their own stories. In these institutions, we can see that when people engage with familiar, everyday objects, they see themselves and nurture their identity and connection with others; where people share objects, they are sharing themselves, processing their grief, and synergizing with others; where people are touching, making, and associating with objects, they are experiencing the creative process and the life process.

As museum professionals, or everyday object carers who engage with museums, we can utilize the Psychotherapeutic Objects Dynamics framework with intention as a tool for creating and evaluating exhibitions and programs that will generate healthful and healing experiences for our participants. This includes:

- Fostering Giving and Receiving; Composing; Releasing/Unburdening; Synergizing and Associating healing Dynamics through creating thematic exhibitions and programs that enable people to donate and share objects that tell their individual and collective stories.

- Creating Touch and Making experiences with objects in galleries and programs that enable visitors and staff to fully experience an object's rich sensory aspects.
- Working with the support of mental health professionals to evaluate existing exhibition object encounters with their visitors and staff to identify the Psychotherapeutic Object Dynamics that are already occurring within their institutions.
- Exhibiting difficult content through object encounters that provide multiple perspectives and multiple points of view using evocative objects as prompts for wonder and empathy.

Every day, museum staff, visitors, volunteers, and communities are thriving through object encounters in sometimes small and unseen ways, and sometimes large and overt ways. In each instance, they are experiencing a journey of health, well-being, and healing. In each instance, they are building awareness of themselves and others, connecting with themselves and others, and seeing and feeling themselves as part of a larger world: a whole world rich with meaning, humanity, health, and oneness.

## Notes


**1** Hannah Arendt, *The Human Condition* (The University of Chicago Press, 1958).

**2** John Dewey, "Having an Experience," in *Art as Experience* (Perigee, 1934), 52–3, http:www.marxists.org/reference/subject/philosophy/works/us/an-experience.htm.

**3** David Abrams, *The Spell of the Sensuous: Perception and Language in a More-Than-Human World* (Vintage Books, 1996), 54–5.

**4** Sherry Turkle, *Evocative Objects: Things We Think With* (Massachusetts Institute of Technology Press, 2007), 9.

**5** Janet Hoskins, *Biographical Objects: How Things Tell the Stories of People's Lives* (Routledge, 1998).

**6** Elizabeth Wood and Kiersten F. Latham, *The Objects of Experience: Transforming Visitor-Object Encounters in Museums* (Left Coast Press, 2014).

**7** Paul K. Piff, Matthew Feinberg, Pia Dietz, Daniel M. Stancato, and Dacher Keltner, "Awe, the Small Self, and Prosocial Behavior," *The Journal of Personality and Social Psychology* 108, no. 6 (2015): 883–99.

**8** K. F. Latham, "Psychological Flow and the Numinous Museum," in *University of Michigan Working Papers in Museum Studies*, No. 11 (University of Michigan, 2016), 1–17.

# 8 Empathy for All Animals

*Jim Wharton*

*Sarah Brenkert*

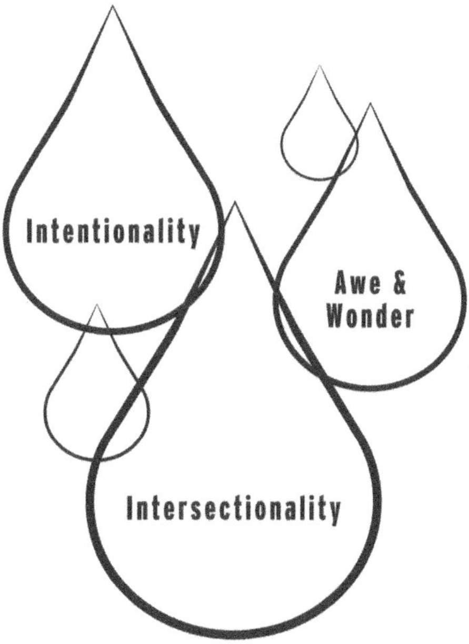


Empathy helps create connections through perspective-taking. In this chapter, we will explore how understanding and connecting with animals can extend to improved human interactions and social and environmental well-being. Although it is sometimes argued that it is easier to feel empathy for animals than humans, the neurological pathways are the same.[1] The authors will discuss how the same strategies that foster empathy for animals can be used to help people feel empathy for other humans that are very different from themselves.

The smartphone in our pocket pings. The tiny super-computer strapped to our wrist buzzes. Headphones conduct vibrations through the bones of our skull, bathing our brains in a constant stream of curated content.

For millions of us, this digital and technological immersion is the reality of our modern lives. We live in a time when we can transmit messages instantly, store infinite data in the cloud, and access all the knowledge that has been accumulated throughout human history with a click. This rapid connectivity has benefited us in innumerable ways but has also come at a price. Despite its promise of connection, the digital world often leaves us feeling isolated, disconnected from other people and from nature.

It is easy to think about the ways our industrial societies have replaced natural rhythms with synthetic systems. Absorbed in the glow of our screens, we miss the subtle changes in the light as the days start to lengthen in early spring. The ease of using GPS technology has made navigation by natural cues or landmarks obsolete. We don't know where our food comes from, or where our waste goes.

But any sense of separateness we feel from nature is an illusion. Humans are as much a part of the living world as the forests, rivers, and oceans. When we're surrounded by urban infrastructure and immersed in streaming media, it's easy to lose sight of this. The illusion of separateness has very real consequences—not only harming our physical and emotional well-being but also shaping our habits and values. When we feel disconnected from nature, we're less likely to care about the urgent challenges facing our planet, like climate change and biodiversity loss.

That's where empathy comes in. Empathy isn't just about kindness; it's about recognizing the deep connections between all living things, *including* humans, animals, and the ecosystems we depend on. It helps us see conservation not as saving "other" species or landscapes but as protecting the systems that make life possible for everyone—including ourselves.

Research has long supported a link between empathy and general prosocial behaviors—actions taken voluntarily with the goal of benefiting others.[2] Additional studies have found that people who feel more empathy for wildlife are more likely to engage in pro-environmental behaviors.[3] Educators in the zoo and aquarium field often seek to encourage empathy for nonhuman animals as one strategy for increasing conservation action among their visitors.

Recently, there is a growing interest in the idea that strengthening empathy in one area (e.g., empathy for animals) can enhance empathy skills generally by encouraging broader, more inclusive ways of thinking. Research by

Adam Galinsky and Gordon Moskowitz supports this link, finding that when study participants were coached in perspective-taking—actively imagining another's viewpoint—they reduced their stereotypic thinking and in-group favoritism (a term that refers to the tendency to treat those we see as part of our own group better than those outside of it). In other words, practicing perspective-taking in one context promoted fairer interactions across social boundaries.[4] Another study found that the practice of focusing on someone's individual characteristics shifts attention from group differences to personal uniqueness.[5] In psychology, this is known as *decategorization,* and it can help reduce biases and enhance understanding between people from diverse backgrounds—and it's similar to what zoo and aquarium educators do when we encourage people to see animals as subjective others rather than generic representatives of their species. The findings from these studies suggest that growing our capacity to feel empathy for animals may support attitudes and mindsets that improve empathy and reduce prejudice in person-to-person social contexts.

As we consider how feeling empathy for wildlife relates to feeling empathy for other people, it's helpful to start with an understanding of the mechanisms that evoke empathy. What is it about nonhuman animals that elicits feelings of connectedness and care, and why do we feel empathy for some animals more readily than others? A summary of the elements that cause us to feel empathy is provided in Box 8.1.[6]

## Box 8.1 What Causes Us to Feel Empathy?

As we consider how feeling empathy for wildlife relates to feeling empathy for other people, it's helpful to start with an understanding of the mechanisms that evoke empathy. What is it about nonhuman animals that elicits feelings of connectedness and care, and why do we feel empathy for some animals more readily than others? Conservation psychologist Gene Myers describes four characteristics that influence the way people relate to other animals: *agency, affectivity, coherence, and continuity.*

- ***Agency*** means an animal takes action to meet their needs; they eat or play or groom or hide. This is easy for people to also recognize in themselves. Recognizing an animal's agency facilitates a feeling of similarity. *Affectivity* refers to an animal's observed behavior from which people might infer the animal's emotional state. In other people, we notice facial expressions, tone of voice, and body language and draw conclusions about how they are feeling. For some animals and some behaviors, we feel confident about the relationship between a given behavior and the emotional state inferred (e.g., a dog's wagging tail or the hiss of a cat). For many, if not most animals, however, that link between behavior and emotional states is unfamiliar or unknown (even to experts). Birds and sharks, to give two examples, do not have expressive faces, and their behaviors are often misconstrued. For other animals, it may not be accurate at all to describe an animal's internal state as an "emotion." In absence of this knowledge, people often make assumptions around an animal's emotions driven by their own experiences. In human care settings like zoos and aquariums, "activity" is often mistaken for affectivity (i.e., sedentary animals are sad, and active animals are happy).

- ***Affectivity*** refers to an animal's observed behavior from which people might infer the animal's emotional state. In other people, we notice facial expressions, tone of voice, and body language and draw conclusions about how they are feeling. For some animals and some behaviors, we feel confident about the relationship between a given behavior and the emotional state inferred (e.g., a dog's wagging tail or the hiss of a cat). For many, if not most animals, however, that link between behavior and emotional states is unfamiliar or unknown (even to experts). Birds and sharks, to give two examples, do not have expressive faces, and their behaviors are often misconstrued. For other animals, it may not be accurate at all to describe an animal's internal state as an "emotion." In absence of this knowledge, people often make assumptions around an animal's emotions driven by their own experiences. In human care settings like zoos and aquariums, "activity" is often mistaken for affectivity (i.e., sedentary animals are sad, and active animals are happy).
- ***Coherence*** means an animal looks like an animal. It has arms and legs and a face. You may have never seen a pangolin before, but when presented with a picture or video, it's easy to accept that this is an animal, if an unfamiliar one. A sea anemone is another story. This is an invertebrate sea creature that looks as much like a flower as a creature.

- ***Continuity*** is simply the time we spend with or around animals. It's the reason we are comfortable believing we know how our pets are feeling.

The reason these characteristics help engender empathy for nonhuman animals in people is because they are characteristics we see in ourselves. We naturally look for ourselves in other animals. As young children, we see other animals as peers and gradually, over time, have that connection "educated" out of us. Eventually, someone explains to us that it is inappropriate to ascribe human characteristics to nonhuman animals, because that's *anthropomorphism*. Some biologists object to anthropomorphic thinking because it gives us an inaccurate and potentially misleading understanding of an animal's needs and behavior. It can lead to feeding wild animals and "rescuing" seal pups from the beach where they are awaiting the return of their parents with food. We should pause before judging these actions too harshly; anthropomorphism is a truly human reaction to the unknown. It's natural for us to use experiences or phenomena that we understand to make sense of new experiences. This is how we learn. The problem occurs when people stop there. When we fail to take the step beyond appreciating similarities to understanding differences we become mired in *anthropocentrism*, assuming all animal experiences are *exactly* like our own.

In that way, anthropomorphism is really about projection: projecting human experiences and norms onto other animals. This tendency isn't limited to our thinking about nonhuman animals; we naturally do it any time we encounter something we don't know or understand, instinctively filling in the gaps with what we are most familiar with—our own feelings and experiences. Engaging empathically asks us to interrupt this intuitive egocentrism and attempt to imagine another's lived reality. In other words, true empathy is less about "walking a mile in someone else's shoes" and more about striving to understand what it is like for them to walk that mile in their own shoes.

The good news is, we have the power to cultivate our capacity for empathy—and the more we practice perspective-taking and cognitive de-centering, the better we get at it. This is true for our connection both with animals and with other humans. In the zoo and aquarium world, we continuously look for ways that we can offer invitations for our visitors to consider animals' perspectives. Toward that goal, the four characteristics mentioned above—agency, affectivity, coherence, and continuity—function like empathy light bulbs: Activating one or more of the characteristics can flip a switch and reveal the individuality of another. It turns out that tuning into the same four characteristics that enhance empathy for animals can help us appreciate the individuality of a fellow human. Learning to look for and pay attention to those four characteristics can illuminate someone as an individual with a unique perspective.

## Effective Practices for Cultivating Empathy

There are specific strategies that can help emphasize or reveal those characteristics, even with others who initially seem alien or unknowable. Our exploration of the literature helped us to identify a set of practices that can help bridge the chasm of "otherness" that we sometimes feel when encountering an animal very different from ourselves. These include: sharing knowledge, effective framing, activating imagination, and offering opportunities to practice empathetic behaviors.[7]

***Framing*** refers to the way information is presented, structured, or contextualized to influence how people perceive, interpret, and respond to it. It's about highlighting certain aspects while downplaying others to scaffold a particular understanding or emotional response. In zoos and aquariums, effective framing for empathy centers on presenting an animal as an individual, with a perspective and a lived experience. Often with the animals in our care, framing can be as simple as using an animal's name or pronouns instead of referring to them as "it." It can also mean telling stories about that individual animal, their preferences, their identity, their quirks, or special qualities.

To cultivate empathy for other people, the same practice of *framing* can apply:

- We can use personalization in our thinking, making an effort to see someone as a unique individual rather than defining them by where they live, what they do for a job, or their political beliefs. Recognizing what someone cares about or values is another way to heighten our appreciation of their individuality.

- Seeking parallels is another *framing* strategy that can help us find common ground or shared experiences, even if they are from very different contexts. In zoos and aquariums, this practice is often called "strategic anthropomorphism," and it involves highlighting similarities between human and nonhuman animals that may be harder to relate to, while holding in mind what makes animals distinct by focusing on key aspects of their natural history.[8] Take the barnacle as an example. Hidden away in a rock-like shell, a barnacle would seem to lack many of the characteristics that naturally engender empathy. However, with guided attention, we notice that barnacles are active at high tide, showing their agency by collecting food from the water with long, thin structures that just happen to be their legs. When we look carefully, the barnacle's agency, activity, and coherence are easy to see. In the same way, in person-to-person contexts, it may require patience and an openness to looking with new eyes to recognize how you might share certain values, like love for family or community, while recognizing your traditions or practices may be very different.

***Activating imagination*** as an empathy practice is closely connected to the idea of perspective-taking. Inviting people to consider another point of view, to try and imagine what it might look like or feel like to experience the world as another being experiences it—these are powerful ways to help people understand the perspective of another. A 2011 study found that participants who imagined a day in the life of a person from a different racial background exhibited less race-based bias compared to those who did not.[9] Activating imagination to empathize with other people might look like the following:

- With other people, *activating imagination* doesn't need to mean wild flights of fantasy, but rather something simple, like imagining their day-to-day life. What might their daily routines be like, their challenges, and joys? What might their mornings look like? How do they unwind or celebrate?
- Sometimes *activating imagination* means challenging our assumptions. It's an interesting exercise to step back from our own thoughts and try to identify and question the preconceived notions we might hold. We might ask ourselves: "Why do I think they act this way?" and "What if my interpretation of their behavior isn't accurate?" In this way, *activating imagination* can help us notice when we might be projecting our biases onto their perspective.

***Sharing knowledge*** is another evidence-backed practice to foster empathy with nonhuman animals. In zoos and aquariums, we strategically share insights about an animal's history or biology to enrich the connection that people might feel and add layers of nuance and accuracy to their understanding. Sharing knowledge helps to counter our tendency to project our own perspectives on someone or something unfamiliar. A visitor might think the giant Pacific octopus is lonely living all alone in her aquarium habitat. But when an aquarium educator shares a bit of knowledge: *"Octopuses live alone in the wild, and they seek solitude and cozy, safe spaces,"* we can help people make the mental leap from what they assume to a more accurate understanding of what someone else might truly be experiencing. And seeking to understand someone's else's hopes, fears and values can make a real difference in our ability to empathize and find common ground. Studies by sociologists Matthew Feinberg and Rob Willer have found that encouraging individuals to engage in perspective-taking can reduce negative perceptions of opposing political groups and reduce polarization.[10] Other research has found that actively taking the perspective of another person can reduce racial and cultural bias toward people we consider "outside" our social identity group.[11] Consider how learning more could reframe your experience with others:

- With fellow humans, we have the unique opportunity to learn directly from them, often in their own words. Interested in having someone *share knowledge* about themselves? Invite them to tell you a story about their life. Ask open-ended questions and be an active listener. When we encourage others to share stories about their perspectives and experiences, it can make abstract ideas like values or beliefs more relatable and can build mutual understanding.

***Practice*** is the final strategy we use to foster empathy for animals, specifically the opportunity to practice empathetic action. Empathy is often thought of as a natural trait, but studies show that it behaves more like a skill—it can be developed with effort and intention. Practicing empathy, even in small ways, strengthens pathways in the brain associated with perspective-taking and emotional attunement. Trying simple exercises, such as noticing your own feelings or state of mind, or acknowledging others' emotions without judgment, can expand our capacity for empathy. We'd like to share a practice that can help cultivate the skills and mindsets that support greater empathy (Figure 8.1).[12]

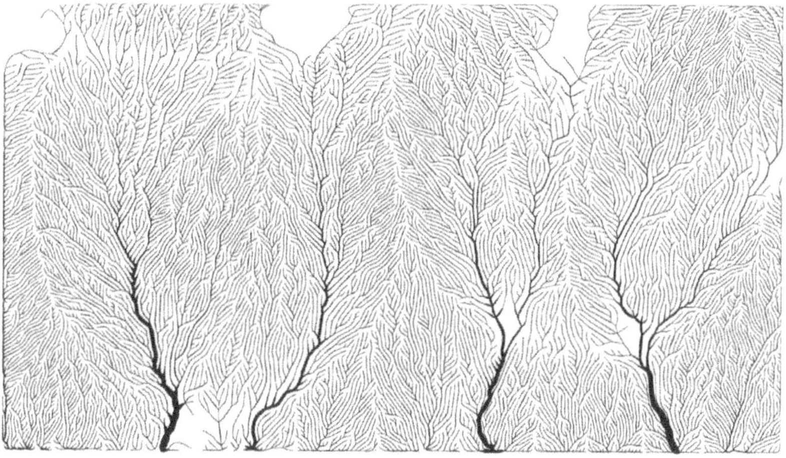

**Figure 8.1** Shinrin-yoku: The art and science of forest bathing. Image Credit: License-free image by Garry Killian on Freepik.

*Shinrin-yoku* or "forest bathing," is a practice that originated in Japan in the 1980s as part of a national health initiative and is the act of immersing oneself in the sights, sounds, smells, and overall sensory experience of a forest or natural space. Shinrin-yoku was developed in response to rising urbanization and the health challenges associated with modern life, such as stress and burnout. It reflects Japan's deep-rooted cultural and spiritual connection to nature. Historically, Shinrin-yoku draws from Shintoism, which honors natural elements like forests, rivers, and mountains as sacred; and Zen Buddhism, which emphasizes mindfulness, presence, and harmony with the natural world. These philosophies center a deep respect for nature as a source of balance and well-being, shaping how Shinrin-yoku is both practiced and understood. Shinrin-yoku incorporates these spiritual foundations with concepts of beauty in imperfection and impermanence (*wabi sabi*), the interconnectedness of nature (*komorebi*), and an inexpressible feeling of awe in nature (*yugen*). Shinrin-yoku encourages a kind of intentional presence that can shift our focus from mere observers of nature to kin. *Shinrin-yoku (Forest Bathing)* can be practiced as follows:

- Find a place in nature nearby where you can sit undisturbed for 5-10 minutes.
- Ground yourself in the place. Place your feet flat on the ground. If you are lying down, lie as flat as you can. Feel the earth beneath you. Feel the ground rise up to meet you.

- You will be engaging all your senses, but individually at first, so close your eyes and take several deep, slow, centering breaths.
- For one minute (or 10 cycles of breath), listen carefully. What sounds do you hear? Which are near and which are far? Which would you call "natural"?
- Add your sense of touch for a second minute. Can you feel a breeze on your face? What do you notice about the ground beneath you? How is your body moving in stillness?
- Spend a third minute with your sense of smell. What does the breeze bring to you? What do you notice right away and what comes with time?
- Finally, open your eyes, but instead of just seeking new things with your sight, look around and allow your vision to weave your experiences together... Take one minute to build a full, rich sensory experience of the nature around you.
- Reflect in a journal, or with a partner or friend later:
  - What was your state of mind before and after your experience?
  - What emotions (feeling states) do you notice? Try and name them. Greet each feeling (whether "positive" or "negative") with gentle awareness.
  - What is different about how your observations compared to other times spend in natural spaces?

## We Are All Animals

It is easy for people to feel separate from other animals. The simple truth is that we have many things in common with even the simplest organisms: the need for energy, safety, a drive to pass our genes to a new generation. With some creatures, the gap is even smaller. Orca whale moms share language and culture with their calves. Our own genetic codes are less than 2 percent different from chimpanzees. Separation changes us. The longer animals spend in isolation, the more likely they are to become different species. In the United States and elsewhere, we are living through increasing political and cultural polarization, actively separating ourselves from those that look, live, and think differently. Empathy is an antidote to polarization. Empathizing with animals can not only inspire care and protection of our shared planet but can also chart a course for increasing connection with other humans. Paying attention to the natural world and considering the individuality of animals can forge a foundation for greater understanding and empathy for people.

## Notes

1 Robert G. Franklin and Robert E. Adams, "Neural Mechanisms of Empathy for Humans and Animals," *ResearchGate*, 2012, https://www.researchgate.net/publication/234259960_Neural_mechanisms_of_empathy_for_humans_and_animals; Claus Lamm, Jean Decety, and Tania Singer, "Meta-Analytic Evidence for Common and Distinct Neural Networks Associated with Directly Experienced Pain and Empathy for Pain," *PLoS ONE* 5, no. 1 (2010): e10847, https://journals.plos.org/plosone/article?id=10.1371%2Fjournal.pone.0010847.

2 C. D. Batson, B. D. Duncan, P. Ackerman, T. Buckley, and K. Birch, "Is Empathic Emotion a Source of Altruistic Motivation?" *Journal of Personality and Social Psychology* 40, no. 2 (1981): 290–302, https://doi.org/10.1037/0022-3514.40.2.290; Nancy Eisenberg and Paul A. Miller, "The Relation of Empathy to Prosocial and Related Behaviors," *Psychological Bulletin* 101, no. 1 (1987): 91–119, https://doi.org/10.1037/0033-2909.101.1.91; Jean Decety and Jean M. Cowell, "The Complex Relation Between Morality and Empathy," *Trends in Cognitive Sciences* 18, no. 7 (2014): 337–9, https://doi.org/10.1016/j.tics.2014.04.008.

3 Joaquin Berenguer, "The Effect of Empathy in Pro-Environmental Attitudes and Behaviors," *Environment and Behavior* 39, no. 2 (2007): 269–83, https://doi.org/10.1177/0013916506292937; K.-P. Tam, "Dispositional Empathy with Nature," *Journal of Environmental Psychology* 35 (2013): 92–104, https://doi.org/10.1016/j.jenvp.2013.05.004; Maddalena Ienna, Ariel Rofe, Mina Gendi, Hayley E. Douglas, and Michael Kelly, "The Relative Role of Knowledge and Empathy in Predicting Pro-Environmental Attitudes and Behavior," *Sustainability* 14, no. 8 (2022): 4622, https://doi.org/10.3390/su14084622; Paul Smith, Jesse Mann, and Adam Marsh, "Empathy for Wildlife: The Importance of the Individual," *Ambio* 53 (2024): 1269–80, https://doi.org/10.1007/s13280-024-02017-4; Abigail Young, K. A. Khalil, and Jessica Wharton, "Empathy for Animals: A Review of the Existing Literature," *Curator: The Museum Journal* 61, no. 2 (2018): 327–43, https://doi.org/10.1111/cura.12257.

4 Adam D. Galinsky and Gordon B. Moskowitz, "Perspective-Taking: Decreasing Stereotype Expression, Stereotype Accessibility, and In-Group Favoritism," *Journal of Personality and Social Psychology* 78, no. 4 (2000): 708–24, https://doi.org/10.1037/0022-3514.78.4.708.

**5** Nurcan Ensari and Norman Miller, "Decategorization and the Reduction of Bias in the Crossed Categorization Paradigm," *Journal of Personality and Social Psychology* 80, no. 5 (2001): 645–61, https://doi.org/10.1037/0022-3514.80.5.645.

**6** This note includes all references for Textbox 8.1. For the four characteristics that engender empathy, please see: Oliver E. Myers Jr., *The Significance of Children and Animals: Social Development and Our Connections to Other Species*, 2nd rev. ed. (Purdue University Press, 2007), (Originally published 1998). For how young children perceive animals as peers, please see: Affrica Taylor and Veronica Pacini-Ketchabaw, "Learning with Animals: Pedagogies of Common Worlds," *Educational Philosophy and Theory* 47, no. 9 (2015): 915–27, https://doi.org/10.1080/00131857.2014.880647; Pauline Born, "Regarding Animals: A Perspective on the Importance of Animals in Early Childhood Environmental Education," *International Journal of Early Childhood Environmental Education* 6, no. 1 (2018): 7–18. For the constructivist model of learning, please see: Saul McLeod, "Piaget's Theory and Stages of Cognitive Development," *Simply Psychology*, 2023, https://www.simplypsychology.org/piaget.html. For a discussion of anthropocentrism, please see: Meredith Root-Bernstein, Liza Douglas, Andrew Smith, and Diogo Veríssimo, "Anthropomorphized Species as Tools for Conservation: Utility Beyond Prosocial, Intelligent and Suffering Species," *Biodiversity and Conservation* 22, no. 8 (2013): 1577–89.

**7** Louise Chawla, "Growing up Green: Becoming Agents of Care for the Natural World," *Journal of Developmental Practice* 4, no. 1 (2009): 6–23; Christopher Blizard and Robert M. Schuster, "Fostering Connections to Natural Places Through Cultural and Natural Storytelling," *Children, Youth and Environment* 17, no. 4 (2007): 171–206; Veronica Ornaghi, Jens Brockmeier, and Ilaria Grazzani, "Enhancing Social Cognition by Training Children in Emotion Understanding: A Primary School Study," *Journal of Experimental Child Psychology* 119 (2013): 26–39.

**8** Ulrich Gebhard, Peter Nevers, and Elke Billmann-Mahecha, "Moralizing Trees: Anthropomorphism and Identity in Children's Relationships to Nature," in *Identity and the Natural Environment: The Psychological Significance of Nature*, ed. Susan Clayton and Susan Opotow (MIT Press, 2003), 91–112.

**9** Andrew R. Todd, Galen V. Bodenhausen, Jennifer A. Richeson, and Adam D. Galinsky, "Perspective Taking Combats Automatic Expressions of Racial Bias," *Journal of Personality and Social Psychology* 100, no. 6 (2011): 1027–42, https://doi.org/10.1037/a0022308.

**10** Matthew Feinberg and Robb Willer, "From Gulf to Bridge: When Do Moral Arguments Facilitate Political Influence?" *Personality and Social Psychology Bulletin* 41 (2015): 1665–81, https://doi.org/10.1177/0146167215607842.

**11** John F. Dovidio, Marleen Ten Vergert, Tiffany L. Stewart, Samuel L. Gaertner, James D. Johnson, Victoria M. Esses, Blake M. Riek, and Adam R. Pearson, "Perspective and Prejudice: Antecedents and Mediating Mechanisms," *Personality and Social Psychology Bulletin* 30, no. 12 (2004): 1537–49, https://doi.org/10.1177/0146167204271177.

**12** Eliot Teding van Berkhout and John M. Malouff, "The Efficacy of Empathy Training: A Meta-Analysis of Randomized Controlled Trials," Journal of Counseling Psychology 63, no. 1 (2016): 32–41, https://doi.org/10.1037/cou0000093; Jean Decety, "The Neurodevelopment of Empathy in Humans," Developmental Neuroscience 32, no. 4 (2010): 257–67, https://doi.org/10.1159/000317771; Kathryn E. Smith, Gregory J. Norman, and Jean Decety, "The Impact of Empathy on Altruistic Behaviors: Evidence from Charitable Donation Studies," Psychological Science 31, no. 6 (2020): 731–41, https://doi.org/10.1177/0956797620916788.

# Part II
# Promoting Understanding Through Perspective-Taking and Thinking Strategies

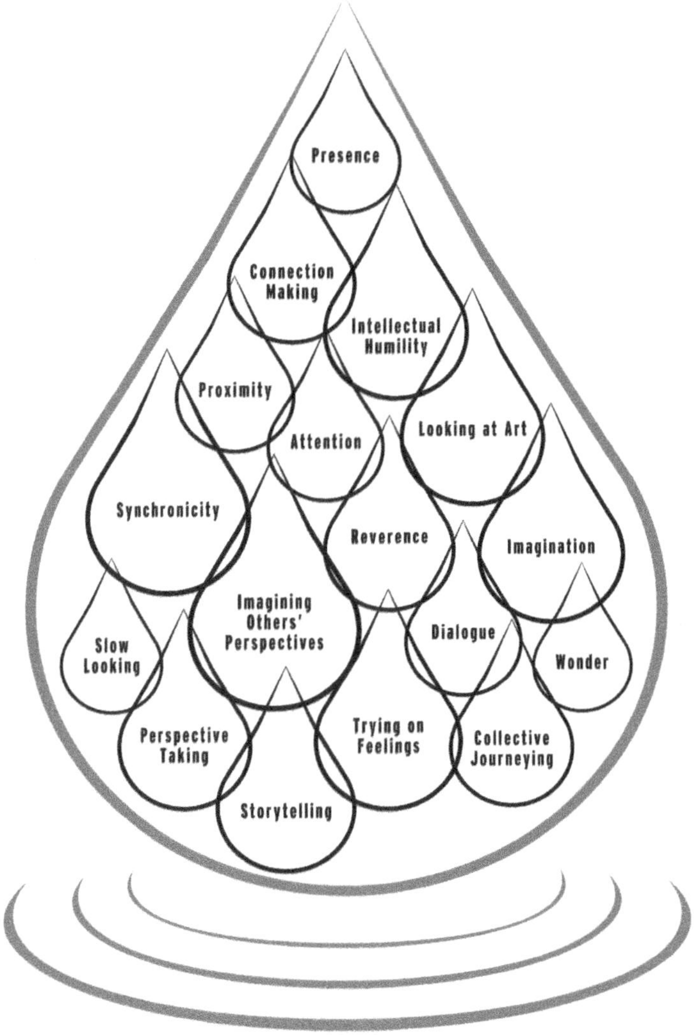

# 9 The World and Our Lenses

## Addressing Wicked Problems Through Imaginative Empathy

*Lidewij Niezink*

*Katherine Train*

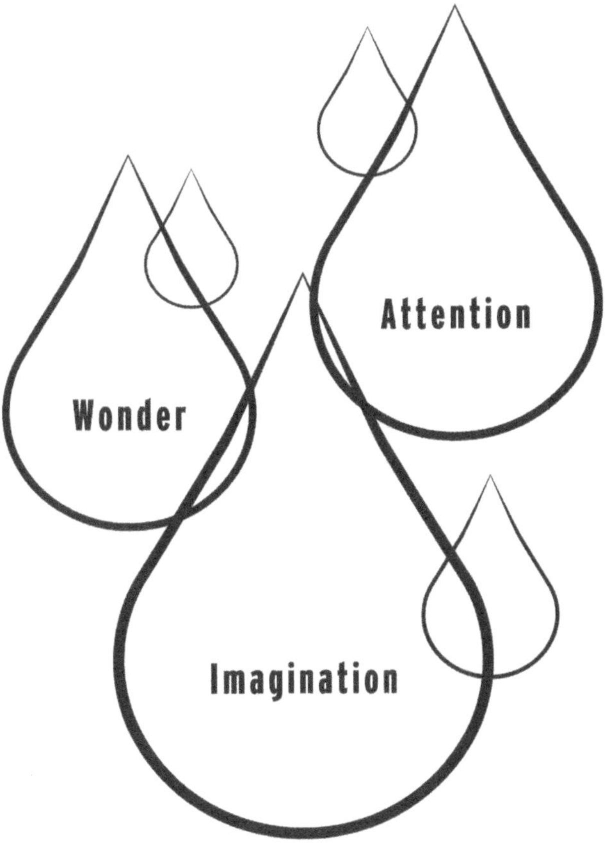

Do you remember that teacher at school who might not have taught the most interesting subject but who did it with such passion that you were captivated by what they said? Maybe it was mathematics. They'd have a whiteboard scribbled with formulas. You might have been gazing out the window, thinking about what you'd do when school was out. But then they said: "This problem can be solved this way, and the results are correct, but it's not very elegant. There is another way." They would wipe out the scribbles and start anew, guiding you through fewer formulas. You'd never considered mathematics like that. They opened your eyes to a whole new world.

What did the teacher elicit in you?

## Troubling Times

Navigating our current time is complex and uncertain. The interrelated challenges of regional conflicts, climate change, and technological ethics demand global cooperation. Geopolitical tensions and regional conflicts, not only cause prolonged and unbearable suffering, but also divert resources from sustainable development. This is especially in areas where the impact of climate change and conflict coincide, disrupting international cooperation.[1] Climate change threatens ecological stability through rising temperatures, extreme weather events, and potential ecosystem collapse.[2] All species are under threat, and the consequences are particularly severe for vulnerable communities and regions. At the same time, technological ethics raises concerns as advancements in areas like artificial intelligence and data privacy pose risks to human rights and autonomy. Responsible development and deployment of technology are crucial, and need systemic global reflection and action. We need to reimagine our collective approach to issues (Box 9.1).

## The Landscape of Imaginative Empathy

**Box 9.1 Imaginative Empathy**

Imaginative empathy is a powerful tool for navigating a complex and interconnected world. By embracing the power of imagination to connect with others, we can foster greater understanding and cooperation in addressing pressing global challenges. But what is imaginative empathy, and how does it work?

The ambiguity of *imagination* has led to interdisciplinary inquiries from fields like philosophy, cognitive science, neuroscience, psychology, and psychopathology. This makes it particularly interesting when trying to integrate these perspectives on imagination into a practice. Imaginative empathy is more than taking the perspective of another person. In imaginative empathy, we use imagination to simulate the experience of others. What is necessary in imagination is that we simultaneously have an experience of what we imagine (*What would it be like to be at the beach right now?*) as well as an experience of the actual situation we find ourselves in (*Sitting at the desk, writing this chapter, hearing a bird outside*). This simultaneous experience is very important in the practice of empathy. We need to constantly hold space for both the imagined reality of the other as well as our own actual presence in the moment. If we lose track of ourselves, we lose our anchor in actual being, and we start dreaming, hallucinating, or projecting. Of course, our experience will never be the actual experience of the other, we cannot inherently know their experience. It will, however, open us up to perspectives and questions that go beyond what we are already familiar with. We learn to hold space for the other.

Imaginative empathy helps bridge divides and foster understanding between conflicting groups. Restorative Justice is an approach that applies principles of imaginative empathy oriented toward repairing harms caused by crime and other transgressions. It brings together and invites perspectives from the victim, offender, and other possible parties involved in the crime. South Africa has a long history of Restorative Justice practices. In 2010/11, the *National Justice Crime Prevention and Security Cluster* (JCPS) endorsed the *Restorative Justice National Policy Framework*. The endorsement of this framework extends the foundations laid at *The Truth and Reconciliation Commission* of 1994. The TRC sought to uncover truths, and allowed individuals to seek amnesty, about human rights violations in the apartheid era.

The understanding, policies, and practices of Restorative Justice in South Africa align with, and are developed in consultation with elders and leaders in traditional African culture. Restorative Justice principles follow the fundamental African principle of *Ubuntu,* in which a person with rights only begins to have meaning in the context of the person within a society of persons. The application of this approach forms the backbone of justice in South Africa and encourages all parties to explore and wonder about motivations and effects of crimes on all parties. Examples such as these highlight how small and individual initiatives, as well as individuals and movements alike, sparked by a sense of wonder and concern, take meaningful steps to improve the world.

In the domain of art, we see artists like Ai Weiwei, using their work to comment on social issues, evoking wonder while raising awareness about human rights abuses. Weiwei's installations challenge viewers to confront uncomfortable truths about society, inspiring them to take action against injustice. His art serves as a catalyst for dialogue and activism, illustrating how creative expressions that elicit wonder can lead to meaningful societal change.

Perhaps, now more than ever, our world needs imaginative empathy (see Box 9.1).[3] The way information is shared in our modern age, funnels us toward more of the things we know and agree with. To widen our worldview, we need to actively reach out, and imaginative empathy can be practiced to do so. We would like to highlight two purposes:

1. As an antidote to polarization and conflict.
2. To boost creativity.

## *The Role of Imaginative Empathy in Resolving Polarization*

Polarization occurs when we rigidly identify with one way of seeing the world while rejecting other perspectives. It arises from our needs and thoughts on the one hand, and our context on the other. As an innately social species, we construct our identities from the groups we identify with. Often, we see those who agree with our worldview as in-group, and those who disagree as out-group. Our need to belong motivates us to hold beliefs that improve our standing in a group.

Our in-group has its own social norms, habits, and social pressures. And communicating with its members often results in convictions more extreme than the beliefs of individual members. We overlook that people hold multiple truths and instead, dig in our heels and stick to our convictions.

Imagine what a little wonder can do in such situations. Lifting us out of the familiar, into mental openness. What would happen if we embraced the mental flexibility to transcend our own thoughts and explore the many ways in which people see the world?

## *The Role of Imaginative Empathy in Generating Creativity*

When we think of creativity, we often associate it with inspiration. It *happens to us* and we're *riding the wave*. But according to the science of creativity, things are not that simple. Creative ideas arise from a combination of spontaneous thought and active, structured deliberation.[4] When we see a stimulus, it elicits one or more automatic, effortless, and often unconscious associations. Think of judgment when confronted with the behavior of others, and the quick, associative thinking we engage in when we brainstorm solutions to problems. It takes divergent thinking, actively exploring different directions, to move beyond first spontaneous thoughts.

Imagination can be the driving force behind divergent efforts. But when the object of our thinking is the mind of other people, the work continues. We might imagine ways in which another person experiences the world, yet these efforts might be nothing like what the person experiences. It takes conscious, deliberate, and goal directed thought, namely: cognitive control, to evaluate the outcome of imaginative efforts. Imaginative empathy allows us to diversify and *live into* the possible experiences of other people. We then check-in with *self-empathy* to prevent projection, and where possible engage in active dialogue to verify the fruits of our efforts. In self-empathy, we direct attention to our world of thoughts, feelings, and behaviors with an empathic attitude to become aware of our state of being. This is done to prepare an inner space for others (Box 9.2).[5]

**Box 9.2 AI and the Limits of Logic**

Artificial Intelligence (AI) is also capable of imagination but AI's "imagination" isn't like human imagination. It is a process of making predictions and generating possibilities based on patterns in the data it has learned. We can think of it as a super-powered tool for pattern recognition and extrapolation, guided by logic and mathematical rules.

Imagine you're teaching someone to cook by showing them thousands of recipes. Over time, they'd notice patterns such as what combinations of ingredients work well together and how different cooking methods affect the final dish. Generative AI does something similar. It "learns" patterns in data (images, text, or music) using a process called machine learning. For example, an AI might learn how colors and shapes combine to make a painting or how words form a meaningful sentence. Once an AI has learned these patterns, it can start to create new things based on them. This is where its "imagination" comes in. AI can "imagine" art by creating a new image that looks like a Van Gogh-style artwork but is completely unique. This artwork, however, is based on the thousands of existing artworks it has been trained on. AI uses probability to generate its creations.

One way AI mimics human imagination is by blending different concepts. An AI might combine features of a mouse and a dragon to create an entirely new, fantastical creature, or it might mix musical styles to create a piece that sounds part jazz, part classical.

The AI does this by mathematically combining features it has learned—like shapes, textures, or sounds—and generating something novel. AI's imagination, however, is different from ours in key ways. It is bound by training data, which means that it can only create based on what it has already been exposed to. If it hasn't seen something similar, it struggles to imagine it. AI also has no notion of intention, ethics, or values. It doesn't create with purpose or meaning; it generates outputs based on patterns, not personal intentions or moral goals. And crucially, AI has no notion of wonder or emotion. Humans do imagine with a sense of curiosity, wonder, and emotion. AI doesn't feel or ask "What if?" in the same way.

However, even though AI doesn't imagine like humans do, its ability to process vast amounts of data and identify patterns, resulting in the generation of multiple possibilities, is nevertheless powerful. When addressing the issue of climate change, AI algorithms can, for instance optimize renewable energy systems or develop predictive models for extreme weather events, allowing for better preparedness and response. AI imagination is a tool, one that amplifies human creativity and problem-solving by rapidly generating possibilities, yet it lacks the emotional depth and capacity for wonder that drives truly transformative solutions. It is up to us, with our sense of wonder, intention, and purpose, to guide AI's outputs toward meaningful and ethical applications.

## The Nature of Wonder

Wonder lies at the heart of imaginative empathy. Through wonder, we open ourselves to unfamiliar perspectives. Wonder is a fundamental element of human imagination. It is the driving force behind our ability to imagine possibilities beyond our immediate perceptions. Perhaps the teacher elicited wonder in us when they spoke of the elegance in mathematics.

Wonder always has an object which can be concrete, such as an instance of natural beauty or an artwork, or abstract, such as the moral law.[6] First intrigue is triggered, slowing us down, wanting to know more. We are often overcome by wonder, allowing ourselves to explore a thought, an experience, or an image with a "beginner's mind." Then, interest needs to be sustained. Wonder activates physiological, perceptual, and cognitive changes that "enlarge the field of peripheral vision" and can direct our attention to a broader range of objects that might otherwise go unnoticed.[7] Since the object of wonder does not necessarily involve other people's experiences, it is interesting in the exploration of solutions to global challenges.

When we wonder, the hairs on the back of our neck might rise, our heartbeat increase, our eyes widen and we might feel connected to something we can't explain. We ask ourselves: Can it be so? Wonder drives us to explore, understand, and connect with the world.[8]

In the medical field, wonder is sought as empathic curiosity.[9] More than intellectual curiosity, empathic curiosity embraces emotions inherent in interpersonal communication. It cultivates openness and resonance to emotional expressions, rather than detaching from them. Cultivating emotional resonance while imagining another's situation guides us to imagine characteristics we might otherwise not notice. Affective attunement prevents us from treating the other as a curiosity in and of itself.

Wonder pushes us beyond the familiar: While curiosity sparks an initial interest in something new, wonder compels us to move beyond superficial observation and explore deeper understanding. Experiencing freshly is something artists strive to cultivate. To imagine beyond what is known, they need to avoid observational and cognitive repetition and stagnation. Here again, human and AI imagination differs. Besides the fact that AI lacks subjective experience or consciousness, its outputs are based on patterns it has learned from past data. It cannot view something as genuinely novel outside this learned framework.[10]

Knowing too much too soon blocks openness to others and can lead to prejudice. Yet given life's pressures, this can be our default response. There are evolutionary explanations for this behavior. We cannot take everything in; we make unconscious selections and are driven by incomplete and often irrational decisions. This makes us adaptive, flexible, and quick to react but keeps us blinkered.

Practicing intellectual humility is a useful antidote to premature evaluations: the acknowledgment that much of what we believe to be true might not be so. With intellectual humility, we challenge our beliefs and opinions, knowing that we often rely on faulty or incomplete information. It might help to wonder whether the meaning of life and our relationship with others is really about *achieving* knowledge or understanding, or rather the *pursuit* thereof.

To imaginatively empathize, we wonder what the other person's experience is like and acknowledge our own reaction to it. Wonder sparks imaginative analogies between our own understanding and what we hear of other's experience. In other words, we compare and then have an automatic imaginative reaction to what we perceive. When we resist the automatic path, reconsider our perspectives with imaginative curiosity we mark the difference between our own experience and the other person's. Then we bring the other person's experience into sharper focus. We correct ourselves, check whether what we understand corresponds with the experience of the other, and seek further cues through observation and dialogue.

Wonder expands our "world of concern." It highlights the interconnectedness of life. It enables us to see beyond ourselves and recognize the inherent value in things we might have overlooked. This expanded perspective, motivates us to act to benefit others and contribute to a greater good.[11]

Wonder can be triggered by a wide range of experiences, from encountering the vastness of the universe to observing intricate details of nature. It plays a crucial role in overcoming intellectual stagnation and fostering creativity. By encouraging us to suspend judgment and embrace new possibilities, wonder serves as a catalyst for personal growth and transformative change.[12]

By nurturing wonder, we tap into a source of inspiration and motivation to help us address wicked problems facing humanity.

## From Imaginative Empathy and Wonder to Action: Addressing Global Challenges

The global challenges we face require that we transcend polarization and apply our combined creative energies. We need to tap into diverse fields of knowledge and experience to foster a holistic understanding of the challenges and their interconnectedness. Different disciplines offer unique perspectives to enrich our understanding of such complex issues. Inviting different perspectives, can help overcome the fragmentation of knowledge that hinders effective problem-solving.[13]

We propose that imaginative empathy, and wonder, provide an effective starting point. By expanding our "world of concern" through imaginative empathy, wonder can inspire a sense of responsibility to address these challenges. It leads to action because it motivates us to venture outward, with rapport for the environment.[14] Wonder deactivates our utilitarian striving, opens a sense of participating in a more general order of life; and can help us realize our interconnectedness with nature. This can lead to sustainable practices and a sense of urgency to tackle the climate crisis.

### *Technological vs. Social Imagination*

There is a growing concern about the dominance of *technological imagination*, focused on envisioning advancements in science and technology. The pervasiveness thereof, fueled by popular culture, science fiction, and substantial investments in research and development, creates a captivating narrative of the future. While technological imagination drives progress in fields like AI, data science, and biotechnology, this focus comes at the expense of *social imagination*: envisioning and working toward a better society. AI and data science have the power to solve complex problems and advance technology, but often sideline ethical implications and societal impacts addressed through social imagination.[15]

The decline of social imagination stems from various factors, including a loss of confidence in progress, the overwhelming complexity of global challenges, and the dominance of technological narratives. This shift results in a lack of compelling visions for the future, leading to pessimism, a sense of lost agency, and fear of the future.

## *The Need for a Dialectical Approach*

We don't propose throwing the baby out with the bathwater. But rather a dialectical approach, integrating both technological and social imagination perspectives. One that acknowledges the potential of technology to drive social progress while also addressing its ethical implications in service of humanity's best interests. A dialectical approach requires going "with the grain" of technological advancements while going "against the grain" to critically examine their societal impact and shape their development to benefit humanity. The potential lies to combine human imagination with AI's imagination to imagine solutions that are feasible from a technological and social perspective.

Rekindling social imagination is crucial to tackle global challenges and create a just and equitable future. A strong social vision that prioritizes human well-being and ethics, and a commitment to address root causes provides a sustainable roadmap. Social imagination guides technological innovation in service of positive transformation rather than exacerbating existing inequalities or creating new ones.

With imaginative empathy, we engage with diverse perspectives: We seek stories from people different from ourselves, challenging our own biases and actively listening to understand rather than judge. We open our eyes to a new way of looking at the world. To navigate the complexity and uncertainty of our times requires the fresh, new eyes that imaginative empathy affords us.

As we strive to foster imaginative empathy as an institutional capacity in museums and the communities we serve, it is useful to consider the capacities required for empathy. We consider empathy as the ability to hold a space for others and their perspectives. Since all people bring a host of personal, social, and cultural considerations, some with sensitivities and defenses to topics, it is necessary to create an environment conducive for the person to feel adequately safe to let go of their defenses. A conducive environment enables a person to open a space in themselves to wonder at other perspectives.

Creating a conducive environment requires building a physical and atmospheric environment to hold the experiences likely to be inspired by the collections, programs, and visitor experiences being offered. To do so, we:

1. Create opportunities to discuss what people need to build trust.

2. Display an openness to acknowledge and allow expressions of thoughts, feelings, and actions brought up by the experience.
3. Build a space in which judgments are acknowledged and suspended.

Once the conducive environment is established, a space for wonder opens. Wonder speaks to each individual. It's not something we can "instill" or "train," but we can create the conditions for it to thrive. In the museum or zoo environment, we are spoiled with expressions of beauty to inspire wonder. Wonder happens when someone is touched by what they perceive. It is felt in moments of inspiration. Imaginative empathy transforms inspiration into tangible outcomes. First, we notice the feeling of wonder and "just be with it." Let it sit, give it a name, highlight how it influences our thoughts, our bodies, our way of being. Then, extend our attention to the moment and bring innocence to see the world "with new eyes." We direct attention toward the objectives we want to accomplish. Wonder helps us to see the previously discussed wicked problems in a new light and imagine creative solutions. There is an opportunity to open our collections through invitations to perceive with something beyond our analytical minds.

What inspires your sense of wonder? How can you use it to contribute to a better world?

## Notes


1 United Nations High Commissioner for Refugees, *Global Trends Forced Displacement in 2023* (UNHCR, 2024).

2 IPCC. *Climate Change 2023: Synthesis Report. Contribution of Working Groups I, II and III to the Sixth Assessment Report of the Intergovernmental Panel on Climate Change.* Core Writing Team, edited by H. Lee and J. Romero (IPCC, Switzerland, 2023), https://doi.org/10.59327/IPCC/AR6-9789291691647.

3 Julia Jansen, "Phenomenology, Imagination and Interdisciplinary Research", in *Handbook of Phenomenology and Cognitive Science*, ed. Gallagher, Shaun and Daniel Schmicking (Springer, 2010), 141–58; Eduard Marbach, *Mental Representation and Consciousness* (Kluwer, 1993); *Restorative Justice National Policy Framework* (Restorative Justice Centre, 2015).

4 Mathias Benedek and Emanuel Jauk, "Spontaneous and Controlled Processes in Creative Cognition," in *The Oxford Handbook of Spontaneous Thought:*

*Mind-Wandering, Creativity, and Dreaming*, ed. Kalina Christoff and Kieran C. R. Fox (Oxford Library of Psychology, 2018); online edn, Oxford Academic, April 5, 2018, https://doi.org/10.1093/oxfordhb/9780190464745.013.22.

**5** Katherine J. Train and Lidewij W. Niezink, *The Self in Empathy: Self-empathy* (Empathic Intervision, 2019).

**6** Martha C. Nussbaum, *Upheavals of Thought* (Cambridge University Press, 2001).

**7** Jonathan Haidt, "The Moral Emotions," in *Handbook of Affective Sciences*, ed. R. Davidson, K. Scherer, and H. Goldsmith (Oxford University Press, 2003), 852–70.

**8** Joyce Ann Konigsburg, "Scientific Wonder, Artificial Intelligence, and Awe of the Divine," *Religions* 15, no. 4 (2024): 442, https://doi.org/10.3390/rel15040442.

**9** Jodi Halpern, *From Detached Concern to Empathy: Humanizing Medical Practice* (2001; online edn, Oxford Academic, May 27, 2015), https://doi.org/10.1093/acprof:osobl/9780195111194.001.0001.

**10** Konigsburg, *Scientific Wonder, Artificial Intelligence, and Awe of the Divine*, 442.

**11** L. Niezink and K. Train, *Integrative Empathy, From Theory to Practice* (Empathic Intervision, 2021); Robert Fuller, "The Wonder of it All: Emotion and Personal Transformation," *Revision*, 29, no. 2 (2006): 24–35.

**12** Alfred Margulies, "Toward Empathy: The Uses of Wonder," *The American Journal of Psychiatry* 141, no. 9 (1984): 1025–33, https://doi.org/10.1176/ajp.141.9.1025.

**13** Mary Midgley, *Wisdom, Information and Wonder: What is Knowledge For?* (1st ed.) (Routledge, 1991), https://doi.org/10.4324/9780203003879.

**14** Margulies, *Toward Empathy: The Uses of Wonder*, 1025–33.

**15** Geoff Mulgan, *The Imaginary Crisis: Web* (UCL, Demos Helsinki, and Untitled, April 2020).

# 10 Mirroring Art

## A Workshop for Building New Understandings Through Engagement with Art

*Zorana Ivcevic Pringle*

*Rebekah Rodriguez-Boerwinkle*

*Pablo P. L. Tinio*

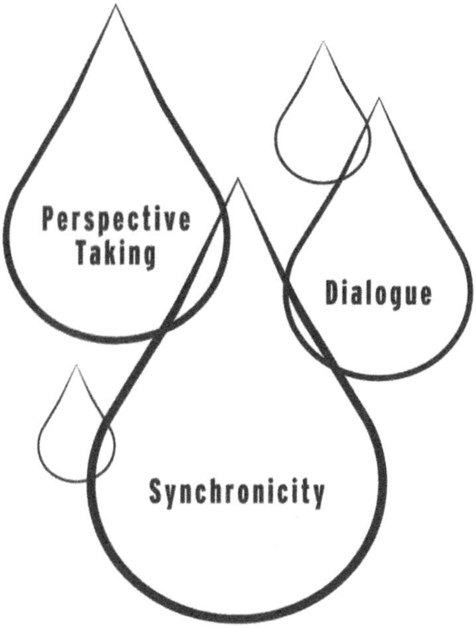

*The state of empathy, or being empathic, is to perceive the internal frame of reference of another with accuracy and with the emotional components and meanings which pertain thereto as if one were the person, but without ever losing the 'as if' condition. Thus it means to sense the hurt or the pleasure of another as he senses it and to perceive the causes thereof as he perceives them, but without ever losing the recognition that it is as if I were hurt or pleased or so forth.*

—*Psychologist Carl Rogers*[1]

In everyday discourse, empathy is often described as walking in another's shoes. This metaphorical definition is an apt one. When we walk in someone's shoes, we sense how they broke them in, whether they favor one side, or how strongly they step. We are walking their routes, possibly in places unfamiliar to us. We are seeing with their eyes in our imagination. In our mind, we perceive the other mirrored, their ideas and ways of understanding reflected in their decisions and actions. As psychologist Carl Rogers, one of the pioneers in championing the study of empathy in psychology, noted, to empathize, we need to intentionally leave our personal frame of reference and enter that of another.[2] Empathy also means sensing feelings of another and imagining those feelings as if our own.

Contemporary theory and research in psychology distinguishes two aspects of empathy: emotional empathy, which refers to concern for others' feelings, and cognitive empathy, which describes intellectual understanding of others' perspectives and viewpoints.[3] Empathy can be studied as a trait (i.e., the tendency of individuals to be habitually attuned to others' feelings and perspectives) or as a process (i.e., how it unfolds in particular interactions). When examined as a trait, empathy is a personality attribute and people vary in how empathic they are. By contrast, when empathy is considered as a process, we can consider how to jumpstart or guide it. In this chapter, we adopt this latter approach to empathy and describe how to engage art museum visitors in the empathic process through which they could gain new understandings and insights.

Research suggests that there is an increasing need to focus on the process of empathy and how to stimulate it. A meta-analysis of studies of American college students between 1979 and 2009 (with close to 14,000 people) showed that both empathic concern and perspective-taking aspects of empathy have declined through time, most prominently after the year

2000.[4] Yet, we know that greater empathy is beneficial to success in social relationships and interactions. For example, more empathetic people act in more prosocial (helping and altruistic) ways, and psychotherapists who are perceived as more empathetic have clients who benefit more from therapy.[5] Furthermore, empathic perspective-taking broadens thinking and enhances original thinking about everyday problems and people's ability to formulate creative solutions.[6]

Psychological research also shows that empathy can be enhanced through training.[7] The most effective programs are those that include a social aspect—building social skills and directly interacting with others (e.g., in service-learning programs for university students).[8] The arts have been long discussed as a means to promote empathy through the provision of new insights about experiences of others or new perspectives and understandings. Recent studies have found support for this function of the arts. Using multiple national datasets in the United States, Kou and colleagues found that engagement with art, including visual arts, performing arts, and literature, was associated with greater empathy.[9]

Here we present *Mirroring Art*, a workshop tool envisioned for use in educational programming or guided tours in art museums or galleries. We were guided by two theoretical approaches. The first is aesthetic cognitivism born in philosophy of art. This theory proposes that a major function and value of art is in its ability to facilitate understanding of ourselves, the human condition, and moral and spiritual concepts.[10] Second, our tool is rooted in the mirror model of art from psychology, which describes how art can serve as a vehicle for building understanding.[11] This theory describes art reception and appreciation as a mirror-reverse of art creation.

## Breaking Down Art Creation and Appreciation: The Mirror Model of Art

The art-making process begins with an idea—a message about the world or spiritual reality—that the artist aims to portray. This idea is not necessarily fully developed or defined. Interviews with artists show that they often start with an incomplete or only schematic vision fueled by a "narrative desire" and "a curiosity to see and express."[12] The process of translating this vision or initial idea into a work of art involves sketching and outlining, experimentation through interaction with physical materials of particular media in which artists work, and adding (or subtracting or simplifying) layers. As the work evolves, compositional elements and other features are defined. Toward the end of the artistic creation process, artists add final highlights and finishing touches.

Art appreciation begins where the artists left off—at the surface of the work. Although it is fundamentally a nonlinear process, here we describe it as a set of stages for the purpose of slow engaging. Viewers first process basic visual features, such as striking contours, textures, or colors. In this stage, what viewers notice depends on what immediately grabs their attention and what perceptual details stand out in some way. As audiences continue to engage with the work, they begin to identify elements of structure and objects (if an artwork is representational). In this stage, processing is memory-based—viewers might recognize places or items based on their prior knowledge, recall memories of their personal past, or make connections with something they have previously seen, learned, or experienced. This is when a viewer relates Georgia O'Keeffe's painting of the Brooklyn Bridge with photographs of this New York landmark they have seen, or when they remember their trip to Venice as they view The Piazza San Marco painting by Pierre-Auguste Renoir. With further engagement, the viewers start processing aesthetic emotions (from interest, wonder, and awe to discomfort, confusion, anger, and disgust), formulate aesthetic judgments, and can begin the process of meaning-making.[13] It is at this stage that audiences start to access the concepts and meanings the artist aimed to communicate. Viewers often find that the artwork helped them reflect on deeper concepts or questions and that it conveyed meaningful themes and understandings.

The mirroring that transpires between art creation and reception, between artist and audience, may be considered an empathy-filled conversation occurring through the artwork. In this process, audience members ask questions and gain understandings pertaining both to the creative process and the ideas artists aim to depict in their work. In a study at the Whitney Museum of American Art in New York, we asked visitors to identify one work of art that was especially meaningful to them and then interviewed them about what they have noticed, associated with, felt, and wondered about as they observed the work. These interviews allowed visitors to describe their lived experience of specific artworks and provide vivid details about what understandings they gained from art. Five groups of understandings emerged from the accounts of the art experience (Box 10.1).

## Box 10.1 Five Groups of Understandings That Emerged from the Accounts of the Art Experience:

1. Visitors described gaining insights about art techniques and materials. They pointed to features of works that drew them in, such as walking closer to one piece because at first glance it looked like a blueprint of a slave ship, and in another case finding red string connecting people in pictures as striking. Being attracted by prominent features of an artwork made viewers additionally engage, appreciate the artistic choices, and ask questions about such choices.
2. Viewers actively wondered about the nature of the artistic process and tried to understand the motivations, intentions, and meanings artists aimed to show through their work. Through this interaction with the art, viewers attempted to understand the artists and gain insights about artists' lives.
3. Audience members came to understand the work by creating an aesthetic narrative. They empathized with depicted protagonists in representational works, built stories around symbols in semi-abstract works, and placed the works in social and historical contexts. Viewers imagined walking into an artwork to get closer to the point of view portrayed. In these ways, audience members grasped insights about the meaning of the work and became able to personally identify with it.
4. When museum visitors gained insights about themselves and their own life history, they made explicit connections between their experiences and what they observed in the artworks. They spoke of works of art providing personal inspiration for a new way of seeing themselves and their situation, either by realizing similarities with what is expressed through the art or by drawing a contrast between their own perspectives and those of the artist. Visitors gained new insights about themselves, learned a new way of seeing their lives, made meaning of personal experiences, and came to understand a need for intellectual humility.

5. Viewers gained understandings about others, relationships, and the world or the nature of existence. Empathic feelings brought out through engagement with art created a state of open-mindedness in which viewers considered different perspectives about society or history, and pondered spiritual or religious questions. In doing so, they reached insights that went beyond the museum and beyond immediate concerns of daily living and approached questions of ultimate meaning.

## How to Facilitate Deep Engagement with Art

To build on the potential for empathy-building through engagement with art, we have developed an art museum or gallery activity that can be run as a standalone workshop or as a part of a guided tour of museum highlights. The workshop is best run for small groups of 5–10 attendees. If there are more participants, they can be split into different groups to facilitate group interaction. The following procedure is written assuming that there are multiple groups of participants, but facilitators can adapt it to use with a single group. The goal of the workshop is for facilitators (museum educators or docents) to engage audience members in directed observation based on the above-described research rooted in the mirror model of art. The workshop can be focused on a single work of art or a series of works. Engagement with each piece should take approximately thirty minutes. This could be shortened to 15–20 minutes for workshops or tours including multiple pieces or expanded to forty-five minutes for an in-depth analysis of a piece.

The facilitator introduces the workshop by sharing that psychology of art has found that people have the tendency to engage with and psychologically process art in a way that connects appreciation to artistic creation. This connection is driven by our senses, thoughts, and emotional responses in our interaction with artworks. Our initial reactions to art objects are very similar perceptually to our initial reaction to non-art objects. It is the later stages of this engagement that set apart appreciation of art and that define the aesthetic experience. The workshop dives into the process of deeply engaging with art, so it is most effective if one of the participants is an artist who created the work around which the workshop is focused (but whose identity is kept secret until halfway through the workshop; see description below). If this is not possible, facilitators should have a lot of information about the artwork—artist's ideas, motivations, inspirations, emotions, and meanings they intended to convey. We have conducted the workshop at the Designing for Empathy Summit at the Phillips Collection (without an artist present) and the event at the Glencairn Museum (with an artist present). This tool was originally developed for use with the visual arts, but it can be adapted and used for other art media or domains (e.g., music, poetry), as long as workshop attendees can freely engage with the work.

The benefit of a workshop based on the mirror model of art is that it slows down the process of experiencing art. Researchers have found that visitors do not spend a lot of time looking at art. Studies in major art museums, such as the Metropolitan Museum of Art in New York and the Art Institute of Chicago, showed that people on average spend about thirty seconds in front of artworks, including those pieces that are considered masterpieces of museum collections, even taking into account reading the label.[14] Applying the mirror model in guiding appreciation of specific works of art provides a formal approach to help visitors experience art deeply and connect art reception and art creation.

## Preparation:

Facilitators distribute several clipboards and writing implements. It is not necessary for everyone in the group to have a clipboard, but it can be useful for participants to be able to take some notes on the discussion. There is also no need to consolidate all notes; this can be a fairly informal process.

## Introduction:

The facilitator should warn participants that the workshop breaks down a process that often happens quickly and in a non-linear fashion. Ask participants to try as much as they can to stay focused on specific questions and avoid the temptation to jump further or deeper into the aesthetic experience. Reassure participants that the workshop will get where they aim to go.

## *The Experience Flow:*

1) **Perception:** Standing in front of a selected artwork, the facilitator starts the engagement by asking participants to focus on perceptual features.

   *Example script:* In your group, discuss what you first notice in the piece. This can involve surface features, dimensions, and physical orientation of the work, texture, colors, contrasts or highlights, or something else that jumps at people. How do these aspects impact your overall experience of the work? It is fine if different people focus on different aspects. Make note of similarities and differences in what you are noticing.

   After several minutes, participants are invited to share what they discussed within their groups. Facilitators point out that art appreciation starts with what is grabbing attention and what might be the finishing touches the artist created.

2) **Memory-based search:** Next, facilitators move the discussion to the memory-based stage of processing.

   *Example script:* In your group, discuss what the work reminds you of. What is being shown? Are there specific depictions or representations (such as people, places, or things)? What do you notice about the composition and structure of the work? Does it remind you of anything? Does the work bring up any experiences from your personal life or something that you have read, heard, or learned about previously?

   Facilitators should provide more time for discussion than in the first step and then provide an opportunity for groups to share. Facilitators point out that after the first and very quick impressions, art appreciation moves to memory associations, both autobiographical and knowledge-based. These associations can generate new questions about the meaning of the artwork and the creative process.

3) **Meaning-making:** Finally, facilitators engage participants in the step focused on aesthetic judgments, emotions, and meaning-making.

   *Example script:* Now we will move to considering the motivations and ideas behind the work. Can you get any clues from the title of the work or style features? Imagine if you were the artist, why would you have created this piece? (If the artwork is a historical piece, the facilitator can also ask participants to consider what they might know about the artist and what they might know about the historical context in which the work was created.)

4) **Group sharing:** As facilitators invite groups to share, they point to similarities and differences in ideas and meanings shared. Facilitators acknowledge that the thoughts shared are hypotheses and they can be tested in relation to what we know about the artist's process and meanings. At this point, there are two routes for the continued engagement, depending on whether the creator of the work is present or not.

## *Option A: If the Artist Is Present*

*Example script:* We have a surprise for you. The artist is among us, and we can ask them directly how close your hypotheses were to their ideas and process. (Before the workshop, the artist should be instructed to minimize their participation in the workshop and act as an observer.)

The facilitator should ask a series of questions from the artist guided by the mirror model stages. After each set of questions, the facilitator points to similarities and differences between the artist's account of their creative process and viewers' aesthetic processing of the artwork.

*Example script, first stage:* Could you tell us what prompted or motivated you to create this piece? What was your inspiration? What ideas or meanings did you intend to portray or communicate?

*Example script, second stage:* How did you go about starting work on the piece? Tell us about the structural composition as it relates to the subject. How did your vision or ideas develop as you worked to create the piece? What was your physical process of working in your medium (with your materials) to complete this work?

*Example script, third stage:* What were the last things you did as you decided the work was near complete? What did you imagine audiences would notice first?

### *Option B: If the Artist Is not Present*

If it is not possible to have the artist present in the workshop, facilitators should use artists' writings on their work, descriptions of their point of view or motivation, and historical analyses of the process of creation of a particular piece to prepare insights into these questions ahead of time. For contemporary artists, or those who worked in relatively recent times, interviews or videos might also be available.

Art has a powerful potential to foster empathy, creativity, and deepened understanding of one's self and others. The design of this workshop provides a counterpoint to the fleeting, unguided art interactions during typical museum visits, and in doing so, bridges the meaning-making gap between artists and audiences. By framing art appreciation as a mirror of the creative process, this workshop reveals the pathways through which audiences can connect sensory impressions to personal memories, construct aesthetic narratives, and grapple with broader existential and societal issues. These layers of engagement not only enhance the art-viewing experience but also offer a structured means to cultivate empathy and open-mindedness, qualities increasingly vital in our interconnected yet often divided world.

## *Acknowledgment*

The authors were supported by a grant funded by the Templeton Religion Trust. The opinions expressed in this publication are those of the authors and do not necessarily reflect the view of the Templeton Religion Trust.

## Notes

1 Carl R. Rogers, "Empathic: An Unappreciated Way of Being," *The Counseling Psychologist* 5, no. 2 (1975): 2–10, https://doi.org/10.1177/001100007500500202.

2 Rogers, "Empathic," 5.

3 Mark H. Davis, *Empathy: A Social Psychological Approach* (Westview Press, 1994).

4 Sara H. Konrath, Edward H. O'Brien, and Courtney Hsing, "Changes in Dispositional Empathy in American College Students Over Time: A Meta-Analysis," *Personality and Social Psychology Review* 15, no. 2 (2011): 180–98, https://doi.org/10.1177/1088868310377395.

5 Yingying Yin and Yong Wang, "Is Empathy Associated with More Prosocial Behaviour? A Meta-Analysis," *Asian Journal of Social Psychology* 26, no. 1 (2023): 3–22, https://doi.org/10.1111/ajsp.12537; Robert Elliott et al., "Therapist Empathy and Client Outcome: An Updated Meta-Analysis," *Psychotherapy* 55, no. 4 (2018): 399–410, https://doi.org/10.1037/pst0000175.

6 Adam M. Grant and James W. Berry, "The Necessity of Others Is the Mother of Invention: Intrinsic and Prosocial Motivations, Perspective Taking, and Creativity," *Academy of Management Journal* 54, no. 1 (2011): 73–96, https://doi.org/10.5465/AMJ.2011.59215085; Sanaa J. Kripal and Roni Reiter-Palmon, "The Role of Empathy in Problem Construction and Creative Problem Solving," *Learning and Individual Differences* 114 (2024): 102501, https://doi.org/10.1016/j.lindif.2024.102501.

7 Emily Teding van Berkhout and John M. Malouff, "The Efficacy of Empathy Training: A Meta-Analysis of Randomized Controlled Trials," *Journal of Counseling Psychology* 63, no. 1 (2016): 32.

8 Xiao Wu et al., "Categories of Training to Improve Empathy: A Systematic Review and Meta-Analysis," *Psychological Bulletin* 150, no. 10 (2024): 1237–60, https://doi.org/10.1037/bul0000453; Chloe S. Gordon et al., "A Systematic Meta-Analysis and Meta-Synthesis of the Impact of Service-Learning Programs on University Students' Empathy," *Educational Research Review* 37 (2022): 100490, https://doi.org/10.1016/j.edurev.2022.100490.

9 Xiaonan Kou, Sara Konrath, and Thalia R. Goldstein, "The Relationship Among Different Types of Arts Engagement, Empathy, and Prosocial Behavior," *Psychology of Aesthetics, Creativity, and the Arts* 14, no. 4 (2020): 481–92, https://doi.org/10.1037/aca0000269.

10 Christoph Baumberger, "Art and Understanding. Defence of Aesthetic Cognitivism," in *Bilder sehen. Perspektiven der Bildwissenschaft*, ed. Michael Greenlee et al. (Schnell + Steiner, 2013), 41–67; Gordon Graham, *Philosophy of the Arts: An Introduction to Aesthetics*, 3rd ed. (Routledge, 2005), https://doi.org/10.4324/9780203696224.

11 Pablo P. L. Tinio, "From Artistic Creation to Aesthetic Reception: The Mirror Model of Art," *Psychology of Aesthetics, Creativity, and the Arts* 7, no. 3 (2013): 265–75, https://doi.org/10.1037/a0030872.

12 Vlad Glaveanu et al., "Creativity as Action: Findings from Five Creative Domains," *Frontiers in Psychology* 4 (2013): 176, https://doi.org/10.3389/fpsyg.2013.00176.

13 Paul J. Silvia, "Looking Past Pleasure: Anger, Confusion, Disgust, Pride, Surprise, and Other Unusual Aesthetic Emotions," *Psychology of Aesthetics, Creativity, and the Arts* 3, no. 1 (2009): 48–51, https://doi.org/10.1037/a0014632.

**14** Lisa F. Smith, Jeffrey K. Smith, and Pablo P. L. Tinio, "Time Spent Viewing Art and Reading Labels," *Psychology of Aesthetics, Creativity, and the Arts* 11, no. 1 (2017): 77–85, https://doi.org/10.1037/aca0000049; Jeffrey K. Smith and Lisa F. Smith, "Spending Time on Art," *Empirical Studies of the Arts* 19, no. 2 (2001): 229–36, https://doi.org/10.2190/5MQM-59JH-X21R-JN5J.

# 11 Exploring Perspectives and Fostering Empathy in Conversations About Art

## Three Learning Experience Models

*Julie A. Carmean*

*Elizabeth H. Diament*

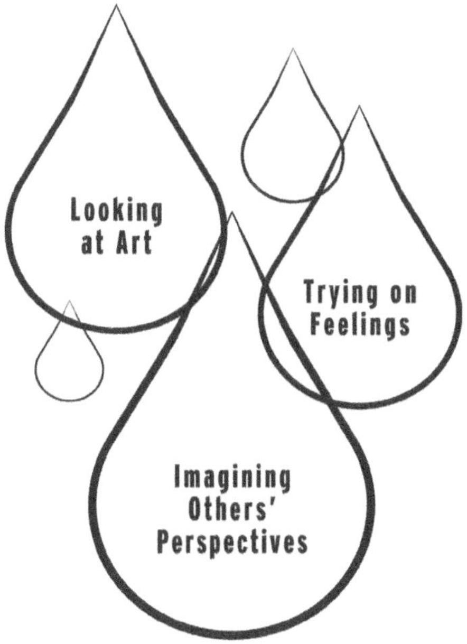

# Introduction

Across time, people have looked to art as a mirror to more keenly understanding themselves and as a window into viewing and connecting with the experiences and perspectives of others. In our modern world, museums have become primary locations in which people seek to see themselves and each other in works of art. At the National Gallery of Art, in Washington, DC, we recognize the power of art for society and aim "to serve the nation by welcoming all people to explore and experience art, creativity, and our shared humanity."[1] One of our institutional core values, "empathy and generosity of spirit," supports this mission, inspiring and grounding our museum work, as we strive to impact culture. In our Division of Learning and Engagement, this value is central to program design and pedagogy. By centering open-ended conversations about art, participant voices are valued and heard, diverse perspectives are shared, and often meaningful emotional connections are made.

The approaches we use for creating museum experiences that foster empathy are largely informed by research developed at Project Zero at the Harvard Graduate School of Education. Researchers at Project Zero, such as Shari Tishman, Ron Ritchhart, and Veronica Boix Mansilla, have examined ideas around slow looking at art, using thinking routines, and perspective-taking, which are foundational to the design and teaching of our programs.[2]

Thinking routines, pithy sets of open-ended questions that can be easily held in mind, target specific thinking dispositions, such as observing and describing, reasoning with evidence, and perspective-taking. They encourage both individual and collaborative thinking and are intended for facilitating respectful group conversations. Thinking routines are often used repeatedly with groups to make complex thinking become second-nature.

For over twenty years, thinking routines have been at the heart of our teaching practice at the National Gallery. We have used and adapted a range of routines and created some new ones to connect various audiences with art in our collection and to structure deep conversations that reveal and unpack layers of meaning. We have found that thinking routines not only support critical thinking, but also yield profound outcomes in social and emotional learning, such as active listening, effectively, and building trust and community.

As part of a response to teacher survey feedback in 2020, in which teachers requested more social-emotional learning (SEL) strategies, we further probed the relationship between SEL and looking at art. We collaborated with several leaders in the field of social-emotional learning and the Project Zero researchers to consider what qualities of SEL could transpire when discussing art. We discovered that thinking routines that target perspective-taking especially promote qualities of SEL, like cultivating self-awareness, trying on new feelings, and demonstrating empathy and compassion.[3] These ideas became central to a wide range of subsequent programs, including the 2021–2023 Summer Institute for Educators, "The Power of Art: Pathways to Critical Thinking and Social-Emotional Learning," and the second edX Massive Open Online Course (MOOC), *Teaching Complex Thinking through Art with the National Gallery of Art*.[4]

In this chapter, we offer three examples that describe the "experiential learning of empathy" through our museum education practice, presented as models that can be replicated elsewhere.[5] Engaging deeply with works of art, particularly those that offer emotionally evocative or ambiguous narratives, can be especially well-suited to having these empathy-building experiences. Each case study highlights a thinking routine in action and aims to foster the capacity for the three types of empathy as defined by psychologist and author Daniel Goleman: Cognitive Empathy (the ability to understand another person's perspective), Emotional Empathy (the ability to feel what another person feels), and Compassionate Empathy (the ability to sense what another person needs from you and to act accordingly).[6]

## Learning Experience Model 1: Circle of Viewpoints

### Practicing Compassionate Empathy with "The Return of the Prodigal Son" by Bartolomé Esteban Murillo

*With this kind of empathy, we not only understand a person's predicament and feel with them but are spontaneously moved to help, if needed.*

—*Daniel Goleman*[7]

Over many years, the National Gallery has partnered with local teachers in the Washington, DC area, including Sacred Heart Bilingual Catholic School, to bring museum experiences into the classroom and support the integration of art in formal learning settings. As part of one of the National Gallery's MOOCs, we collaborated with a fifth-grade teacher from Sacred Heart School on a lesson about teaching perspective-taking and empathy using a work of art. Before this filmed lesson, the educator had been teaching units in both Religion and Language Arts classes on the theme of forgiveness. She had read the Biblical parable "The Return of the Prodigal Son" with her students, and together they discussed lessons from the story.[8]

The educator brought the characters to life by introducing the painting *The Return of the Prodigal Son* by Spanish artist, Bartolomé Esteban Murillo (1667/1670), who uses a large canvas—roughly nine feet square—to invite viewers into the story (Figure 11.1).[9] It's as if the viewer is present experiencing the father's compassion toward his wayward son, at the very moment he returns home after squandering his inheritance.

Murillo sets the story in seventeenth-century Seville, relating the image to a contemporary audience who might have identified with the characters. Dressed in rags with dirty bare feet, the son kneels before his father and begs for forgiveness. We witness his father lovingly embrace him. Murillo places these two figures in the center of the painting, within a triangular composition, highlighting the central message—the emotional and physical expression of full forgiveness as illustrated through the father's leaning down, toward his kneeling son.

Well-dressed servants present the Prodigal Son with luxurious new clothes, shoes, and a ruby ring. Murillo makes it clear that the son will be accepted back into the family and the community. However, the artist seems to acknowledge the tension in the parable. The character with a confused expression on his face staring at the ring might be the older brother who jealously questions his father's acts of compassion and generosity.[10]

In the lesson, after careful looking at the work of art, students observed elements, such as composition, body language, and facial expressions. The teacher then introduced the thinking routine *Circle of Viewpoints* which students used to brainstorm the many perspectives represented and to connect and empathize with the characters (Box 11.1).[11] Before embarking on the discussion, she reminded them that although they can imagine

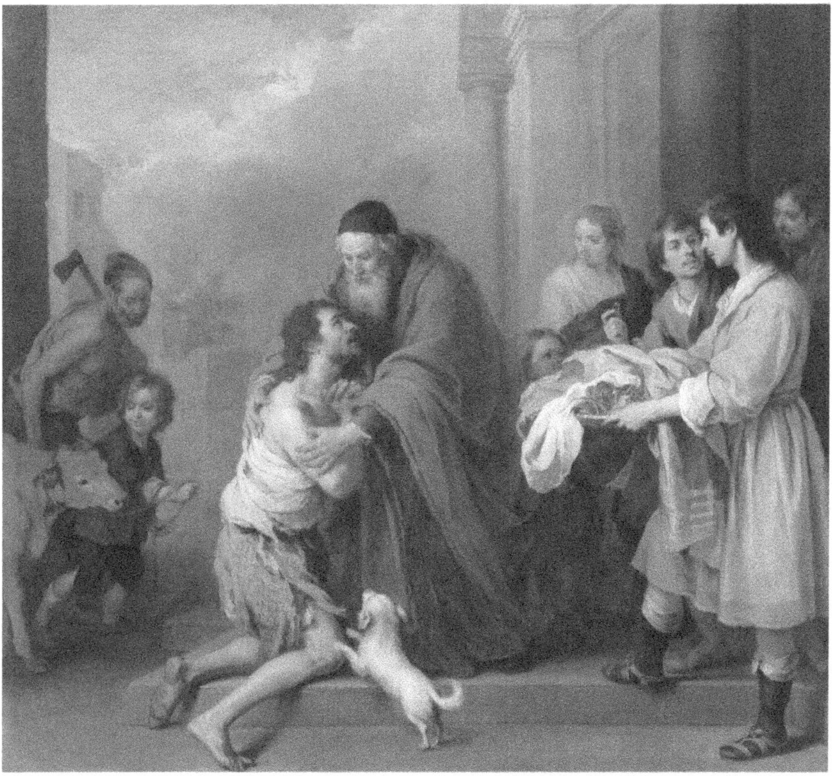

**Figure 11.1** Bartolomé Esteban Murillo, *The Return of the Prodigal Son,* (1667/1670), oil on canvas, 93 1/16 x 102 3/4 in., National Gallery of Art, Gift of the Avalon Foundation, 1948.12.1. Credit: Courtesy of The National Gallery of Art, Washington, DC.

perspectives, no one can ever fully know what it is like to be in someone else's shoes, and they must imagine with care and sensitivity.

**Box 11.1 Circle of Viewpoints Thinking Routine Steps**

1. *I am* . . . (name of character/person/viewpoint) (OR) *I am thinking of* . . . (the topic/story/event) *from the point of view of* . . . (the viewpoint you've chosen).
2. *I think* . . . (describe your thoughts about the topic/story/event from the character's viewpoint).
3. *I wonder* . . . (OR) *A question I have from this viewpoint is* . . . (ask a question from this viewpoint).

To begin the routine, students listed, in a pie chart format (the "circle of viewpoints"), all the characters represented who would have had a point of view, and even perspectives outside the painting, such as the mother and the artist Murillo. Then each student chose a character and considered the story from that perspective, imagining their character's thoughts and questions. Finally, they each created an "I Am" poem from their character's perspective and shared these aloud.

The "I Am" poem gave students a creative way to record their thoughts, feelings, and wonders from their characters' points of view. The words students used in their poems—*unfair, jealous, angry, sad, happy, excited, wasteful, kind, poor, disappointed, confused, hungry, blessed, safe*—expressed the wide-ranging emotions and viewpoints of the characters—and by extension, of these imaginative students. The final move in the routine "I wonder . . . (or) A question I have from this viewpoint is. . ." led to curiosity and openness as to what that character was thinking and wondering about. One student imagined the older resentful brother asking: "Why would my father treat my brother so well and make him a whole feast after wasting all my dad's money?"

Then, to illuminate the perspective of the artist, the teacher shared that Murillo was orphaned as a young boy and, in adulthood painted several versions of the Prodigal Son. The artwork students were discussing was originally in the Chapel of St. George in the Hospital de la Caridad, a charity hospital dedicated to supporting those in need. It was one of six works commissioned by the hospital that Murillo painted between 1667 and 1670 depicting the stories of mercy and charity, to inspire viewers to open their hearts toward acts of compassion. These works include acts of kindness, such as feeding the hungry, giving drink to the thirsty, visiting the imprisoned, and providing clothes to those without.

The teacher concluded with one of the most meaningful aspects of the lesson—a time for reflection on how student thinking shifted after looking at this artwork while using the *Circle of Viewpoints* routine. She asked them: "What new ideas do you have about the story that you didn't have before? What new questions do you have?"

Students responded with profound insights and personal growth:

> *Maybe I should be less judgmental. Maybe I should take a deeper dive and ask questions, ask why they did it.*
>
> *You can't look at a person and say it is just a person. You have to look closer and think what they're thinking.*

*Everyone makes mistakes. We should be given the chance to correct mistakes and make better choices. (Translated from Spanish)*

*The brother didn't deserve [to be forgiven] but he really does need help, so even if [I were] mad, I would help.*

*Be grateful for what you have and appreciate what parents give you. Because not all [of us] have things to survive.*[12]

Not only did students practice cognitive empathy in *Circle of Viewpoints* and articulate emotional empathy in their "I Am" poems, but their reflections indicated that they were moved toward taking compassionate empathic action: to be less judgmental, to ask questions, to correct mistakes and make better choices, to help those who need it, and to be grateful for what they have been given.

Murillo's *Return of the Prodigal Son* is a powerful painting both in the expressive way it is painted and the story it tells. With its central tenet of Compassionate Empathy, it gives us a clear example of what it looks like to forgive wholeheartedly when wronged and to care for the suffering of another person. The painting also suggests the opposite of Compassionate Empathy, which one might describe as enmity and jealousy, suggested by the facial expression of the returning son's brother. Seeing Murillo's imagination on display sparks our own imagination toward a more complex understanding of the painting's narrative.

The *Circle of Viewpoints* thinking routine gave students a framework to take perspectives and give voice to multifaceted emotional responses. After moving through the steps of the routine, students often expanded their original perspectives and empathized with the characters in the painting. As one teacher remarked after trying this lesson: "We can see ourselves in every character–we can stretch and imagine ourselves in all these roles."

## Learning Experience Model 2: Three Details / Three Feelings

### Practicing Emotional Empathy with "A Sunburst Restrained" by María Berrío

*Emotion is the moving and cementing force.*

–*John Dewey*[13]

As part of the 2022 Summer Institute for Educators, an annual week-long intensive, researcher Shari Tishman, who specializes in slow looking and thinking routines, presented on the theme of "Building Emotional Capacity through Slow Looking at Art." Together with Tishman, we developed a new thinking routine titled *Three Details / Three Feelings*, which she showcased in her presentation. We designed the new routine with two goals in mind: to build awareness of the feelings that surface when engaging with a work of art and to strengthen the dispositions of perspective-taking and emotional empathy by "trying on" the feelings of others. We recognized the value of cultivating awareness of our own feelings in order to imagine what someone else might be feeling. Ultimately, for people to practice empathy, we need to be able to "try on" the feelings of others. Works of art can provide a powerful point of reference for accessing our own emotions and those of others.

In a subsequent teacher professional development workshop, we used the *Three Details / Three Feelings* routine with the artwork *A Sunburst Restrained* (2019) by Colombian American artist María Berrío (Figure 11.2).[14]

Berrío created this 5-by 6-foot artwork using her signature collage process of combining Japanese paper and watercolor on canvas. Her luminous painting features two female figures reclining in a pastel tile setting. Branches of leaves and lemons cut across a pink foreground. This work was partly inspired by a poem by Pablo Neruda called "Ode to a Lemon," in which he finds beauty in everyday objects, such as a simple lemon.[15]

We selected this painting to pair with our new thinking routine because its intrinsically ambiguous and complex qualities invite exploration of feelings and perspectives. Although it is replete with recognizable elements, its mood and facial expressions are enigmatic, suggesting multiple interpretations and evoking a range of emotional responses.

The facilitator began the *Three Details / Three Feelings* routine by inviting the group of educators to look slowly and closely at the work of art (Box 11.2). Observations were shared before moving to the first prompt of the routine: "Name one feeling that this work of art suggests for you. What are three details that you see that evoke this feeling?"

To allow for varying comfort levels in discussing feelings evoked, the facilitator offered options: **(1)** What feeling(s) do you perceive being portrayed within

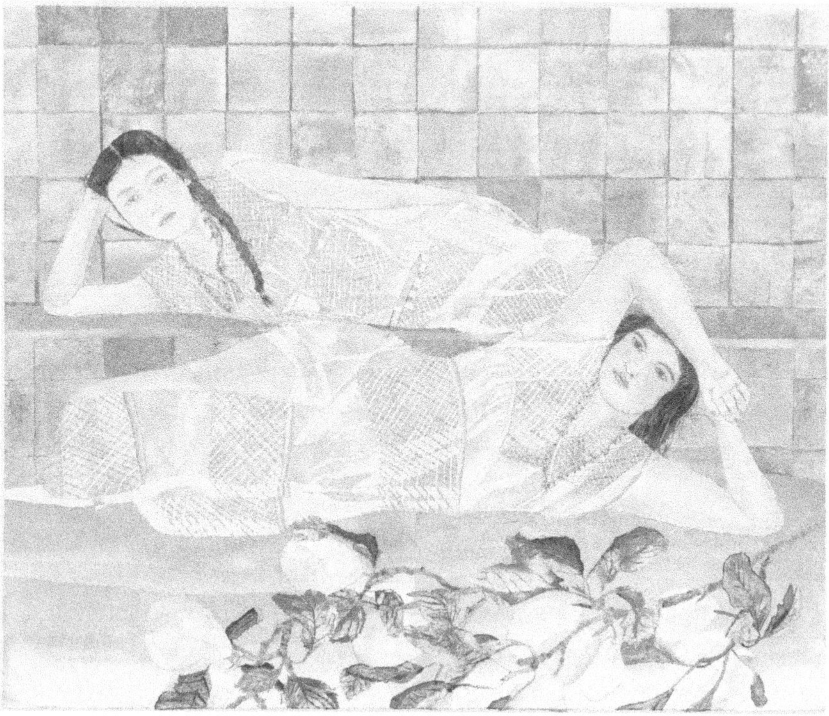

**Figure 11.2** María Berrío, *A Sunburst Restrained* (2019), collage with Japanese paper and watercolor on canvas, 152.4 x 182.9 cm. (60 × 72 in.), Gift of Erika and John Toussaint, 2020.2.1. Credit: Courtesy of The National Gallery of Art, Washington, DC.

the work of art? **(2)** What feeling(s) does this work of art evoke for you personally? Participants chose how they preferred to engage—whether expressing feelings in the artwork or their personal feelings toward it, and whether to keep private or share them aloud.

## Box 11.2 Three Details / Three Feelings Thinking Routine Steps

1. **1 Feeling / 3 Details:** Look slowly and carefully at the work of art. Name one feeling that this work of art suggests for you—a feeling portrayed within the art or a feeling the art evokes for you personally. What are three details you see in the artwork that evoke this feeling?

2. **1 Detail / 3 Feelings:** Choose one of these details and think of three more feelings that this detail could evoke. What three additional feelings might this detail evoke?
3. **Stretch:** Now stretch yourself and try on somebody else's feeling, one that wasn't a first response for you. Look again at the work of art through the lens of that new feeling. Now, what do you notice? How does this feel?

Responses ranged from projected feelings of detachment based on the women's half-closed eyes and languid positions to a personal feeling of invigoration from the iridescent colors, repetition of squares, and vibrant lemons.

The facilitator invited the group to consider the second prompt: "Choose one detail you noticed and think of three more feelings that this detail could evoke." At this juncture, she introduced the *Hoffman List of Feeling Words* as a reference for identifying more nuanced feelings.[16] Some participants focused on the women's seemingly blank gazes and attributed various feelings: determination, entrapment, or satisfaction. Others noticed the prominence of the lemons and imagined the contrasting feelings of bitterness, freshness, and abundance.

Next, the facilitator asked participants to stretch themselves and try on someone else's feelings and look at the artwork through the lens of that new feeling. After considering this quietly, participants discussed in pairs how it felt to look through someone else's emotional response. One person originally sensed tension in the work but "tried on" her partner's feeling of "contentment." She described that as she "tried on" contentment, her whole body relaxed, her way of seeing the painting changed, and she noticed more color. Others expressed:

> *It's challenging to stretch and use that muscle because we know what is true to us and feel it in our bodies.*

> *This was hard to do, but very rewarding . . . Sometimes our perspectives are more rigid because we know and can feel our emotions. But the artwork or situation has more nuance, and we can discover more flexibility in our thinking.*

The facilitator then shared some contextual information, such as the voice of the artist, María Berrío, and concluded with the following questions: "Are there any new feelings or thoughts coming to mind now that you've heard a bit about the artist and her work? What does this leave you wondering about the painting or other things?"

Berrío's quote about the women in the painting, "the ghostly pallor of their skin suggests another worldliness; they are more spirit than flesh," led one participant to notice the translucent appearance of the women in the painting, sensing a spiritual quality and a feeling of their inner strength.

The *Three Details / Three Feelings* routine encouraged participants to identify their feelings, connect those feelings to evidence within the painting, and use them as a lens to make meaning of the art. By also using the language of "trying on" someone else's feelings, they expanded their range of emotional responses, experimented with affective perspective-taking while maintaining the freedom to hold onto their own perspectives. Additionally, as the museum educator shared the artist's voice and contextual information, yet another perspective was revealed. This further stretched participants to reexamine their original feelings and thoughts about the painting. In conclusion, participants summarized the impact of this routine:

> *We can grow from sitting with uncomfortable feelings and learn how to handle them.*
>
> *We can build empathy through exploring other peoples' emotions.*

Practicing the dispositions of articulating feelings and exploring viewpoints can reveal as much about ourselves as it can about those we are seeking to understand.

Opportunities to pause, to allow art to move us, to identify our feelings, and to try on the feelings of another are few and far between, both in formal learning settings and in life. Yet conversations like this, with art as the centerpiece, hold immense potential for expanding a disposition toward honoring what it means to be human, practicing vulnerability and empathy, and valuing the power of art. These conversations give us a template for the heart and mind to imagine the varied perceptions of others and to care to relate to one another with curiosity and openness. Through this work, we broaden our capacity to "be" with each other and to express emotional empathy—sharing in the feelings of another person. Like Berrío's art, we too can enact the dignity and inner strength of being together in connection.

## Learning Experience Model 3: Step Inside

### Practicing Cognitive Empathy with "Kitchen Table Series" by Carrie Mae Weems

*Under the gaze of each group's observant eyes, the characters and places within the depicted scenes come alive and the viewer may live a little in them, moved—and even transported.*

—*Rika Burnham*[17]

For several years, we have offered perspective-taking tours for high school students. Docents and staff have employed thinking routines that promote perspective-taking through art, facilitated with an emphasis on self-awareness, respect, and empathy. In this final case study, we highlight a perspective-taking tour which took place with a group of eleventh and twelfth-grade art students from the Washington International School and focused on the *Kitchen Table Series* by Carrie Mae Weems.[18] A museum educator led students in looking and discussing what they saw and then guided them through a *Step Inside* routine to explore the viewpoints of the characters represented in the photographs. This lesson was captured on video and is featured in the "Exploring Viewpoints" unit in our online course *Teaching Complex Thinking through Art.*[19]

The lesson began in the East Building of the National Gallery with the museum educator inviting students to take a walk around a large gallery exhibiting the special installation of the twenty platinum/palladium prints and fourteen screenprints of text that comprise Weems' *Kitchen Table Series*.

Weems used her own kitchen table to tell stories of family, friendship, gender roles, race, and interpersonal power dynamics using black-and-white photography. She chose the kitchen table as a relatable setting for exploring these themes through the multiple perspectives of her "characters." She posed herself as the "main character" and recruited neighbors, friends, and colleagues to be the other "characters."

Weems portrayed interconnected scenes in the series. While she, the table, chairs, and lamp are constants (though her clothing, expressions, and body language are ever-changing), the other characters and props invite the viewer to imagine a variety of dramatic interactions and conversations—based both on what they see in the photographs and on what they've experienced at their own kitchen tables.

The museum educator asked students to work in small groups to discuss: "What do you think is going on in this artwork? And what do you see that makes you say that?" Students looked together, identifying the different characters and poses of a mother and daughter, a woman and man, and a woman with friends. They also noticed the props—posters, a telephone, makeup mirror, birdcage, books and papers, and playing cards—which suggested different narratives.

The educator contextualized the work of art by asking students to read aloud quotes from the artist, such as: "I use my body as a stand-in, but I never think of it as being about me. Rather, the character helps to reveal something that is more complicated about the lives of women," and "[*Kitchen Table Series* is] not simply a voice for African American women, but more generally for women."

Next, the museum educator introduced the high schoolers to the *Step Inside* routine, designed to teach how a viewpoint is formed and how to explore someone else's viewpoint.[20] Aligning with the language of the routine, she explained how people's viewpoints develop—from what they perceive with their five senses, what they know about or believe, and what they care about, value, hope, and fear. The routine examines these three aspects of a viewpoint through specific thinking moves: **(1)** Step Inside the Body, **(2)** Step Inside the Heart, and **(3)** Step Inside the Mind (Box 11.3).

### Box 11.3 Step Inside Thinking Routine Steps

1. **Step Inside the Body:** What might the person or thing perceive with their five senses?
2. **Step Inside the Mind:** What might the person or thing know about, understand, or believe?
3. **Step Inside the Heart:** What might the person or thing care about, value, hope for, or fear?

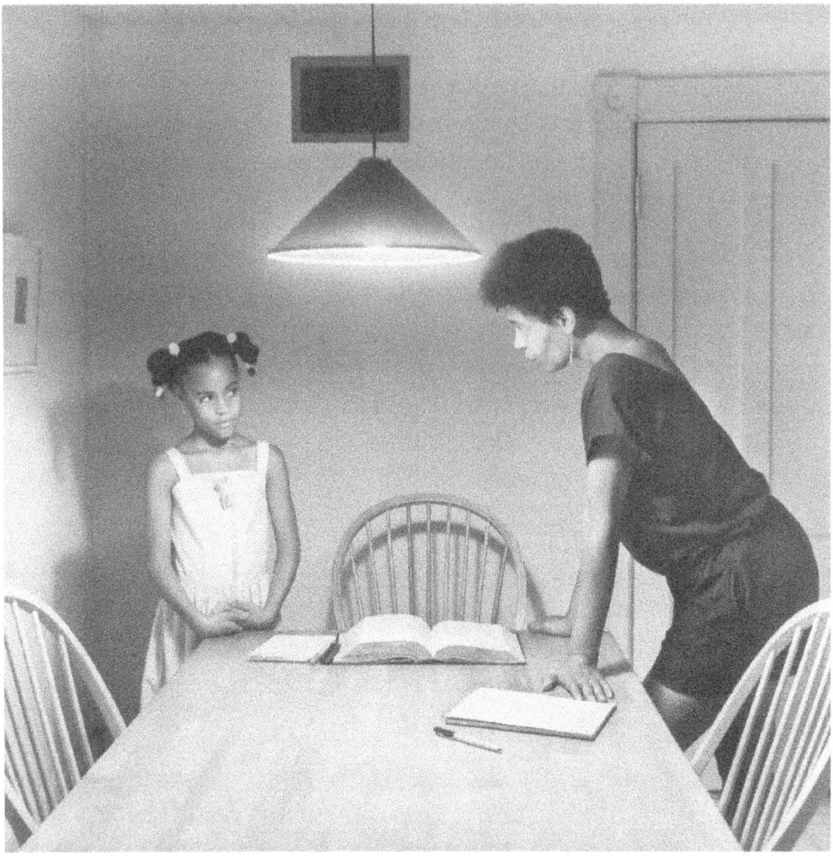

**Figure 11.3** Carrie Mae Weems, *Kitchen Table Series* (1990, printed 2003), Number 22, portfolio of 20 platinum/palladium prints and 14 screenprints (20 × 20 in.), Gift of the Collectors Committee; and Robert B. Menschel and the Vital Projects Fund, 2017.4.1.1–34. Credit: Courtesy of The National Gallery of Art, Washington, DC.

The museum educator modeled the routine with one of the photographs, Number 22, which presents an interaction between the adult female figure and the young girl (Figure 11.3). She prompted the students to focus on the young girl's facial expression, gesture, and interaction with the other figures and to imagine what the girl might be perceiving, thinking, and feeling. Students inferred that the adult figure was the mother, and that the young girl is seeing "a stern look on the mother's face." The students related to a parent-child dynamic and imagined that the girl might have done something wrong and is wondering about the consequences. They inferred that she might also "feel respect for her mom and value the relationship."

Next, students were eager to try the routine with another photograph working in pairs. They noted the similarities and differences in their interpretations. Many focused on the perspective of the main female adult character. Some felt the woman demonstrated confidence. To support their claim, they noted the symbolic use of the mirror in photograph Number 1, connoting self-care and self-assuredness. Another perspective was that her robe's soft fabric represented her tenderness and vulnerability. Students began to understand that interpretations vary as each person brings different backgrounds, identities, and experiences to examining the character. Here the students demonstrated "the complexity of perspective," defined by researcher Shari Tishman as a quality of thinking in which "students become aware of their own perspectives, recognizing that they have a relationship of familiarity or unfamiliarity with the time and place and people depicted in the picture."[21]

After doing the routine, the educator gave students a taste of Weems' process of perspective-taking. She invited students to use their perspectives from the *Step Inside* routine to each write a monologue in the voice of their chosen character. Then, working in small groups, they created a tableau performance of their written monologues.

One of the student's monologues animated the relationship between woman and the girl:

> *We sit in comfortable silence; she aware of my space, and I aware of hers. . . . There are a thousand things you are too young to know, complex and simple things, but for now I can show you what it means to be a woman. . . .*

The performance became a capstone for the entire experience, as students embodied empathetic monologues.

Finally, the museum educator encouraged students to reflect on how their own experiences, beliefs, and feelings form their perspectives. She then asked: "What do you notice about your own perspective and what it takes to imagine somebody else's?" They reflected:

> *Through perspective-taking, I realized my own assumptions. Hearing other ideas helped me appreciate that there's always more to the story.*

> *Artistic choices affect the way we perceive the artwork. It makes me as an artist more conscious of how every choice that I make affects the viewer's perspective.*

*Focusing on a character's experience helped us shape distinct thoughts about that character, to understand their emotions and what would lead them to feel this way.*

The fictional drama of Carrie Mae Weems' *Kitchen Table Series* gave students the impetus and space to envision the stories of characters within a familiar setting. Each picture held a narrative that connected to the others but was always changing with its cast and symbolic props. The *Step Inside* routine gave opportunities for students to make authentic connections, unpack the nuances of perspectives, and build elaborate, imaginative stories around the artwork. Ultimately, students were able to practice cognitive empathy, reading visual cues in the photographs to imagine possible perspectives of another. Learning experiences like these create pathways that can expand students' capacity to think through another's perspective, not only in art but also in the world around them.

## Conclusion

The three learning experiences we have described need not be relegated to national museums and veteran educators. The central components of these facilitated conversations include slowing down and lingering with works of art in community with others and sharing ideas and feelings using the structures of open-ended perspective-taking routines. Additionally, being guided by a willing facilitator who caringly allows the group time for processing and communicating ideas and feelings can stretch us further toward a transformative experience.

When we began to intentionally use thinking routines to cultivate social-emotional learning and empathy through art, we knew that both thinking routines in their simplicity and works of art in their complexity were uniquely suited to the task. Art can be ambiguous and open-ended. It invites multiple interpretations and perspectives. It presents stories—stories from history, stories of emotion, stories of imagination, and biographical, personal stories. It captures our attention and provides a sense of awe through beauty, novelty, artistry, and creativity. It pushes us to think critically and creatively. It pulls at our heartstrings, creates emotional connections, and at times moves us to action. It grapples with aspects of what it means to be human and beckons us to care and empathize—to imagine what it might feel like to be the other, whether a returning errant son, a woman gazing into the distance by the lemon branches, or a young girl asserting her independence.

# Notes

1 National Gallery of Art website, "About the National Gallery," https://www.nga.gov/about.html.

2 Project Zero website, Harvard Graduate School of Education, https://pz.harvard.edu/; Shari Tishman, *Slow Looking: The Art and Practice of Learning Through Observation* (Routledge, 2017); Ron Ritchhart, *Creating Cultures of Thinking: The 8 Forces We Must Master to Truly Transform Our Schools* (Jossey-Bass, 2015), 45; Verónica Boix Mansilla and Anthony Jackson, *Educating for Global Competence: Preparing Our Youth to Engage the World,* 1st ed. (The Asia Society, 2011).

3 Collaborative for Academic, Social, and Emotional Learning website: https://casel.org/fundamentals-of-sel/what-is-the-casel-framework/.

4 *Teaching Complex Thinking through Art with the National Gallery of Artwebsite* (edX, 2024): https://www.edx.org/learn/art/the-smithsonian-institution-teaching-complex-thinking-through-art-with-the-national-gallery-of-art.

5 Elif Gökçiğdem, *Designing for Empathy* (American Alliance of Museums, 2019).

6 Daniel Goleman, *Social Intelligence: The New Science of Human Relationships* (Bantam, 2006).

7 Goleman, *Social Intelligence*, 38.

8 Gospel of Luke 15:11-32.

9 Bartolomé Esteban Murillo, *The Return of the Prodigal Son* (1667/1670), oil on canvas, 93 1/16 x 102 3/4 in, National Gallery of Art, Gift of the Avalon Foundation, 1948.12.1, https://www.nga.gov/collection/art-object-page.34956.html.

10 Jonathan Brown and Richard G. Mann, *Spanish Paintings of the Fifteenth through Nineteenth Centuries*, The Collections of the National Gallery of Art Systematic Catalogue (National Gallery of Art, 1990), 109–10, color repro. 111, https://www.nga.gov/content/dam/ngaweb/research/publications/pdfs/spanish-painting-15th-19th-centuries.pdf.

11 "Circle of Viewpoints," Artful Thinking, Project Zero, Harvard Graduate School of Education: http://pzartfulthinking.org/?p=42 and https://pz.harvard.edu/sites/default/files/Circle%20of%20Viewpoints_0.pdf.

12 *Teaching Complex Thinking through Art with the National Gallery of Art*, "Circle of Viewpoints: Imagining Diverse Perspectives" video (2024): https://www.youtube.com/watch?v=1QZiel7XeWo&list=PLErBGbWC2wSMSf2E1QkFUGoM-OnrkGkwN&index=12.

13 John Dewey, *Art as Experience* (Milton Balch, 1934), 35–45.

**14** María Berrío, *A Sunburst Restrained* (2019), collage with Japanese paper and watercolor on canvas, 152.4 x 182.9 cm. (60 × 72 in.), Gift of Erika and John Toussaint, 2020.2.1, https://www.nga.gov/collection/art-object-page.221464.html.

**15** Pablo Neruda, Ferris Cook, and Ken Krabbenhoft. *Odes to Common Things: Bilingual Edition.* "Ode to a Lemon." Hardcover ed. May 1, 1994, 54.

**16** Hoffman Institute Foundation, *Hoffman List of Feeling Words* (2013).

**17** Rika Burnham and Elliott Kai-Kee, *Teaching in the Art Museum: Interpretation as Experience* (J. Paul Getty Museum, 2011),15.

**18** Carrie Mae Weems, *Kitchen Table Series* (1990, printed 2003), portfolio of 20 platinum/palladium prints and 14 screenprints (20 × 20 in.), Gift of the Collectors Committee; and Robert B. Menschel and the Vital Projects Fund, 2017.4.1.1-34, https://www.nga.gov/collection/art-object-page.209288.html.

**19** *Teaching Complex Thinking through Art with the National Gallery of Art.* Massive Open Online Course videos, "Step Inside: Exploring Viewpoints" and "Step Inside: Extending through Monologues" (2024): https://www.youtube.com/watch?v=ELgkTVSlqeg&list=PLErBGbWC2wSMSf2E1QkFUGoM-OnrkGkwN&index=10 and https://www.youtube.com/watch?v=xyuvXUYr7yE&list=PLErBGbWC2wSMSf2E1QkFUGoM-OnrkGkwN&index=11.

**20** "Step Inside," Artful Thinking, Project Zero, Harvard Graduate School of Education: http://pzartfulthinking.org/?p=40 and https://pz.harvard.edu/sites/default/files/Step%20Inside_2.pdf.

**21** Shari Tishman, *Slow Looking: The Art and Practice of Learning Through Observation* (Routledge, 2017), 134.

# 12 Seeing Differently

## Fostering Connections and Perspective-Taking through Slow-Looking

*Claire Bown*

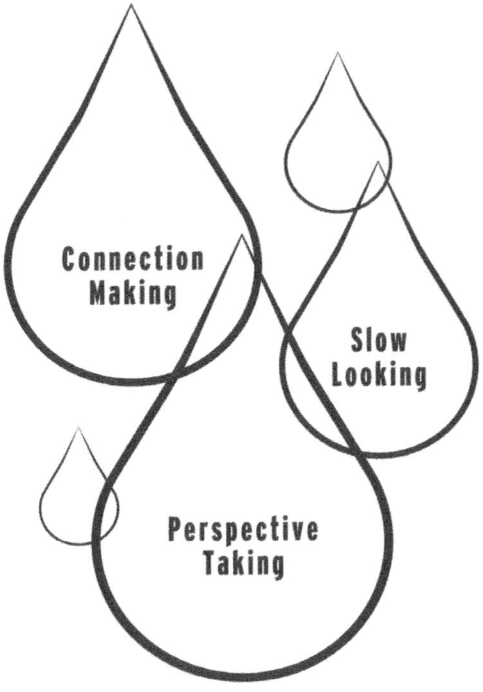


"I don't like museums, *generally,*" one of the IT managers said with a faint smile as the group gathered in the entrance hall of the museum. "I don't know anything about art," another added quietly, looking nervously around the space. I'd just explained to the group of IT managers that we'd be spending the next ninety minutes looking closely at artworks in the museum galleries and asked them to share their expectations for our time together.

We started slowly, with simple exercises designed to help them feel comfortable in the space. They began noticing small details, making connections between what they saw. Their initial hesitancy gradually gave way to curiosity. By the middle of our session, the group had settled into both the museum environment and each other's company, allowing us to move into more complex discussions.

When we reached the exhibition featuring Canadian photographer Jeff Wall's large scale, cinematic photographs, the group was immediately drawn in. The same managers who had been uncertain in the entrance hall were now fully absorbed, discussing their thoughts, ideas, and theories for what they saw in the images. They happily explored the perspectives of different figures, imagining their stories, and predicting what might happen next. "I never knew you could do this in a museum," one commented happily as our session drew to a close.

The way the group moved from initial hesitation to shared discovery that afternoon is something I've seen happen again and again. Over the past decade, this practice of careful, sustained observation has become increasingly valued, not just in museums but in many different environments. Slow looking has a unique ability to bring people together and open up new perspectives, helping us see situations and each other in different ways.

In this chapter, I will explore how slow looking can be a powerful tool for building empathy, transforming not only how we see, but how we engage with art, objects, ideas, and, crucially, each other. I will examine what slow looking is, how it naturally leads to connection-making and perspective-taking, and provide practical tools for facilitating these experiences in various settings.

At first glance, slow looking might seem to be simply a different way of engaging with art or objects in museums. But what if it offers something more profound? How might the act of looking carefully together create bridges between different ways of seeing? What makes slow looking such a powerful tool for developing empathy?

## What Is Slow Looking?

When I first started exploring slow looking in the museum environment more than twelve years ago, it was relatively unheard of, and few books had been written about it, although there were certainly researchers and educators who were exploring the benefits of a slower approach to art or object engagement. While the exact origins of the term "slow looking" remain unclear, the practice seems to have emerged from a variety of influences. John Berger's *Ways of Seeing*, invited viewers to take time engaging with artworks and look beyond the surface, while the Slow Movement that began in the 1980s and was popularized in Carl Honoré's *In Praise of Slow*, emphasized the value of slowing down in our fast-paced world.[1] These ideas found their way into cultural organizations through initiatives like Slow Art Day, a yearly event which encourages people to spend extended time engaging not only with artworks, but also with objects, historical sites, and even sacred spaces such as churches.[2]

In my own research I was drawn to David Perkins' 1994 book, *The Intelligent Eye*, in which he warns against "audience impressionism" where visitors spend mere seconds with paintings and advocates strongly for "giving looking time".[3] Most recently, Shari Tishman has defined slow looking as a "mode of learning" and a way of "gaining knowledge about the world", outlining four simple strategies to approach observation: Categories, Open Inventory, Scale and Scope, and Juxtaposition.[4] Notably, Tishman also points out that learning through slow looking can occur through any or all of the senses, not just sight.

While these foundations have definitively shaped our understanding of slow looking in theory, it is the experience within the gallery that is invaluable in developing how to design and facilitate it in practice. In 2011, in response to teachers' requests, I designed a museum program (called *Stories around the World*) that had participants as young as six looking intently at objects in the museum for 15–20 minutes at a time.[5] I've been practicing slow looking ever since, with all age groups, a variety of objects and artworks, and in a range of situations and places.

I have come to understand slow looking as a practice, mindset, and approach involving the study of something with intention and attention. The experience can unfold in various ways, shaped by what you are seeking, your goals, or how you wish to engage. Slow looking can be deeply *introspective*, focusing inwardly on your personal connection to the artwork or object, perhaps using mindfulness or meditation, or *extrospective*, broadening outward to consider its context, meaning, and interpretation. While distinct, these approaches can also complement each other within a single slow looking experience.

Slow looking can be an individual pursuit or a shared experience—and everything in between. Sometimes, slow looking is quiet and contemplative, while at other times it is alive with chatter, wondering, and discovery. You might come to it seeking pleasure, learning, or a deeper understanding of art and objects. Some find it brings moments of calm and enhanced well-being and enjoy incorporating elements of mindfulness or meditation. You are free to explore slowly through discussion, sketching, movement, making, writing, or simply observing. All you need is the willingness to linger a little longer with what catches your eye. While regular practice helps to make it easier to look for extended periods, slow looking welcomes everyone, from first-timers to seasoned observers. Whether we are exploring art in a museum, looking at nature on a walk, or studying everyday objects in our homes, slow looking opens up new possibilities for connection and understanding. It reminds us that there's always more to see, more to discover, if we just take the time to really look.

## Social Connection

The practice of slow looking takes on a deeper meaning through the lens of human connection. As social beings, we thrive on community and shared experience, something that feels particularly relevant in our digital age, where screens often replace face-to-face interaction and feelings of disconnection have become commonplace. Additionally, we know that social interactions are essential for sustaining our mental and emotional well-being. In *Your Brain on Art* by Susan Magsamen and Ivy Ross discuss the powerful effects of art and social engagement on the brain.[6]

In museum spaces, slow looking brings people together. Even when we come from different backgrounds and life experiences, all types of museum collections—whether art, historical objects, scientific specimens, or cultural artifacts—have the ability to unite us in moments of collective wonder. As people share their observations and insights, they build on each other's ideas, and these collective discoveries foster connections and bonds among participants. One person might notice the subtle patterns of light, while another picks up on hidden symbols or unexpected surprises. Through slow looking, a relationship with the artwork and, importantly, each other gradually unfolds. Initial observations lead to deeper discoveries, questions arise naturally, and personal meanings and associations may emerge. Something in an artwork might remind us of a place we've been, a story we've heard, or a feeling we've had. These connections—between educators and participants, among the participants themselves, and with the artwork or object being explored—help us to feel that we belong in these spaces, are part of a shared experience, and that museums can be places of meaningful connection.

Recent research backs up the power of these social connections in slow looking experiences. A study at Manchester Art Gallery, UK, had participants slowly look at artworks for ten minutes with guided prompts.[7] Groups who discussed the artworks together reported significantly higher levels of engagement, emotional connection, and enjoyment compared to those viewing art silently or alone. Importantly, the social interactions also increased their sense of connection to society at large, with many continuing their conversations long after the formal viewing ended. This research confirms what many museum educators have long observed in practice. However, creating these meaningful social connections through slow looking requires thoughtful facilitation.

## Facilitating Connections

For facilitators, it's important to intentionally create the conditions where people feel comfortable to practice slow looking together. By attending to physical space, trust-building, pacing, and group dynamics, we can foster a community where looking, thinking, and sharing flourish.

Listening lies at the heart of meaningful slow looking experiences and requires us to tune in completely to what others notice and observe, letting go of our own thoughts about the artwork or object before us. The quality of listening shapes the depth of engagement and richness of shared discovery. Equally important are the moments of silence *between* contributions, where thoughts settle and new ideas surface. The facilitator's role is to hold these moments with confidence, creating a natural flow between individual discovery and shared inquiry.

Through carefully crafted questions, we can unlock new ways of seeing and open up new lines of discussion. While open-ended exploration has value, slow looking becomes more intentional through structure, starting with observation and description, moving through interpretation and significance, before finally, drawing conclusions. Without a plan, questioning can become scattered, making it harder for participants to move beyond surface observations. Over the past decade, I've developed Questioning Practices to support inquiry and guide discussions around artworks and objects. These structured sets of questions or prompts are used to guide inquiry, stimulate critical thinking, and facilitate learning.[8] The next section looks at one of these: The Perspectives Triangle, which supports discussions that progress from careful observation to rich perspective-taking. But before we continue, we should first explore what perspective-taking means and why museums provide an ideal environment for developing this capacity.

## Perspective-Taking

Our perspective—how we uniquely see and make sense of the world—is formed by our lived experiences, cultural background, knowledge, and values. Through *perspective-taking*, this unique way of seeing the world becomes a powerful tool for relating to and understanding others.

Perspective-taking is the "mental flexibility to intentionally adopt the perspective of the other".[9] It invites us to move outside our own viewpoint and imagine: *What might someone else be thinking or feeling? What experiences have shaped their view of the world?* It asks us to temporarily see the world through another's lens, rather than attempting to completely step into their experience. Understanding this distinction is important, as research shows maintaining some distance while understanding others' viewpoints reduces the emotional stress that can come with complete emotional immersion.[10] By seeing the world through another's lens, we create the space to build empathy—a deeper connection that allows us to better understand and relate to others' experiences.

Museums offer unique opportunities for developing the skill or capacity for perspective-taking. When we take the time to explore objects and artworks carefully, we're presented with tangible connections to other times, places, and cultures. The challenge comes in moving beyond initial observations to deeper understanding. Research shows that without proper historical and cultural context, our attempts at perspective-taking often fall back on assumptions or stereotypes rather than leading to genuine understanding.[11] This is why situating an object within a specific context by sharing information—about the creator, the cultural significance, the historical period, and contemporary meaning for source communities—is essential for thoughtful perspective-taking in museum settings.

The Perspectives Triangle offers a structured approach to guide slow looking discussions that acknowledges and addresses these challenges. This Questioning Practice guides both facilitators and participants from careful looking through to exploring multiple perspectives, ensuring that crucial contextual information can be shared at the right moment.

## The Perspectives Triangle

The Perspectives Triangle (Figure 12.1) encourages three types of perspective-taking in three simple stages. The process begins with careful observation to stimulate curiosity. Before asking any questions, participants spend time looking at the artwork or object. This might be in silence, in pairs, or with gentle guidance from the facilitator. After this period, two simple questions open the discussion: *What do you see? How does it look and feel?* and participants are invited to describe the object fully.

As looking continues, participants are encouraged to voice their questions: *What questions come to mind?* This mirrors the brain's natural response, acknowledges participants' interests and creates opportunities for the facilitator to share relevant information in response to the group's curiosity. These "Look" and "Inquire" stages set the foundation for meaningful perspective-taking.

## The Perspectives Triangle

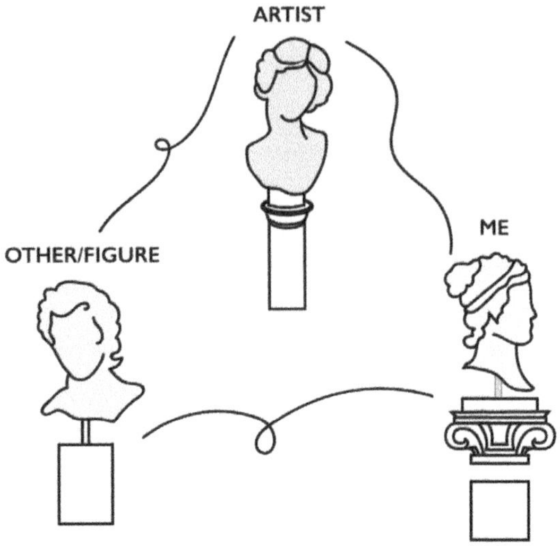


- LOOK: **What do you see?**
- INQUIRE: **What questions come to mind?**
- PERSPECTIVE-TAKING: **Explore and centre a range of different perspectives. Choose from:**

  - ARTIST:
    What's the artist, photographer, or maker's perspective?
  - OTHER/FIGURE:
    What other perspectives are involved?
    or
    What is the perspective of a figure in the artwork?
  - ME:
    What's my perspective?

- **How do they/you feel? What do you see that makes you say that?**

**Figure 12.1** The Perspectives Triangle Questioning Practice from The Art Engager: Reimagining Guided Experiences in Museums. Credit: Artwork by Çiğdem Güven / crocusfield.com, from *The Art Engager: Reimagining Guided Experiences in Museums* by Claire Bown.

The final stage asks participants to explore a range of different perspectives as shown in Figure 12.1. asking: *How do they/you feel? What do you see that makes you say that?* When looking at a painting, for example, participants might begin with the artist's perspective before considering the viewpoints of different figures in the piece. With historical objects, groups might brainstorm a list of various perspectives to explore—from curators and collectors to past users and owners—before choosing which perspectives they would like to discuss further, adding valuable agency to the experience too.

Our personal perspective is intentionally the final of the three questions. Our brains naturally place our own perspective at the center, so by first exploring other viewpoints, we create space to appreciate and understand *other* perspectives before finally examining our own response. The goal of the Perspectives Triangle is not to reach definitive answers but to foster a deeper understanding of how others see the world, while also inviting us to reflect on our own lens.

At the start of this chapter, we met a group of IT managers whose initial response to being in an art museum was uncertainty and disconnection. Through a series of slow encounters with different works of art, their hesitation gave way to curiosity, engagement, and connection. When we take time to look carefully together, share our observations, and explore different perspectives, we begin to see in new ways—discovering fresh possibilities in both the artworks or objects and in how we understand each other. This is the real magic of slow looking: by opening ourselves to different ways of seeing, we forge connections and insights that enrich how we experience the world.

## Notes

**1** John Berger, *Ways of Seeing* (The Schools, 1972); Carl Honore, *In Praise of Slow* (National Geographic Books, 2004).

**2** "Slow Art Day," *Slow Art Day*, https://www.slowartday.com/. Accessed February 4, 2025.

**3** David N. Perkins, *The Intelligent Eye : Learning to Think by Looking at Art* (Getty Center For Education In The Arts, 1994), 36.

**4** Shari Tishman, *Slow Looking: The Art and Practice of Learning through Observation* (Routledge, 2018), 2.

**5** Claire Bown, "Stories around the World - Interview with Claire Bown," *Thinking Museum*, last modified February 7, 2013, https://thinkingmuseum. com/2013/02/07/stories-around-the-world-interview-with-claire-bown/.

**6** Susan Magsamen and Ivy Ross, *Your Brain on Art: How the Arts Transform Us* ([S.l.]: Random House, 2023), 203.

**7** Aleksandra Igdalova, Safiyyah Nawaz, and Rebecca Chamberlain, "A View Worth Talking About: The Influence of Social Interaction on Aesthetic Experience and Well-Being Outcomes in the Gallery," January 15, 2025.

**8** Claire Bown, *The Art Engager: Reimagining Guided Experiences in Museums* (Amsterdam Academy, 2024).

**9** Jean Decety, "Perspective Taking as the Royal Avenue to Empathy," in *Other Minds: How Humans Bridge the Gap between Self and Others.*, ed. Bertram F. Malle and Sara D. Hodges (The Guilford Press, 2005), 143–57.

**10** Anneke E.K. Buffone et al., "Don't Walk in Her Shoes! Different Forms of Perspective Taking Affect Stress Physiology," *Journal of Experimental Social Psychology* 72 (September 2017): 161–8, https://doi.org/10.1016/j.jesp.2017.04.001.

**11** Nancy Marie Mithlo and Aleksandra Sherman, "Perspective-Taking Can Lead to Increased Bias: A Call for 'Less Certain' Positions in American Indian Contexts," *Curator: The Museum Journal* 63, no. 3 (July 2020): 353–69, https://doi.org/10.1111/cura.12373.

# 13 Religious Objects as Portals to Connecting and Seeing Humanity

*Amy Glenn*

*Leah Smith*

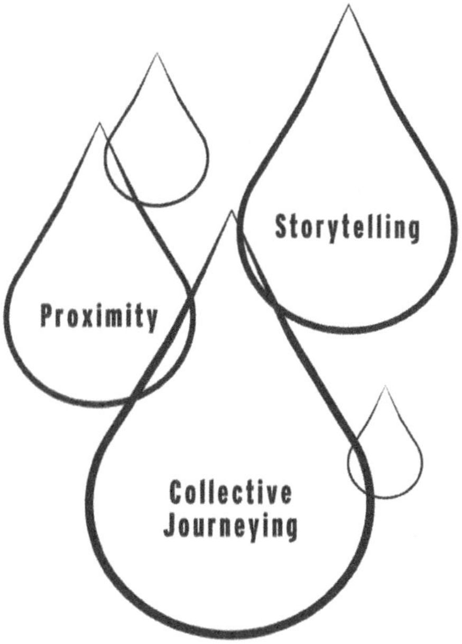


This chapter offers Glencairn Museum's Object Portal Process (the Process) as an example of empathy-building through museums. Glencairn Museum is a museum of religious art located in Bryn Athyn, Pennsylvania. Glencairn, a medieval-style castle, was the home of the Pitcairn Family from 1939 to 1979 before becoming a museum in 1982.[1] The mission of the Museum is to create an intentional space that invites visitors to encounter religious art and artifacts as expressions of spiritual beliefs and practices.

The mission and the desired impact of the Museum bear the fingerprints of the Pitcairn Family's faith and values, reflecting New Church (Swedenborgian Christian) beliefs while also presenting the history of Glencairn, a National Historical Landmark.[2] Glencairn Museum seeks to ignite curiosity, facilitate exploration, and inspire reflection on spiritual beliefs and practices through material objects. Specifically, the Museum hopes that visitors will:

- Recognize the similarity of certain spiritual concepts within the human desire to find meaning and purpose in their lives,
- Respect differences in how religions answer spiritual questions common through time and across cultures,
- Practice empathy by engaging with alternative perspectives, and,
- Reflect on the role of religion and their own spiritual beliefs and practices.[3]

## The Object Portal Process and the Visitor Experience at Glencairn Museum

The Process aims to activate an object as a device to connect humans with one another across time and space. Glencairn Museum's interpretive approach considers art and artifacts as doorways to understanding the total religious experience of the people who created and used them.[4]

Glencairn Museum's use of the Process intends to facilitate personal connections between the visitor and the story told by the object, offering visitors the opportunity to look, understand, and reflect while suspending judgment and seeking shared humanity apart from their own religious ideas. Currently, the Process is primarily used to develop guided tours for groups of about twelve visitors and one museum guide, however it informs all interpretive products at Glencairn. When using the Process, we focus on proximity, storytelling, and collective journeying as the *alchemic ingredients* for building empathy.[5] The Museum facilitates a dialogue between object and viewer, focusing on how objects reveal the beliefs of their creators and users, and the ways in which they expressed those beliefs through their practices. Glencairn Museum is committed to interpreting religious traditions in a way that is:

- Acceptable to, and whenever possible informed by, adherents of the religion in question,
- Informed by the professional community of scholars,
- Comprehensible to the visiting public.[6]

We are aware that tools like the Process exist by different names and in other forms in other institutional contexts. Our experience in utilizing it for a particular focus on religious art suggests that it could also be transferable in spaces that deal with other forms of powerful and personal content such as aspects of identity, politics, and relationships.

The Process includes the following steps designed to pave the way for a visitor's journey toward self-reflection, inner transformation, and a more empathetic approach to interpersonal interactions:

- *The Object*: This step opens the portal, relies on the power of proximity to objects, and is activated by observation. It includes a description of the object, draws attention to observable details, and answers questions. What materials were used? What details can be observed?
- *The Adherent*: This next step invites a visitor to be curious about the life of the object's owner or user. Who was the group or individual that created or used the object? What do we know about them and their culture and time? What were their concerns?
- *The Belief*: This third step invites the visitor to understand the object as an important physical representation of its owner's beliefs. What story of faith does the object tell? Does the object give us information about a religious idea, myth, legend, moral behavior, code, or law?
- *The Practice*: The fourth step brings the use of the object to life for the visitor. How did the adherent use the object in the practice of their faith? Was it used in a religious rite or ritual?
- *The Question*: This is the step that invites the visitor to move from observation and learning into reflection and possible transformation. It draws in the visitor so closely to the object that the object itself is no longer in focus and instead another human being and a shared human experience are visible through the portal created by the object. In the case of guided tours at Glencairn, the script includes a carefully crafted series of questions to achieve this. Questions include: Have I ever felt like the person who owned this object felt? What fear

or dream does this object reflect? What does the object show me about the diversity of human experience, and where do I fit? Does it matter that this object was made and used, and do the objects that I use matter?

The goal of the Process is for the visitor to be successfully transported from their daily experience, through the object portal, into the lived experience of another human. Ideally, they see themselves reflected in this portal, and through this journey gain understanding about the motivations and intentions of humans of the past, resulting in increased empathy for the humans of today.

## An Example of the Process in Practice

Let's see the Object Portal Process in action with an object from the Glencairn collection found on display in the Ancient Near East gallery—the Foundation Deposit of Nabu-kudurri-uşer II (Figure 13.1).[7] The information below would form the building blocks for the script that a guide would deliver aloud to visitors.

- *The Object*: This eight-inch-tall, cylinder-shaped object is made of terracotta. Dating to the early sixth century BCE, it was created during the reign of the Babylonian King Nabu-kudurri-uşer II (605—562 BCE), and is covered with cuneiform script in Akkadian.[8]
- *The Adherent*: In Biblical scripture, King Nabu-kudurri-uşer II is known as Nebuchadnezzar. The Biblical account of his life describes him as responsible for the Babylonian exile of the Jews and the destruction of the first temple in Jerusalem. Beyond these accounts, he was known as a great king of the Ancient Near East who, among his many accomplishments, rebuilt the walls of the city of Babylon, including the Ishtar Gate.
- *The Belief*: King Nebuchadnezzar commissioned the creation of this object to ask for protection from the gods and to secure his place in history. The Akkadian inscription on the foundation deposit lists Nebuchadnezzar's accomplishments. He boasts of the power of his gods and their love and favor for him. He believed that the gods would read it and would protect him as well as the palace or temple where it was buried.

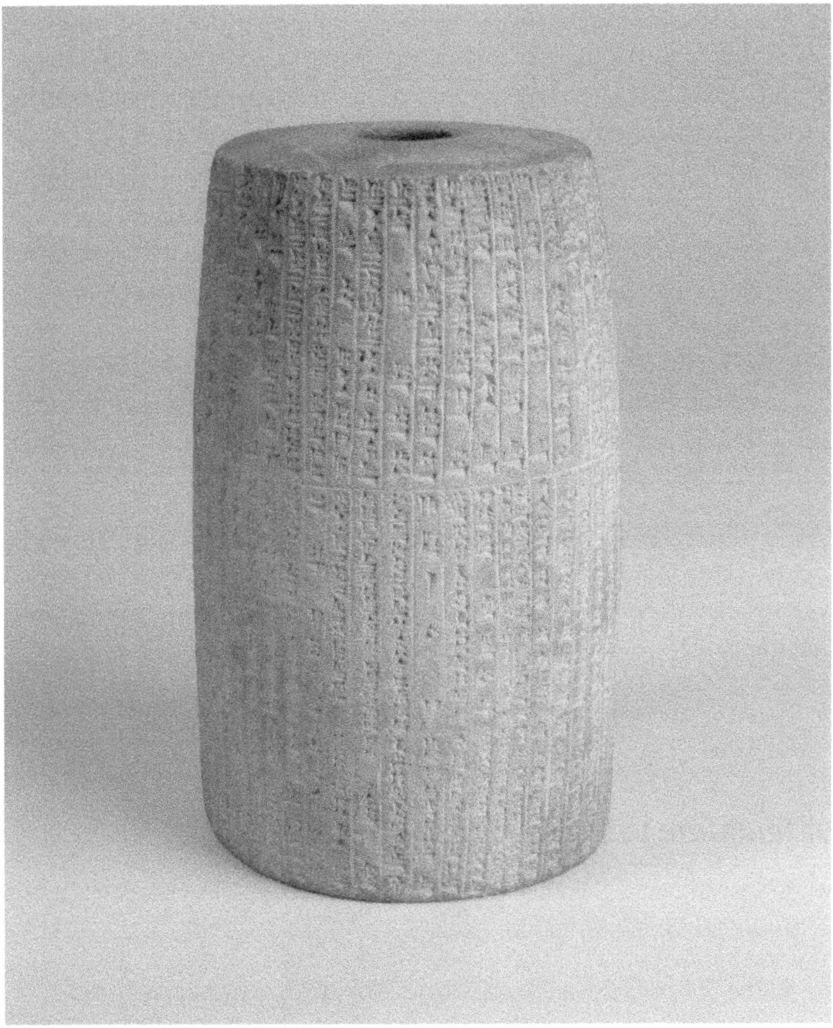

**Figure 13.1** Cylinder foundation deposit of Nebuchadnezzar in Glencairn's Ancient Near East Gallery. Terracotta, Neo-Babylonian, early sixth century BCE (01.IS.77). Credit: Image courtesy of Glencairn Museum.

- *The Practice*: The Glencairn foundation deposit is one of many identical objects that were ritually buried for the gods to read. This was a common practice for religious adherents in the Ancient Near East. Kings would search for deposits buried by former rulers and bury their own objects next to them to honor previous rulers. Written warnings were included to "future proof" the deposits, discouraging future rulers from destroying them or they would be punished by the powerful gods of the kings who buried them. These deposits connected kings to gods, protected sacred spaces, and had a powerful impact even if no human eyes could read them.

- *The Question*: Despite knowing that the future is uncontrollable and unpredictable, humans have made efforts for thousands of years to hold a place for themselves among future generations. There is a strong human desire to leave a legacy. What are the ways that we as modern humans attempt to "future proof" our own legacy? How do we honor ancestors while also adding our own stories? What objects, beliefs, or traditions have been passed down that reflect the continuity of your family legacy? How will you continue that legacy? What will you leave behind?

While visitors are welcome to share their answers to these questions, we do not require visitor participation as we have noticed it can often be stressful. Guides are trained to pose the questions and pause to allow time for visitor reflection. Some guides share their own answers to the questions.

Every object portal can tell many stories. It is the responsibility of the Process user to decide on the most effective empathy-building story to choose.

## A Template to Try the Process

The following is a practical way to try the Process for yourself. Here is a template for experimentation:

- *The Object*: Choose the object, get close to it. Activate the object portal by observation. Describe the physical attributes like color, size, substance, texture, age, notable details, etc.
- *The Adherent*: Begin the journey through the portal by telling the story of the adherent. You could choose to tell the story of the object's owner, creator, or user. What do we know about them and their culture and time?
- *The Belief*: Move deeper into the portal by describing how the object is an important physical representation of its owner's beliefs. Can we guess the purpose of the object by its appearance? Does the object give us information about a myth, legend, or moral behavior? What is the understanding between the object and the creator or viewer?

- *The Practice*: Bring the object to life! Paint the picture of how this object was handled, carried, venerated, buried, protected, worn, burned, or any other action that showed its importance. What is the physical, intellectual, or emotional transaction that takes place between the object and adherent?
- *The Question*: Step past the object. Search for yourself in this new world opened by the object portal. How does the historic experience of this object relate to your own experience today? Do you recognize the practice in your own life? Do you hold a different belief yet still recognize the question that the adherent's belief answers? Do you feel emotionally moved?

Now that you've done the behind-the-scenes work to develop the building blocks of the visitor experience, you are ready to write the script that the guide will deliver.

## *The Facilitator's Role*

The collective journey of the guide and the visitors through the portal created by the object requires human facilitation. While the steps and questions of the Process could be presented as written text, we have found that human interaction breathes the most life into the object. This means that the guide or educator needs to be a skilled facilitator of the visitor's encounter with an object if the process is to be effective. The following socio-emotional skills are helpful:

- *Mastery of the Facts*: Training starts with mastering the script content. For a powerful and maybe vulnerable experience to take place, the guide must be the safe, reliable expert in the room. Once the facilitator is comfortable with these parts of the script, they can progress to asking the questions for reflection which are mastered through mentorship, certification, and assessment.
- *Personal Connection without Judgment*: During training, guides are asked to reflect on the scripted questions for themselves. This creates a personal connection to the Process and helps guides to create an authentic visitor experience. It is critical that guides are mentored to maintain neutrality, hold space for visitors, and see themselves in the process.

- *Engaging, not Entertaining*: Guides report often feeling pressure to create a good visitor experience by prioritizing entertainment over engagement. At Glencairn we train our guides and educators to center their delivery on the objects and artwork.
- *Visitor Sensitivity*: Guides benefit from knowing the different motivations of museum visitors.[9] Every tour group is diverse, and guides are trained not to assume any prior knowledge of a faith. The goal is to provide unbiased, inoffensive, and accurate education about the faiths represented in the collection.
- *Accommodating Visitor Reactions*: Guides are trained to discuss objects within their specific religious context and not to generalize or speak on behalf of contemporary adherents. With religion being such a personal and powerful topic, we prioritize equipping our guides with the awareness and skills to expect and manage all manner of visitor reactions. Confidence is fostered through observing experienced guides, regular debriefing after visitor interactions, and ensuring clear and accessible managerial support.
- *Flexibility of Delivery*: Guides are trained to begin with questions about what visitors can observe, not what they know. This builds a shared foundation from which to launch the object portal experience. To ensure success with every tour group, the guide must maintain flexibility for many reasons, including accessibility, age ranges, time constraints, visitor interest, or discomfort, etc. Their ability to "read the room" and gauge the physical, intellectual, and emotional state of the group is a critical skill that is honed through mentorship, training, and practice. Without effectively building safety and community within the tour group, the guide runs the risk of creating an experience that is boring at best and unsafe at worst.
- *Being Human*: It can be easy for new guides in training to imagine that they must present a flawless, encyclopedic presence for visitors, but that isn't going to engage visitor's hearts and minds in transformative change. Encouraging guides to be warm and candid in a professional way builds rapport and community with visitors and an environment that feels safe for exploration, play, and vulnerability.
- *Seeking a Positive Museum Experience*: At the core of the Process is a desire to facilitate a positive museum experience. Not every visitor walking through Glencairn's doors will be taken on a

worldview-altering journey during their visit and leave a completely empathetic and changed person. But if they leave after having a positive museum experience, we have provided them with a positive feeling toward the invitation to connect with other humans and to see their value.

## *Notes on Impact Evaluation*

We have examined the success of the Process in two main ways: Survey feedback, and anecdotal evidence or, "magic museum moments."

Survey results from our Highlights Tour in 2024 show that 58 percent of tour attendees agree or strongly agree that they feel more likely to respect and empathize with people whose beliefs and practices are different from their own. 67 percent agree or strongly agree that they reflected on the similarities between their values and those of people holding differing religious beliefs. Over 80 percent agree or strongly agree that they better understand how works of art can convey messages.[10]

In addition to this encouraging survey data, many staff members have powerful stories of visitor interactions, often with students. The development of empathy in the moment is hard to measure, and we have found that often it looks like an emotional response that presents an opportunity for empathy to grow. In the following anecdote, an educator has felt a "magic museum moment" take place:

*Glencairn Museum offers a program where students encounter authentic medieval European manuscripts, learn about the hard work and devotion of the monks who created them, and explore the precious and treasured ideas that are reflected in their pages.[11] The program concludes with an art project where students are asked to create a manuscript page about something treasured in their own lives. On one occasion a fourth-grade student began crying quietly while creating her manuscript. She was comforted by her friends and teacher. Despite her emotions, she chose to participate when it was time to share their creations. For her project, she had chosen to focus on a treasured clay imprint of her dog's paw who had died earlier that year. Throughout the rest of the visit, her classmates continued to check in with her and comfort her. This "magic museum moment" is an example of how a student was effectively transported through the portal created by the medieval European manuscript. She saw herself in the questions posed by the Process and felt safe and supported enough to be vulnerable. Both the student and her classmates took part in affirming her humanity.*

## Challenges and Opportunities

In our use of the Process at Glencairn, we have found success and challenges, some with possible solutions:

- The lack of open discussion in our guided tour experience: We have found that adult visitors are not expecting or immediately open to discussion about personal, deeply held values, let alone in-person, real-time reflection. We anticipate more staff training and explicit marketing of the tour experience and its format.
- Limitations to use the Process only during in-person guided tours: This means that only visitors who are physically, financially, and geographically able to visit Glencairn can participate in it. We would like to work toward a translation of the process into self-guided, digital, and off-site forms to allow more people to engage in it.
- Measuring success: While we have survey data and staff anecdotes as shared above, we would like to develop more targeted assessment methods to help inform the development of the Process.
- Updating the Museum's interpretive approach: Including questions that spark empathy-building and reflection in the visitor requires significant staff time and collaboration to develop content. Continuous cross-departmental collaboration is critical to the longevity and the success of the Process.

The Object Portal Process remains open to creativity and interpretation in different contexts. We would be excited to hear about your experience with the Process.

# Notes

**1** "History," Glencairn Museum, https://glencairnmuseum.org/history. Accessed January 31, 2025.

2 "Core Beliefs," New Church, https://newchurch.org/about/core beliefs. Accessed January 31, 2025.

3 "About Us," Glencairn Museum, https://www.glencairnmuseum.org/about-us. Accessed December 1, 2024.

4 James Cox, *An Introduction to the Phenomenology of Religion* (Continuum, 2010).

5 Elif M. Gökçiğdem, ed., *Designing for Empathy: Perspectives on the Museum Experience* (American Alliance of Museums, 2016), xviii.

6 Glencairn Museum, "About Us."

7 Eva Miller, "Future-Proofing Kingship: Mesopotamian Foundation Deposits in Glencairn Museum," *Glencairn Museum Newsletter*, October 12, 2018, https://www.glencairnmuseum.org/newsletter/2018/10/11/future-proofing-kingship-mesopotamian-foundation-deposits-in-glencairn-museum?rq=foundation.

8 "Inscribed Cylinder of Nebuchadnezzar King of Babylon from 605 to 562 B.C.," from a letter to Reginald W. Brown from Edgar J. Banks, October 21, 1927, curatorial file No. 01.IS.77, Glencairn Museum, Bryn Athyn, PA.

9 John H. Falk, *Identity and the Museum Visitor Experience* (Left Coast Press, 2009).

10 "Highlights Tour Survey Results," April 2024 to November 2024, Glencairn Museum, Bryn Athyn, PA, Jahnna Henderson, 2024.

11 "Medieval Life Program," Glencairn Museum, Bryn Athyn, PA, Amy Glenn, 2023.

# Part III
# Creating Space for Perspective-Expanding Social Encounters

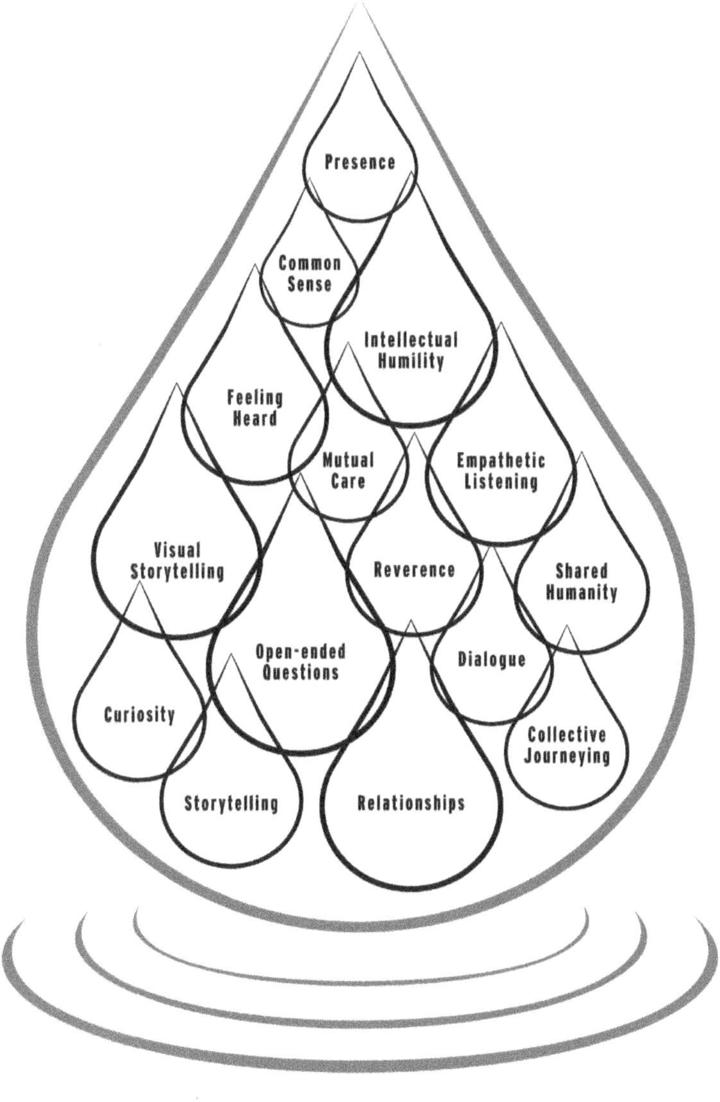

# 14 The Only Way to Learn Is Through Encounter!

*Hakan Elbir*

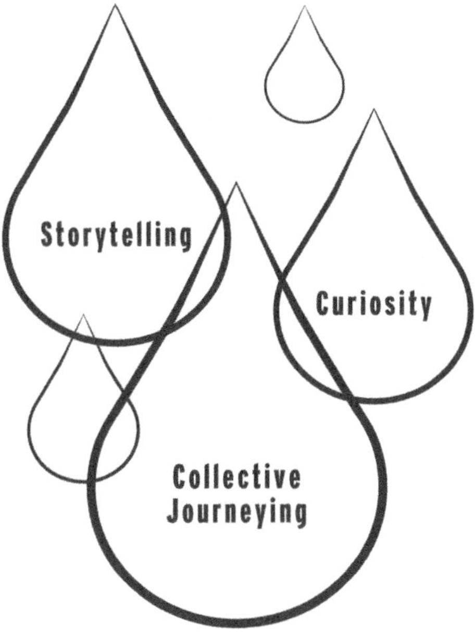


## The Empathy Deficit in a Fragmented World

In today's hyperconnected yet increasingly fragmented world, people are engaging less with those outside their immediate circles, preferring to build relationships only with those who share similar values, beliefs, or backgrounds. The Covid-19 pandemic amplified this trend as physical and social distancing measures forced many into isolation, further diminishing the likelihood of encountering people with differing life experiences. This shift emphasizes an urgent need for experiential learning spaces where individuals can connect with people unlike themselves, fostering empathy and understanding that are essential for social cohesion.

Museums, once primarily regarded as places for preserving, storing, displaying cultural heritage, are evolving to meet this need. In 2022, the International Council of Museums (ICOM) introduced a redefined vision of museums as inclusive, participatory spaces committed to serving communities by preserving both tangible and intangible heritage.[1] This contemporary approach positions museums as community-focused institutions that go beyond conserving artifacts, emphasizing their roles in fostering empathy, inclusivity, and accessibility. This chapter delves into how museums can act as powerful tools for building empathy, utilizing immersive experiences to bridge divides and connect people from diverse backgrounds. Specifically, I examined the London Dialogue Hub (LDH) and Istanbul Dialogue Museum (IDM), as well as their Sign Language Cafés (SLC), as institutions that use transformative experiences to help visitors confront and challenge their constructed biases.[2] Both the LDH and the IDM, along with their respective SLCs, were created and run by a social entrepreneur with the aim of providing transformative experiences that help visitors confront and challenge their constructed biases. These institutions are interconnected through their shared vision of promoting understanding, inclusivity, and the breaking down of prejudices, using dialogue and cultural exchange as key tools to foster empathy and social change. The cohesion between these initiatives strengthens their impact, ensuring a holistic approach to tackling issues of discrimination and promoting diversity across different communities.

## *Origins and Inspirations: Theory U and the Dialogue Museums*

At the core of these museums' approach to empathy-building is Otto Scharmer's Theory U, a social change model that suggests transformative learning occurs when individuals open their minds, hearts, and wills to embrace new perspectives.[3] Theory U proposes that authentic change happens through a "U-shaped" journey: beginning with suspending preconceptions, moving through sensory awareness, and ending with

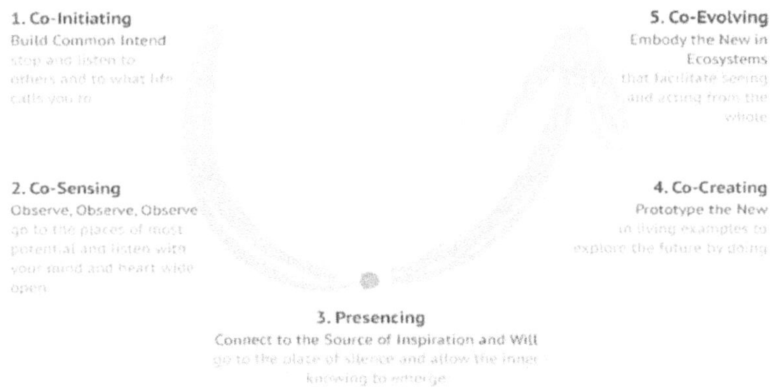


**Figure 14.1** Otto Scharmer's *Theory U*, a social change model. Credit: Otto Scharmer, *Theory U*.

connecting to a more profound understanding of others (Figure 14.1). In this framework, empathy is not merely an intellectual exercise but a deeper shift in consciousness that fosters genuine understanding and compassion.

The LDH and IDM are inspired by this idea. Both institutions use Theory U's principles to craft experiences that guide visitors through immersive, self-reflective engagements. Rather than presenting facts or artifacts, these museums offer structured interactions, often with individuals from marginalized or underrepresented communities. These encounters invite visitors to practice deep listening, awareness, and openness, facilitating profound shifts in perception and empathy. Grounded in a range of fields—including sociology, psychology, and education—these museums exemplify how spaces can be designed to foster empathy by breaking down prejudices and inviting open, meaningful encounters.

While the LDH, the IDM, and the BSL Dialogue Café in the UK are ideas and concepts that were developed entirely by the author of this chapter, the Dialogue in the Dark (DID) and the Dialogue in Silence (DIS) experiences within IDM are inspired by the Dialogue Social Enterprises (DSE) founded by Orna Cohen and Andreas Heinecke. These specific experiences from DSE serve as examples and models for creating transformative, empathy-building environments within the museum.

## *Dialogue in the Dark and Dialogue in Silence as Immersive Empathy-Building Experiences: A Walkthrough*

At the LDH and IDM, visitors embark on a transformative 60-minute journey through DID and DIS, two immersive experiences that prioritize human connection over traditional exhibits. DID immerses visitors in complete darkness, guided by blind or visually impaired facilitators, while DIS removes spoken communication entirely, fostering interactions led by deaf or hard-of-hearing guides. These experiences challenge participants to engage with the world using alternative senses and perspectives, creating a powerful platform for empathy-building and self-reflection. Unlike traditional museums that present exhibits or displays, these museums center the experience on dialogue with human guides. Visitors are greeted by blind/visually impaired and deaf/hard-of-hearing facilitators, often individuals who may differ from them significantly in terms of background or life experience. These guides serve as living exhibits, sharing personal stories that challenge visitors to examine their own assumptions.

Both the DID and DIS experiences begin with a short orientation, where visitors are asked to set aside their biases and enter with an open mind. From here, they are led through a series of interactive, often sensory-driven exhibits. In the DID exhibition, for instance, visitors are immersed in complete darkness, compelling them to navigate their surroundings without sight. This exercise is designed to challenge their reliance on visual cues, encouraging them to connect with their surroundings in new ways. By experiencing vulnerability and interdependence, visitors become more receptive to others' perspectives. Following this sensory exercise, visitors engage in structured dialogues with their blind and visually impaired guide, where they can ask questions and learn about the guide's life experiences. Facilitators are trained to create a safe, judgment-free space that encourages visitors to explore their own biases. The discussions are modeled after empathy-building practices such as active listening, which teaches participants to listen without interruption or judgment.[4] These dialogues can reveal blind spots and help visitors form a deeper connection with others' perspectives.

The experience concludes with a debriefing session, where visitors reflect on their reactions and insights. This reflection process solidifies the empathy-building experience, enabling visitors to internalize what they have learned.

By the end, many participants report a heightened sense of connection and a new understanding of people they might otherwise have ignored or dismissed.

## Sign Language Cafés: Bridging the Gap Through Everyday Interaction

One innovative extension of empathy-building spaces beyond museums is the concept of Sign Language Cafés. These establishments provide an everyday setting for meaningful interactions between hearing visitors and deaf or hard-of-hearing individuals. In LDH and IDM, the SLCs serve as an integral space where Theory U principles are applied, transforming a simple café into a dynamic experience area for mutual learning and interaction. Similarly, the first Turkish Sign Language (TSL) Café in IDM and the first British Sign Language (BSL) Café at LDH illustrate how simple, yet intentional environments can foster profound cultural and personal connections.

At the Istanbul TSL Dialogue Café, baristas fluent in TSL interact with customers, encouraging them to use sign language to place their orders. Visitors are presented with interactive screens and tablets displaying basic TSL signs, such as "coffee," "tea," or "thank you." Similarly, the BSL Dialogue Café in London integrates short instructional videos or tablets to teach visitors the fundamentals of BSL. These cafes create a welcoming atmosphere where mistakes are part of the learning process, allowing visitors to approach the experience with curiosity rather than fear of judgment.

The impact of these initiatives is evident from visitor feedback and media coverage. One visitor to the BSL Café remarked: "I had never interacted with a deaf person before, but ordering my coffee using basic sign language was surprisingly rewarding. It broke the ice and made me want to learn more." Similar sentiments are echoed in a social impact assessment conducted by the Dialogue Hub, where 86 percent of surveyed visitors reported feeling "more confident" about engaging with the deaf community after their visit.[5] In an article by *Time Out*, the BSL Dialogue Café was described as a "groundbreaking initiative that bridges communication gaps in a fun, inclusive way."[6]

The cafés' designs are intentionally inclusive, with open layouts that prioritize visibility, a critical factor for effective sign language communication. In both cities, the deaf and hard-of-hearing baristas often share their stories, providing visitors with a glimpse into the lived experiences of the deaf communities. This direct interaction fosters a deeper sense of empathy, as visitors realize the challenges and joys of navigating a hearing-dominated world.

Encouraging meaningful engagement at SLCs requires active facilitation. Café staff are trained to guide visitors gently, offering tips and corrections when necessary. For visitors, the experience goes beyond ordering a cup of coffee; it becomes a small but impactful step toward bridging communication barriers. The moments of shared laughter and understanding that arise during these interactions highlight the universal nature of connection, transcending language and cultural divides.

## *Evaluating the Impact: The Social Return on Investment (SROI) Methodology*

One of the most compelling ways to measure the success of empathy-building initiatives like the LDH and IDM is through the *Social Return on Investment (SROI)* methodology. Unlike traditional cost-benefit analyses, SROI assigns monetary value to intangible benefits, such as improved quality of social interactions, inclusion, and overall community well-being.

The SROI method is particularly valuable because it incorporates a multi-stakeholder approach, ensuring the perspectives of all who experience or influence the social change are considered. By quantifying outcomes and comparing them to investment costs, SROI produces a ratio that reflects the social value generated. For instance, a 2:1 ratio signifies that for every unit of investment, two units of social value are created.

In the case of the Dialogue Hub, an SROI analysis conducted for the period between July 2021 and June 2022 revealed that an investment of £298,660 generated a social value of £738,804.67 - equating to a return of £2.47 for every £1 invested. Similarly, the IDM's analysis between August 2016 and August 2017 highlighted a cumulative social value of 15,512,323 TL, representing a return of 4.07 TL for every 1 TL invested. These findings not only underscore the tangible impact of these projects but also validate their role as powerful tools for fostering empathy and social cohesion. Furthermore, by addressing social inequalities and promoting inclusion, these initiatives have the potential to ease the financial burden placed on the state, particularly under current laws in Turkey that mandate public support for disabled people.[7]

The SROI methodology is not merely a measurement tool but also a *strategic framework* for future planning, enabling organizations to track progress, refine objectives, and amplify their social value over time. By examining specific projects, such as the Dialogue in the Dark and Dialogue in the Silence exhibitions, the methodology provides nuanced insights into how these initiatives transform the lives of participants and stakeholders alike.

## *Integrating Storytelling, Curiosity, and Collective Journeying*

The success of empathy-building programs like the LDH, IDM, and SLCs is not only reflected in numbers but also in the intangible ingredients that drive their transformative potential. At the heart of these initiatives are storytelling, curiosity, and collective journeying, which serve as powerful tools in bridging divides and fostering understanding:

- Storytelling: By sharing personal narratives, participants connect on a human level, breaking down stereotypes and fostering mutual respect.
- Collective Journeying: Immersive activities, such as navigating darkness or interacting with deaf baristas, create shared experiences that deepen understanding and empathy.
- Curiosity: Encouraging visitors to explore different perspectives sparks dialogue and fosters a willingness to embrace new ideas.

These elements work in harmony, creating an "alchemy of empathy" that transforms casual encounters into meaningful connections.[8] The impact of these tools is further validated through visitor testimonials, such as those from Dialogue Hub participants who described their experiences as "profoundly moving" and "life-changing."

## *Expanding the Sign Language Café Model to Other Contexts*

The success of SLCs in Istanbul and London demonstrates the potential for replicating this innovative model to foster empathy in various informal learning environments. By adopting thoughtful strategies and inclusive practices, communities can create impactful spaces that bridge communication gaps and promote mutual understanding through the SLCs:

1. *Partnering with Local Deaf Communities*: To ensure authenticity and meaningful engagement, it is essential to collaborate with local deaf organizations and community leaders. This step establishes trust and ensures the café reflects the community it aims to represent. These partnerships can help: Recruit qualified deaf or hard-of-hearing staff who reflect the local community. Co-design educational materials tailored to the unique linguistic and cultural needs of the region.
   - Recruit qualified deaf or hard-of-hearing staff who reflect the local community.
   - Co-design educational materials tailored to the unique linguistic and cultural needs of the region.

2. *Designing Inclusive Spaces*: The physical layout of the café plays a critical role in fostering communication and inclusivity. Consider these design principles: Prioritize Visibility: Open layouts with minimal visual obstructions enable clear sight lines, which are essential for sign language communication. Use Tactile Menus: Menus with raised text, Braille, or textured elements can make the café more accessible to visually impaired visitors. Incorporate Visual Aids: Interactive screens, instructional posters, or videos can guide visitors on basic sign language usage, creating a supportive environment for learning.
   - Prioritize Visibility: Open layouts with minimal visual obstructions enable clear sight lines, which are essential for sign language communication.
   - Use Tactile Menus: Menus with raised text, Braille, or textured elements can make the café more accessible to visually impaired visitors.
   - Incorporate Visual Aids: Interactive screens, instructional posters, or videos can guide visitors on basic sign language usage, creating a supportive environment for learning.

3. *Providing Educational Tools*: Education is central to the café's mission of promoting interaction and understanding. These resources ensure that visitors, regardless of prior exposure, feel equipped to participate. Effective tools include: Digital Resources: Short instructional videos or apps teaching basic signs can prepare visitors

for their experience. Printed Materials: Pocket-sized printed sign language alphabet, pocket guides, or table posters with common signs for words like "coffee" or "thank you" can empower visitors to engage confidently with staff.

- Digital Resources: Short instructional videos or apps teaching basic signs can prepare visitors for their experience.
- Printed Materials: Pocket-sized printed sign language alphabet, pocket guides, or table posters with common signs for words like "coffee" or "thank you" can empower visitors to engage confidently with staff.

**4.** *Emphasizing Storytelling*: Personal narratives are a powerful way to foster connection. Their storytelling transforms a simple café visit into a deeply enriching cultural exchange. Baristas can: Share stories about their experiences as deaf or hard-of-hearing individuals. Highlight cultural aspects of the deaf community, providing insights into their challenges and achievements.

- Share stories about their experiences as deaf or hard-of-hearing individuals.
- Highlight cultural aspects of the deaf community, providing insights into their challenges and achievements.

**5.** *Celebrating Mistakes*: Creating a safe, judgment-free environment is crucial for encouraging visitors to step out of their comfort zones. This approach helps visitors shed anxieties and builds confidence in their ability to communicate. The café should: Embrace errors as part of the learning process, reinforcing that making mistakes is natural and acceptable. Foster a playful atmosphere where staff and visitors can share moments of laughter and understanding.

- Embrace errors as part of the learning process, reinforcing that making mistakes is natural and acceptable.
- Foster a playful atmosphere where staff and visitors can share moments of laughter and understanding.

SLCs offer a scalable and adaptable model that can be extended to schools, universities, workplaces, and community centers. Integrating these experiences into corporate diversity training, for instance, can help employees develop greater cultural awareness and communication skills. Similarly, educational institutions can introduce SLCs as part of their curriculum to promote inclusivity and foster empathy among students. Notably, the increasing recognition of BSL in British society is reflected in its inclusion as a General Certificate of Secondary Education (GCSE) subject in the British curriculum starting in September 2025.[9] This development is expected to enhance the visibility of BSL and foster greater linguistic and cultural understanding among younger generations.

## *Challenges in Empathy-Building Programs*

While the potential for empathy-building programs is significant, practitioners often encounter specific challenges.[10] One common obstacle is resistance to vulnerability. Engaging in meaningful dialogue or empathy-building activities requires participants to step out of their comfort zones, which can feel uncomfortable or intimidating for some. Facilitators play a crucial role in creating an atmosphere that encourages openness without pressuring participants. Introductory activities designed to ease individuals into the experience can be particularly effective in overcoming this barrier.

Another challenge arises from cultural differences in dialogue norms. Communication styles and expectations vary widely across cultures, which can sometimes lead to misunderstandings during interactions. To address this, facilitators should be trained in cultural sensitivity, equipping them to navigate these differences effectively and promote inclusive dialogue.

Lastly, skepticism or preexisting biases among visitors can hinder engagement. Some participants may approach these programs with reservations or strong preconceived notions. In such cases, facilitators can use empathy-building practices such as nonjudgmental listening and reframing techniques to foster an environment of openness and trust. The following two primary empathy-building strategies help participants challenge their assumptions and embrace new perspectives:

1. Nonjudgmental Listening,
2. Reframing Techniques.

These strategies are aimed at breaking down skepticism and fostering an atmosphere of trust and openness, which is crucial for transformative and empathetic engagement.

## *Expanding Beyond Museum Walls: Applications in Broader Contexts*

The empathy-building tools developed by the LDH and IDM have applications that extend well beyond museum settings.[11] Schools, for example, can adapt these tools to foster empathy among students from different backgrounds. Structured dialogues and sensory experiences can teach students to appreciate different perspectives, promoting social harmony within diverse educational settings.

Community organizations can also benefit from these tools, especially in intergenerational contexts or areas with diverse socioeconomic backgrounds. Such programs help build bridges across generations and social classes, fostering mutual respect and understanding.

Corporations and workplaces may likewise find value in these empathy-building exercises, particularly in diversity and inclusion training. Encouraging employees to connect through structured dialogues and sensory experiences can create a more inclusive environment, helping colleagues understand each other beyond superficial assumptions. In healthcare, empathy-based training can lead to more compassionate care by helping providers understand diverse patient experiences.[12]

## *The Future of Museums as Empathy-Building Spaces*

In a world where division often outweighs connection, the need for empathy-building spaces is critical. Institutions like the DHL, IDM, and SLCs demonstrate how museums can foster empathy and promote inclusivity through structured, immersive experiences. These experiences encourage visitors to set aside preconceived notions and engage with others in ways that challenge and enrich their worldviews.

As museums continue to evolve, they have the potential to become even more powerful tools for social change. By embracing their role as empathy-building spaces, museums can help build more connected, compassionate communities, inspiring others to adapt similar tools in varied settings.[13] The future of empathy-building in museums is bright, and as institutions refine and expand these methods, they can play a crucial role in creating a more empathetic and inclusive society.

# Notes

1 In 2022, the International Council of Museums adopted a new definition of museums, emphasizing inclusivity and community engagement. This redefinition aligns with the role of museums as empathy-building spaces. For the official definition, see ICOM, https://icom.museum/en/resources/standards-guidelines/museum-definition/.

2 Both institutions are designed to challenge biases through immersive, dialogue-based experiences. For information on their approaches, see Dialogue Hub, https://dialoguehub.co.uk. See also Istanbul Dialogue Museum, https://www.istanbuldiyalogmuzesi.org/en/.

3 Otto Scharmer's Theory U is discussed extensively in his work *Theory U: Leading from the Future as It* Emerges. For details on the stages of the U-shaped process and its application to social change, see Otto Scharmer, *Theory U: Leading from the Future as It Emerges* (Berrett-Koehler Publishers, 2009).

4 Active listening fosters empathy by encouraging participants to suspend judgment and fully engage with others' perspectives. For foundational principles, see Carl R. Rogers and Richard E. Farson, "Active Listening," in *Communications in Organizations*, ed. David W. Johnson (McGraw-Hill, 1995), 88–96 and Oscar Trimboli, *Deep Listening: Impact Beyond Words* (Oscar Trimboli, 2021), 35–42.

5 Dialogue Hub Social Impact Assessment September 2022, prepared by S360UK.

6 Time Out accessed September 22, 2021 https://www.timeout.com/london/news/at-this-waterloo-cafe-you-order-in-sign-language-092221.

7 "Sosyal Yardimlar," Turkiye Cumhuriyeti Aile Ve Sosyal Hizmetler Bakanligi, https://www.aile.gov.tr/sss/engelli-ve-yasli-hizmetleri-genel-mudurlugu/sosyal-yardimlar/.

8 This term which was first used in Elif Gökçiğdem, "Preface" in *Designing for Empathy: Perspectives on the Museum Experience* (Arlington, VA: American Alliance of Museums, 2019), xviii.

9 Department for Education, "British Sign Language: A New GCSE Qualification," https://educationhub.blog.gov.uk/2023/12/21/british-sign-language-gcse-everything-you-need-to-know/.

10 Resistance to vulnerability is a common challenge in empathy-building activities. For a discussion of creating safe spaces for vulnerability, see Brené Brown, *Daring Greatly: How the Courage to Be Vulnerable Transforms the Way We Live, Love, Parent, and Lead* (Penguin Random House, 2012), especially Chapter 4.

**11** Empathy-building tools can transform educational environments, helping students develop social-emotional skills. See Daniel Goleman, *Emotional Intelligence: Why It Can Matter More Than IQ* (Bantam Books, 1995), 269–76.

**12** Healthcare providers benefit from empathy training that improves patient care and communication. See Helen Riess, *The Empathy Effect: Seven Neuroscience-Based Keys for Transforming the Way We Live, Love, Work, and Connect Across Differences* (Sounds True, 2018).

**13** Museums worldwide are reimagining their roles as agents of social change. For examples of innovative programs, see Richard Sandell and Eithne Nightingale, eds., *Museums, Equality and Social Justice* (Routledge, 2012), 45–72.

# 15 Empathy Circles

## Learning and Practicing Mutual Empathy in Small Groups

*Edwin Rutsch*

*Rosa Zubizarreta-Ada*

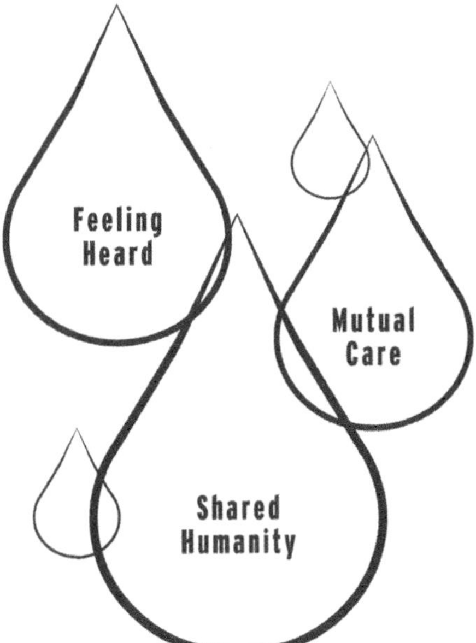


The Empathy Circle is a simple yet powerful practice of deep listening and mutual empathy; it builds capacity for considering multiple perspectives and deepens interpersonal understanding, while generating a sense of community. Empathy Circles can be offered in museum settings to museum visitors for the purpose of enhancing visitor experience and engagement; they can be offered to museum staff, to support internal communication and inclusion; and they can also be part of strengthening relationships within the larger community.

Many valuable approaches for developing empathy exist, as detailed in this volume and elsewhere.[1] Among them is empathic *active listening*: whenever we engage in conversation with another person, we have the opportunity to "listen to understand"—a basic empathy-building practice with strong interpersonal benefits for all involved.[2]

While apparently simple, "listening to understand" is not so easy to enact. While many of us know "about" active listening, without a strong practice we are unlikely to engage in it, especially in difficult situations where it could be particularly beneficial. In many contexts, the norm is to compete for attention, rather than to take turns and listen deeply. Even when we do take turns, it's unusual to begin by reflecting back what the previous person has said, with enough patience to create real connection. Instead, we tend to offer our disagreements quite quickly, usually before having fully empathized with the previous speaker's contribution.

An unexpected aspect of Empathy Circles is how deeply relaxing it can be, to participate in a small group where each person is being fully heard to their satisfaction. Of course, we may feel a tinge of anxiety at first, while learning something unfamiliar. Yet this quickly dissipates, as participants experience the supportive context of the group.

The Empathy Circle supports freedom of speech. When it is our turn to speak, we are free to disagree with anything that anyone else has said. We can speak about our own beliefs and experiences, knowing that our listener, instead of arguing with us, will be focused on understanding what we have said. The experience of being heard helps us be more open to listening to others when it is their turn to speak, even to those with very different experiences and perspectives than our own.

Group contexts can be a powerful format for learning. Young people often come to a museum in groups, and even adults are often predisposed to join a group (e.g., an exhibition tour) as part of their museum experience. The authors have conducted Empathy Circles in structured settings as part of our work with organizations (Rosa), and also in more tumultuous settings such as highly polarized demonstrations and counter-demonstrations (Edwin).

We have seen, over and over again, how the desire to feel deeply heard and understood is a basic human need, and how empathic active listening is a much-needed skill, mindset, and Way of Being.[3] Given that museums can be such a rich location for developing empathy, we share our work here with the intention for it to be usefully adapted to museum contexts.[4]

## Background and Applications

The Empathy Circle is an experiential learning framework designed by Edwin Rutsch based on the empathic active listening at the heart of Carl Rogers' psychotherapeutic approach.[5] Rogers saw empathy, unconditional positive regard, and authenticity as the three core factors of both healing and human development more generally; he also wrote about how deep attentive listening can be helpful in organizations.[6] Many classroom teachers found Rogers' person-centered approach very helpful in their work.[7] Yet while it seems like the logical next step, Rogers did *not* explore how small groups could be designed for mutual empathy by having participants take turns engaging in active listening.

Between us, the authors have a combined total of over twenty years of working with the Empathy Circle and training others in this practice. When working with large groups, we host Empathy Cafés, which are a collection of smaller Empathy Circles (further described below). One particularly memorable experience was an online community-police dialogue in April of 2022, co-sponsored by the organization "Police 2 Peace" and The Empathy Center, founded by Edwin for the purpose of raising the level of empathy in the world.[8] At the end of this Empathy Café, participants from all sides expressed appreciation for the constructive climate they had just co-created, experiencing it as a hopeful alternative to a very tense national situation.[9]

The Empathy Circle and Empathy Café formats are also very useful for in-person gatherings. Lou Zweier and John Crowley of Aqus Community Foundation host in-person Empathy Cafés in Petaluma, California, for building community across differences. Edwin and his colleagues have brought Empathy Circles to the activist realm by bringing the Empathy Tent to charged political demonstrations and counter-demonstrations and offering empathic listening to both sides.[10]

In Europe, Prof. Dr. Katrin Valentin, a Professor of Education in Nuremberg, Germany, has worked with Empathy Circles in the context of supporting municipal processes of transformation toward sustainable communities.[11] She has spread Empathy Circles to others working in higher education, teacher education, organization development, and churches. Meanwhile, Minter Dial, leadership consultant and author, invites business executives to participate in Empathy Circles in his leadership seminars.

## Preparing to Host an Empathy Circle

Trying an Empathy Circle out with a few friends can be an invaluable learning experience. You can also find free Empathy Circles online at EmpathyCircle.com.

### *Format of the Empathy Circle*

The format of the Empathy Circle may seem quite structured, yet within this basic format participants are free to speak about whatever they would like. This balance of structure, openness, and nonjudgmental context creates a high degree of psychological safety (Box 15.1).

**Box 15.1 Empathy Circles: Overall Duration, Appropriate Space & Basic Materials**

The duration of an Empathy Circle depends on how many participants there are, and how many practice rounds you want. For example, if there are 4 participants, one practice round with four 5-minute turns will take about 20 minutes. Ideally, in an Empathy Circle, participants will be able to experience three go-rounds, which adds up to an hour. Having 10 minutes at the start for a welcome and introductions and 10 minutes at the end to debrief the circle, adds up 1 hr 20 min. If less time is available, having only two go-rounds condenses the Empathy Circle experience to one hour. This would be an absolute minimum, as it takes time to relax our nervous systems and enter into another way of being.

When hosting an in-person Empathy Circle, it helps to find a quiet place away from distractions, where people can hear one another and have a reasonably comfy place to sit. If we are including a few minutes of journaling at the start, we will also want a paper or pen for each person and something to write on. If people are new to the practice, you may want to print a handout for each person. (See endnote 15 for the link to a one-page handout.)

*Group Size*: The circle size is between 3–6 participants, including the Facilitator with 4 participants being ideal. For larger groups, we offer the Empathy Café, which consists of simultaneous Empathy Circles (from 2 to 16 or more), each with its own facilitator. Since the basic building block of a larger Café is the smaller Empathy Circle, we begin by describing this basic form.

- *Roles*: In an Empathy Circle, participants rotate among three different roles:
    1. Speaker,
    2. Active Listener,
    3. Silent Listeners.

  This threefold aspect of ***receiving*** active listening, ***offering*** active listening, and ***witnessing*** active listening makes for a rich learning experience. A designated Facilitator also participates in the process, rotating through these roles, holding the practice and serving as a time-keeper throughout. More on this below.
- *Structure of the Rounds*: The Empathy Circle structure consists of a series of timed turns, where one person is Speaking, another person is engaging in Active Listening, and the rest of the circle are in the role of Silent Listeners. Each turn is typically 3–5 minutes long. Once all participants have had the opportunity to speak, we have concluded our first round. Ideally, we have at least three rounds; this means each person will have three speaking turns and three active listening turns.

## *The Role of the Facilitator*

After a brief overview of the process, the first thing the Facilitator does is model being an Active Listener. They do this by offering to be the first Listener, for whomever would like to be the first Speaker: *"I'm volunteering as the first Listener here, so you can get an idea of how this works. Who would like to be the first Speaker?"*

The Facilitator/Active Listener will ask the person who has volunteered as Speaker, to "pause" after expressing an idea or two, for the Facilitator/Active Listener to reflect back what they have understood so far. If the Speaker forgets to pause, the Active Listener can remind them, sometimes simply by holding up their hand.

For participants in the role of Active Listeners, asking Speakers to "pause" can be one of the most challenging aspects of this practice. We have often been taught that to be polite means to "not interrupt." Here, the purpose of "interrupting" is to offer a tentative active listening response back to the speaker. This may sound something like: *"Here's what I've heard you say: (. . .), is that close?"*

Throughout, the Facilitator is also serving as time-keeper. When the first speaker has completed their turn, the Facilitator introduces the second turn by explaining that, *"Whoever has been Listening, will be the next Speaker. So now it is my turn to Speak."* As facilitators, we choose another participant to be our Active Listener for this next turn. As we model Speaking, we will pause every few sentences, and invite the Listener to reflect back their understanding of what has been said.

In the remaining turns, the Facilitator will be in the role of Silent Listener, while still available to offer help as needed. The Facilitator might remind participants that each pair in a given turn—both Speaker and Active Listener—are working together to help the Speaker feel heard to the Speaker's satisfaction. Meanwhile, the Silent Listeners in the circle are offering their caring attention to support the process. Each time, the most recent Active Listener becomes the next Speaker.

We hope this brief description illustrates the key role of an experienced Facilitator, at least for the first few times that participants are learning this format. Once participants are familiar with the practice, all that is needed is for someone to volunteer as time-keeper. This simple graphic illustrates the changing roles of each participant (Figure 15.1).

# The Empathy Café: Overview and Useful Tips

To work with larger groups, Edwin developed the *Empathy Café* format; after an initial whole-group introduction, participants reconfigure into several smaller Empathy Circles. In the context of a museum, holding an Empathy Café is something that a museum can "grow into," once enough staff have had experience with Empathy Circles. While the Café model does *not* require the participants to have previous experience with the Empathy Circle, it does require having an experienced facilitator for each of the small groups.

## *Why a Facilitator for Each Empathy Circle?*

From a number of experiments in scaling the Empathy Circles, we've learned that the most important factor for setting up concurrent Empathy Circles is for each small group to have an experienced Facilitator to hold the process. While the Empathy Circle format is quite simple once one has experienced it, we've found that when left to their own devices, small groups unfamiliar with the process will tend to revert to informal conversation, regardless of any clear instructions we may have given them. Of course, there's nothing wrong with informal conversation! At the same time, it precludes engaging in a new and different experience. Instead, when each Empathy Circle has a Facilitator who can start the circle off by volunteering as the first Active Listener, the small groups will step more easily into the practice.

## *Preparing for an Empathy Café*

In addition to having a facilitator for each Empathy Circle, here are some other things to keep in mind:

- *Crafting the larger theme or question*: We find it helpful to spend time beforehand carefully crafting the overall question, in consultation with the organizational sponsors, so the experience can be as relevant as possible to each particular context. The question or theme is always intended as an invitation, not a constraint: in the Empathy Circles, participants are welcome to speak to whatever is on their mind. However, we've found that when offered a meaningful question, many participants will choose to address it. In the next section, we include additional information on how to approach the selection of

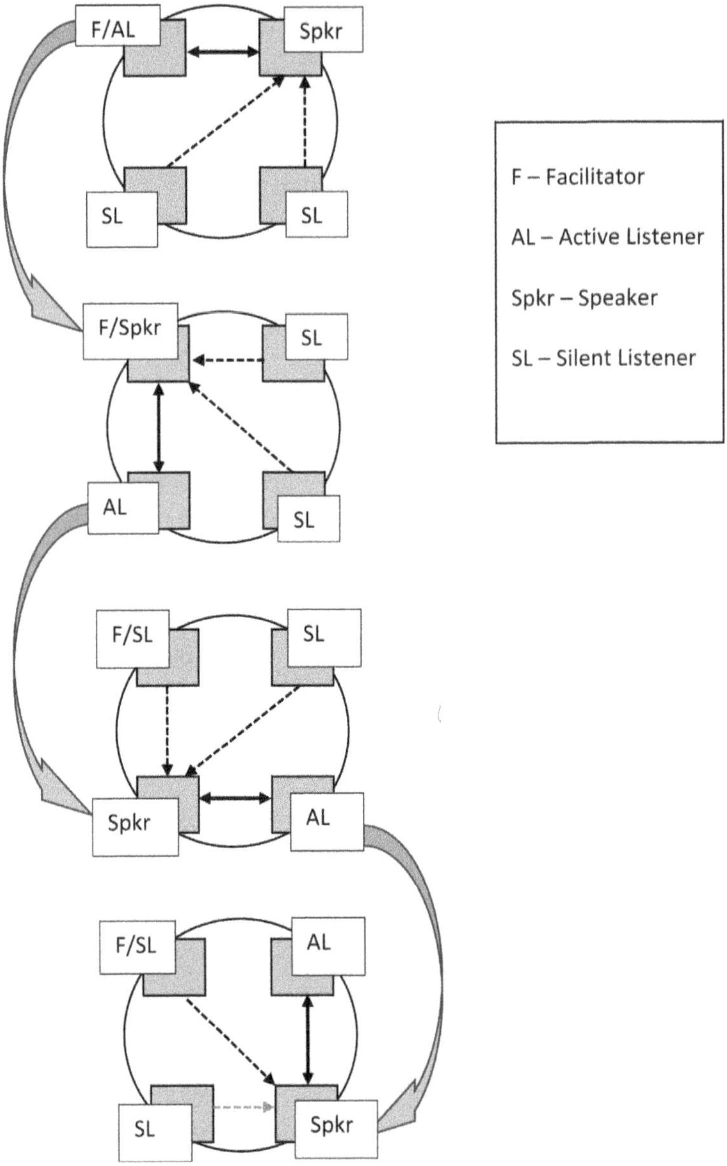


**Figure 15.1** Empathy Circle Roles and Flow. (1) Whether we are doing an Empathy Circle online or in-person, the participants remain in their same seats throughout. Only their roles change. (2) The Facilitator always starts in the role of the first Active Listener, to model Active Listening. (3) The person who is Active Listener in one turn, becomes the Speaker in the next turn. (4) Thus in the second turn, the Facilitator becomes the Speaker. As Speaker, the Facilitator takes a pause every so often, so that the Active Listener can reflect back. (5) The person who is Speaker in one turn, becomes a Silent Listener in the next turn. (6) The Facilitator serves as time-keeper throughout. Credit: Illustration by Rosa Zubizarreta-Ada, 2024.

a theme, and why it can be useful to begin with less controversial themes and questions.

- *Introduction*: Whenever we host an Empathy Café, we like to start and end with some large-group time. At the beginning of the Café, we talk about the purpose of what we will be doing together, and may invite a bit of individual journaling on the theme.
- *Journaling*: In Rosa's work with organizations, she has found it helpful to invite participants to begin by journaling for a few minutes in response to the given topic. In an Empathy Café, we do this together, before reconfiguring into smaller groups. The purpose of journaling is to decrease participants' anxiety about what they might say once it is their turn to speak; this allows them to be more present while listening to others. Of course, once it is their turn to speak, participants can always choose to speak about what is alive for them in the moment.
- *Debrief*: At the end of the Café, we bring participants back together for a debrief. In some cases, this might be a brief 30-second turn per person, where participants can offer a comment about their experience or about the topic. However, when working with an organization on an internal improvement or organizational learning topic, we plan a more extensive debrief to address both participants' learnings on the topic, as well as, any insights and learnings about the communication process itself.

## Empathy Circles and Empathy Cafés in a Museum Context

### *Fostering Internal, Institutional Empathy*

One application of this work to a museum context can be for museum staff, including curators, educators, and docents, to work with Empathy Circles as a means to strengthen mutual understanding and collaboration among staff members. This format offers a supportive space for building community and exploring differences within the team, while also strengthening communication skills.

### *Public Programs Relevant to Visitor Needs*

Another application is for museums to organize Empathy Cafés for their visitors, as a way to build upon exhibitions or guided tours. An Empathy Café offers visitors an opportunity to enjoy deep listening practice in small groups while sharing their own perspectives and experiences related to the art or artifacts they've just seen. Once museum staff have gained some experience facilitating this format, they might host Cafés that help visitors engage with more controversial exhibits, or even host "listening for understanding" sessions on challenging community issues.

Yet while museums often deal with controversial subjects, we would not recommend beginning with the most challenging topic possible. Instead, it makes sense to build our muscles as Empathy Café organizers and hosts by starting with a topic that is somewhat less charged. For example, while working with school staff who were experiencing strong interpersonal difficulties, one of us (Rosa) designed the first communication workshop to begin with an Empathy Café where participants explored what they had found most meaningful or joyful about their recent summer vacation. In that case, the operating principle was to offer an opportunity for participants to build more connection and trust before moving on to explore areas of difficulty. This progression gives participants an opportunity to become familiar with the format before delving into a challenging topic. We find that participants value opportunities to feel deeply heard about things that are meaningful to them, including both positive experiences as well as difficult ones. This example illustrates how it sometimes makes sense to begin with an appreciative theme.

### *Augmenting Online Programs*

While Empathy Cafés work quite well in person, they also work well online, as in the earlier example with Peace 2 Police and community activists. Thus, museums could host Empathy Cafés as a helpful way to augment online programs, offering participants the opportunity for meaningful connection.

## Challenges and Further Learning

Empathy Circles and Empathy Cafés are a great place to begin developing our empathy skills. At the same time, our learning can always deepen. The more skills and training we have, the more we can work effectively in highly contentious situations. Nonetheless, the Empathy Circle, as described here, remains a highly useful "beginner-level" practice, a valuable and highly accessible entry point that can serve as useful grounding for more advanced work.

We hope to have sparked your curiosity about experiencing an Empathy Circle for yourself. After doing so, you'll be in a better position to decide how this work might be of benefit to your organization, as the best way to learn is through direct experience.

To make this work accessible, free Empathy Circles are available online.[12] Free facilitator trainings are also available online.[13] We are delighted that the Empathy Circle facilitator trainings have been so well-received.[14] In addition, you'll find additional "open source," DIY learning resources online.[15] One good place to start is our simple one-page handout.[16]

Ideally, over time organizations will develop their own internal team of trained Empathy Circle facilitators. However, if you'd like to host an online Empathy Café and don't have enough internal facilitators yet, we have a community of practitioners who are available to host online Empathy Circles; contact Edwin to learn more.[17] In sum, we wish you all the best with your projects to strengthen our society's capacity for empathy, and are honored to contribute in whatever way we can, to this valuable work.

## Notes


**1** Susan Lanzoni, *Empathy: A History* (Yale University Press, 2018).

**2** Stephen R. Covey, *The 7 Habits of Highly Effective People: Powerful Lessons in Personal Change* (Simon & Schuster, 2013).

**3** Carl R. Rogers, "Empathic: An Unappreciated Way of Being," *The Person-Centered Journal* 5, no. 2 (Summer 1975), https://doi.org/10.1177/001100007500500202.

**4** Rogers, "Empathic: An Unappreciated Way of Being."

**5** Rogers and Richard E. Farson, "Active Listening," in *Communicating in Business Today*, ed. R. G. Newman, M. A. Danzinger, and M. Cohen (Heath & Company, 1987), https://tinyurl.com/EmpathyC101.

**6** Rogers, *Freedom to Learn for the 80's* (Charles E. Merrill Publishing Company, 1983).

**7** https://EmpathyCircle.com/how-to-empathy-circle.

**8** A special thanks to board members, Kathy Kidd, Lou Zweier, Bill Filler, Ingird Hirtz, and William Kingsbury. For more info, see http://TheEmpathyCenter.org.

**9** Elizabeth Svoboda, "The Empathy Incentive," *Scientific American*, October 2024, https://tinyurl.com/EmpathyC102.

**10** E. Svoboda, "The Empathy Incentive," See also the Empathy Tent website at: https://EmpathyTent.com.

**11** For more info, please visit: http://katrin-valentin.de/?page_id=13.

**12** https://EmpathyCircle.com.

**13** https://BestEmpathyTraining.com.

**14** Zaina Kakai, "Learning on the Go: My Experience with Empathy Circles for System Sensing and Building Connection," Linked-In blog post, January 18, 2021, https://tinyurl.com/EmpathyC103.

**15** https://EmpathyCircle.com.

**16** https://EmpathyCircle.com/how-to-empathy-circle.

**17** edwinrutsch@gmail.com.

# 16 Hey, We Need to Talk!

## Designing Social Sculptures to Encourage Relational Dialogues That Increase Civic Engagement and Social Repair

*Philippa Pham Hughes*

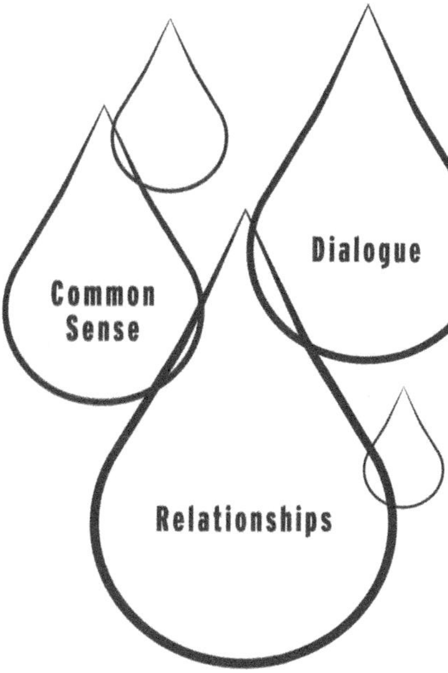

America's social and civic fabric is unraveling as we increasingly refuse to engage with those who hold different beliefs. We sort ourselves into ideological bubbles, dehumanize those who disagree with us, and lose the ability to collaborate on solving our shared challenges. This unwillingness to participate in genuine dialogue across differences has profound consequences: when we stop talking to each other, we stop caring about each other, and when we stop caring about each other, our democratic institutions begin to crumble.

A decline in empathy and compassion can significantly erode civic engagement by weakening the emotional bonds that motivate people to participate in community life. When individuals become less attuned to the struggles and experiences of their neighbors, they are less likely to volunteer, vote, attend community meetings, or support local initiatives that could benefit others.[1] This emotional disconnection can create a self-reinforcing cycle: As people participate less in civic activities, they have fewer opportunities to understand different perspectives and develop empathy, which in turn further reduces their motivation to engage in collective action. The result is a community where people become increasingly focused on their individual concerns, and the concerns of those who think and look like them, rather than the common good, which includes people who look and think differently from one another, ultimately weakening the social fabric that sustains democratic society.

At the University of Michigan in 2024–2025, I approached this challenge through two interconnected initiatives: an exhibition at the University of Michigan Museum of Art (UMMA) and a course at the Ford School of Public Policy. Both were designed to demonstrate how art can serve as a powerful catalyst for civic engagement and social repair by creating spaces for authentic dialogue across difference. The exhibition, "Hey, We Need to Talk!" (HWNTT) transformed a traditional museum gallery into a laboratory for democratic engagement, while students in my Ford School course learned to design and implement their own projects aimed at conversations around specific policy topics (Figure 16.1). Together, these initiatives explored how cultural institutions can move beyond being passive repositories of art to become active spaces for civic engagement and social repair.

## Theoretical Framework

This work builds on three foundational elements: the tradition of socially engaged art, research on political polarization, and established frameworks for democratic flourishing. Socially engaged art represents a radical reimagining of art's role in civic life. While traditional art objects might hang on museum walls awaiting viewers, social sculptures use human interaction itself as their primary material. In these works, the quality of dialogue and depth of connection between participants form the artwork's core. Artists in this field design frameworks that enable meaningful interaction and potential social transformation, often working far beyond traditional art spaces.

Despite narratives of deepening political division in the United States, research reveals a more complex and hopeful picture of how Americans view contentious social issues. Research from More In Common called "The Hidden Tribes of America" reveals that America isn't simply split into two opposing camps. Rather, a vocal minority at the extremes (33 percent of Americans) dominates national conversation while an "Exhausted Majority" (67 percent) demonstrates more nuanced views and a greater flexibility in their positions. This group feels frustrated with political polarization but is often overlooked and even scorned in public discourse. The study shows more potential for agreement on specific issues like racism and immigration policy than often portrayed in media, which suggests significant potential for dialogue across difference.

The conceptual core of "Hey, We Need to Talk!" was inspired by Professor Jenna Bednar's framework for human social flourishing.[2] Bednar suggests that we can create a society in which every human flourishes by reorienting public policy away from the transactional toward the relational. The application of relational thinking to policy and to every aspect of society is at the core of HWNTT.

Bednar also proposes four pillars of flourishing that are at the core of HWNTT:

**1)** Dignity: Ensuring meaningful participation and mutual respect.

**2)** Community: Fostering social bonds and shared spaces.

**3)** Beauty: Embracing cultural expression and wonder.

**4)** Sustainability: Addressing climate change through collective local action.

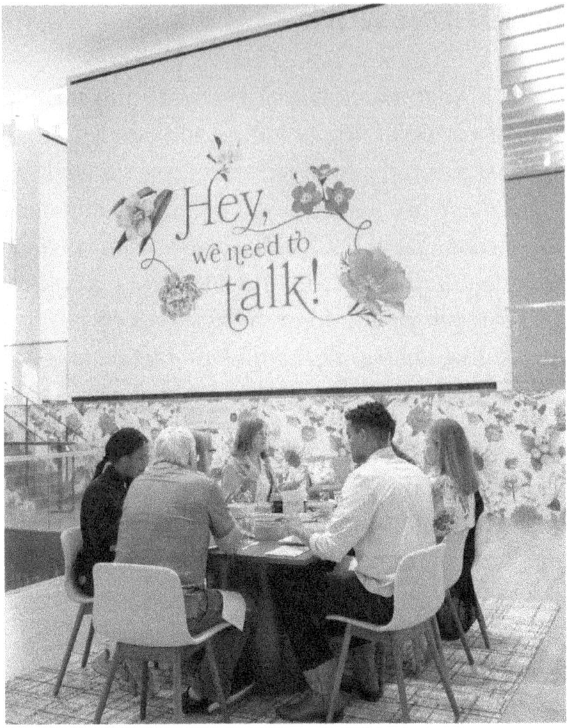


**Figure 16.1** Common Sense Diner, "Hey We Need to Talk!" at the University of Michigan Museum of Art. Credit: Photography by Daniel Ribar. Courtesy of the University of Michigan Museum of Art.

The exhibit's design is supported by research on the relationship between arts participation and civic engagement. Studies show that people who engage with the arts demonstrate higher rates of volunteering, voting, and community involvement. The impact is particularly powerful when individuals actively participate rather than simply observe, as creative engagement develops crucial civic qualities like empathy and the ability to imagine different perspectives.

HWNTT elicits a feeling of awe, which triggers profound changes in how we think and behave. According to Dacher Keltner, when people feel awe, they become less focused on themselves and experience what he calls "the small self" effect, feeling part of something larger. This leads to increased prosocial behavior, generosity, and cooperation with others.[3] People in a state of awe report feeling more connected to humanity, more humble, and more open to new ideas and perspectives. They also experience reduced stress, enhanced curiosity, better learning capacity, and a greater sense of presence in the moment. Keltner's work shows that even small daily experiences of awe can significantly improve both psychological well-being and social bonds, suggesting that awe plays a crucial role in binding communities together and facilitating cultural learning.

Dialogue is the foundation upon which both personal relationships and democracy are built and sustained. Through meaningful conversations, people develop understanding and empathy for one another, building the bonds of trust and care that motivate them to consider others' well-being alongside their own.[4] This web of caring relationships creates the social fabric necessary for democracy to function—when people care about their fellow citizens, they are more likely to support policies and compromises that serve the broader public good rather than just their narrow self-interests.

Meaningful dialogue builds the relationships and mutual understanding that are essential foundations for democratic society.[5] When people engage in authentic conversations, particularly across differences, they begin to see one another as full human beings rather than abstract opponents. These personal connections foster empathy and care—it becomes harder to dismiss or demonize those we know as neighbors, colleagues, and fellow community members. Through sustained dialogue, people develop the capacity to hold multiple perspectives and consider how policies and decisions affect others' lives, not just their own.

Dialogue is also essential in creating informed citizens, a core component of any thriving democracy. When people have the opportunity to openly discuss policies, social issues, and public concerns with others who hold different views, they develop a more nuanced understanding of complex issues. These conversations help people move beyond simplistic positions to grapple with the real challenges of governing a diverse society. The relationships built through dialogue, in turn strengthen democracy by fostering the mutual respect and consideration necessary for collaborative problem-solving.

Sharing stories forges human connections and builds empathy between people.[6] When we tell stories, our brains actually synchronize with our listeners, creating a shared emotional and cognitive experience. This neural synchronization allows us to feel what others feel as they share their experiences, helping us relate to different perspectives and find common ground even with those who may seem quite different from us. Storytelling helps break down barriers between people by revealing our shared humanity and creating moments of genuine understanding and emotional resonance. This innate human capacity for story-sharing builds bridges between individuals and communities, making it a powerful tool for strengthening social bonds and fostering meaningful connections.

## Design Elements and Implementation

"Hey, We Need to Talk!" translates these theoretical foundations into an awe-inspiring physical and social environment designed to foster authentic dialogue. Every element serves both aesthetic and civic purposes, creating a space that simultaneously evokes the transcendent wonder of a traditional museum while fostering the comfortable intimacy of a living room.

### *Physical Design*

The centerpiece is an immersive wallpaper featuring all fifty state flowers, created in collaboration with Detroit-based artist Louise Jones. This dramatic treatment covers every wall surface, with a soaring 40-foot title wall creating an immediate sense of awe upon entry. The flowers are a symbol of our national unity and they serve as a metaphor for flourishing.

The gallery space is organized into four distinct living room areas and a dining room, each carefully furnished to feel like corners of an extraordinary home. Each area corresponds to one of Bednar's pillars of flourishing, with curated artworks from UMMA's collection supporting themes of community, sustainability, dignity, and beauty hung directly over the wallpaper.

Story-sharing prompts in each space invite visitors to reflect and contribute:

- Beauty: Share a story about a time when you felt transformed by something beautiful.
- Community: Share a story about a time when you felt a sense of belonging.
- Sustainability: Share a story about a memorable outdoor experience.
- Dignity: Share a story about a time when you witnessed or experienced an act of dignity.
- American Identity: What does it mean to be American?

Visitors record their responses on perforated postcards, which are collected in photo albums within the gallery. The albums are an evolving archive of shared human experience that future visitors can explore, building layers of connection over time. The gallery guide includes a black-and-white outline of the wallpaper's flower pattern that visitors can color, encouraging meditative engagement with the space.

## *Programmatic Elements*

The heart of the social sculpture is the weekly Common Sense Dinners, where seven people representing different political perspectives share a meal. The conversation format follows carefully considered guidelines while maintaining elements of casual hospitality. The goal is to begin to build trust and connection before entering a conversation about politics.

- *Opening Phase*: These gatherings begin in the community-themed living room area, often requiring extra chairs pulled from the dining table—intentionally recreating the familiar feeling of a spontaneous home gathering.
    - Moderator provides a brief historical overview of HWNTT. Moderator reminds participants that we aren't going to debate issues with talking points and facts; we are simply going to try to understand each other through personal narrative and to learn from each other. We may not find common ground, but the goal is to see each other as humans. Emphasize personal experience over political positions.
    - Participants are invited spend a few minutes gazing at the artworks selected to evoke a conversation about community.
    - Each person shares a story of community or belonging, beginning with the moderator who sets the tone for the type of vulnerable and deep storytelling that is necessary to open people up to one another.
    - Participants are asked to listen to each story without questions.
- *Shared Guidelines*: Before moving to the dinner table, we agree on a few ground rules:
    - Listen with the amount of compassion with which you wish to be heard.
    - Listen without thinking about how you will respond.

- Be mindful of your air time. Create space for people who might speak slowly or briefly, which may create long pauses that feel awkward. Let's be okay with the awkwardness.
- Most importantly: Assume best intentions. If something rubs you the wrong one, ask one more question, maybe two.

*The group is empowered to enforce the guidelines and to speak to one another and not only to the moderator. There won't always be a moderator in every difficult conversations so this is an opportunity for each participant to practice being an active participant in a difficult conversation.*

- *Dinner Dialogue*: After serving dinner family style, the conversation begins with questions that focus on American identity: What does it mean to be American? What is the American Dream? Without prodding, the conversation naturally turns toward a myriad of political issues, often race and immigration. Reminders to share only personal experiences are often necessary. By the end of the short meal, participants have usually opened up to one another and want to continue. They sometimes exchange contact information, some groups immediately creating text message threads, while others documented their experience through selfies. These are all tangible evidence of new bonds formed across traditional social and political boundaries.

  *Between November 2024 and February 2025, second-round dinners were offered exclusively to previous participants, allowing them to deepen connections and practice dialogue skills. These conversations focused on taking action beyond the museum walls.*

- *Informal Use*: The space remained active between formal programs, with visitors using it for studying, meetings, and casual gatherings. This ongoing informal use helped normalize interactions between people who might not normally meet in what became a truly public space.
- *Implementation Challenge:* Our greatest challenge was ensuring political diversity, particularly engaging right-leaning participants. We dedicated a part-time staff member to building trust and relationships

with conservative communities through direct outreach to churches and community organizations.

## Integration with Policy Education

Parallel to the exhibition, Ford School students learned to design their own dialogue-based interventions through hands-on engagement with the social sculpture. Through a series of readings and class discussions, students gained a foundational understanding of socially engaged art. Working in teams, they identified specific policy concerns and created socially engaged artworks for conversations that addressed issues like food access, housing, and social isolation.

Course Description:

> This course is designed for politically diverse and civic-minded students who are concerned about the deepening divide and fraying social fabric in the United States and who wish to take action by creating courageous and relational spaces in which people who disagree with one another can enter into meaningful, respectful, honest, and relational dialogue. The course will include exposure to artworks, reflective writing, multi-disciplinary readings from social psychology and public policy, and relational conversations. We will explore the ways in which art can be used as a tool and a framework for understanding ourselves, our society and where we belong in it, and how we engage in civic life. The class will emphasize active participation, critical thinking, and learning through direct experience and thoughtful dialogue, rather than through traditional lecture-based teaching methods. We will learn by doing, by curious inquiry, and by experimenting with ideas and actions. Students will learn how to develop a program that invites relational conversations and the course will culminate with the implementation of that program.

## Outcomes

The success of "Hey, We Need to Talk!" emerged through individual transformations and ripple effects rather than traditional metrics. After shared meals and honest conversations, participants often formed ongoing connections, documented through text message groups and shared photographs. Many reported that these conversations eased their fear of engaging with people outside their political bubble. Even when groups struggled to find common ground, they demonstrated the capacity to maintain dialogue. A majority of participants indicated a positive shift in how they viewed folks from the "other side."

Jean's story exemplifies the project's potential for catalyzing small but significant changes. After expressing fear of her neighbor because of his Trump flags at one dinner, Jean was moved by Trump supporters in the group who expressed empathy for her perspective. One person with whom Jean had made a connection said, "I voted for Trump. Are you afraid of me?" This encouraged her to initiate contact with her neighbor, suggesting they exchange phone numbers for emergencies. Jean was surprised that he agreed readily and was friendly. She reported that not long after that exchange, she saw him joining an outdoor community music event that he'd never attended before in their liberal community. She invited him to sit next to her. They didn't speak much beyond commenting on the quality of the music. She reports that she no longer fears this neighbor and continues having small neighborly interactions with him that do not involve politics. Their subsequent interactions, while brief, transformed their relationship from one of fear to neighborly cooperation. Like ripples in water, this shift affects not just their relationship but potentially their broader community's social fabric.

## Hope For the Future

The success of *Hey, We Need to Talk!* suggests that solutions to our current political division might be found not entirely in traditional political discourse, but in shared creative experiences that remind us of our common humanity. By breaking down the conventional barriers between museum space and social space, we created something more than an art installation—we created a laboratory for civic engagement and social healing. Key insights include:

- The power of beauty and awe in creating openness to dialogue.
- The importance of careful attention to both physical and social design.
- The value of structured yet natural conversation formats.
- The need for sustained engagement over time.

The project provides a framework that other institutions can adapt to their own contexts. Rather than prescribing a rigid formula, it demonstrates principles for creating spaces where meaningful cross-political dialogue can occur.

Looking ahead, several opportunities emerge for expanding this work:

- Academic Integration: Develop required courses in civic dialogue across university departments. Create interdisciplinary programs combining art, policy, and social practice.
- Institutional Implementation: Establish permanent social sculptures with long-term programming. Build networks of cultural institutions hosting dialogue programs. Support small cohorts dedicated to relationship building.
- Research and Development: Study long-term impacts on participants and communities. Refine methods for facilitating cross-political dialogue. Develop training programs for cultural institutions.

This experiment raises important questions for cultural institutions: How might we reimagine our spaces to better serve democracy? What role can art play in bridging seemingly insurmountable divides? How can we create more opportunities for authentic human connection?

The answers to these questions may help shape the future of both museums and civic life. In our increasingly divided society, we need spaces that serve not just as repositories of culture, but as active participants in rebuilding civic bonds. While a single dinner conversation or art exhibition won't solve systemic polarization, these accumulated moments of genuine human connection demonstrate how art can help repair our torn social fabric, one conversation at a time.

Please contact me at hello@WeShouldTalk.today if you wish to design a social sculpture or academic course, or both, in your institution!

## Notes

**1** "Touching Hearts and Minds and Strengthening Communities," James Irvine Foundation, https:// www.irvine.org/wp-content/uploads/Nick_Rabkin_Civic _Engagement_Report_April_2017.pdf. Accessed December 25, 2024.

**2** Jenna Bednar, "Governance for Human Social Flourishing," *Daedalus* 152, no. 1(2023): 31–45.

**3** Dacher Keltner, *Awe: The New Science of Everyday Wonder and How It Can Transform Your Life* (Penguin Press, 2023).

**4** Grant Kester, "Conversation Pieces: The Role of Dialogue in Socially-Engaged Art," in *Theory in Contemporary Art Since 1985*, ed. Zoya Kucor and Simon Leung (Blackwell, 2005).

**5** R. D. Putnam, *Bowling Alone: The Collapse and Revival of American Community* (Simon & Schuster, 2000).

**6** Joshua Gowin, "Why Sharing Stories Brings People Together." *Psychology Today*, June 6, 2011.

# 17 **Museum Sage**

## Personalizing the Museum, One Artwork at a Time

*Laurie Phillips*

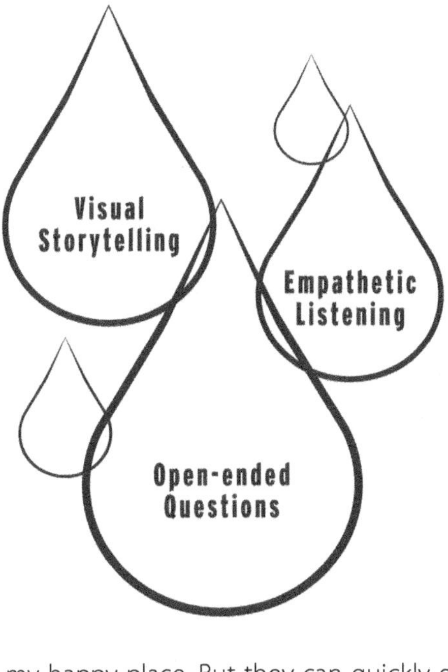


Art museums are my happy place. But they can quickly overwhelm me—I shut down after half an hour and my eyes glaze over. I've tried rushing through exhibitions, spending only a few seconds on each piece, only to leave feeling drained.

This challenge inspired the creation of a meditative, energizing, and deeply personal experience of museum art called Museum Sage®. It cultivates a profound sense of empathy and connection with others.

In Museum Sage, artworks become Tarot-like oracles by offering insights into personal questions. A questioner, called a Sage, approaches an artwork with a question about their life; anything from what color they should paint their bedroom to finding a sense of their life's purpose. A helper, called the Guide, aids the Sage in teasing out how the work's subject, style, colors, mood, material, and any other elements might suggest answers to the question. Anyone else who may be accompanying the Sage on the museum visit also has a chance to help interpret the art's "response" to the question.

In the twenty-plus years since Museum Sage was invented, I've seen hundreds of people learn about themselves and even change their lives with its help. I've also seen the experience bond people and build relationships. Guides and Sages learn about each other through the process of asking personal questions and finding answers together. They share their aspirations in a safe, structured environment, fostering empathy between colleagues, friends, or even strangers. And when it's practiced by families, the results can be especially powerful and moving.

## The Journey of Museum Sage®

One Sunday in 2000, my husband Jon and I visited the Walker Art Center in Minneapolis. Halfway through, I caught myself rushing from artwork to label, speeding through the exhibit. Suddenly, my inner artist urged, "Stop! Slow down and engage with the art." But I couldn't do it. I mentioned my dilemma to Jon, who immediately suggested making up a game that could help me.

Jon had been reading André Breton's Surrealist classic *L'Amour Fou* (*Mad Love*) and recalled a chapter in which Breton and sculptor Alberto Giacometti sought out unintentionally surreal objects at the Paris flea market. Breton believed that chance finds of strange things could unlock poetic inspiration. Jon thought the exhibition we were visiting could do something similar for me—free my mind from compulsive "art shopping" and help me connect with each piece on a deeper level.

Jon asked me to close my eyes and let him guide me through the museum, trusting my body to know when I should stop. (For safety reasons, we later switched to eyes open and looking at the floor.) When I felt ready, we paused, and Jon encouraged me to open my eyes and ask the nearest artwork a question. I had one in mind: When could I leave my unfulfilling graphic design job?

In front of me was an abstract marble sculpture. Jon encouraged me to describe it in detail. I focused on the contrast between the hardness of the marble and the softness of its gently rounded contours. The shapes seemed to suggest I could soften my "hard edges" by being more forgiving and generous with my coworkers. Jon noted its ball-like form and suggested I adopt a more playful attitude toward my job. I took the "advice" of the sculpture by committing to take a small, spontaneous, and generous action in the coming days. Museum Sage was born. Its basic elements are:

1. A personal question.
2. A work of art chosen through chance/random means.
3. A verbal description of the art by the questioner ("Sage").
4. Asking the art for its "advice" on the question.
5. Others commenting on what insights they see the art offering the Sage.
6. A commitment to a small, positive action step by the Sage.

My action step was to have lunch with a co-worker who was going through a divorce. I listened with a soft heart as she talked about her sadness and confusion. Having been through a divorce myself I was able to share that everything she felt was normal, and that it would pass with time. We both seemed lighter by the end of our lunch together, and I had a new friend.

I was soon feeling better about my work life. The success I'd had with the process Jon created of combining physical experience with the power of metaphor led me to wonder if it could work in the wider world. I was training as a life coach at that time, and I decided to try this new art inquiry with my practice clients. I guided someone who ended up in front of a powerful piece of African art. We stood there for two hours as her life story unfolded. The four other practice clients I guided had the same kind of deep, resonant experience.

Months later, I was at a life-coaching convention in Chicago where I'd shared stories about Museum Sage. Several coaches asked me to train them so they could use it with their clients. When we met up at the Art Institute of Chicago, I was the Sage for my new trainee, Louise, to practice on. Despite my improved attitude toward my job, I was still feeling the urge to leave. Again I asked the question, "When will I get to leave my job?"

I ended up in front of a large painting that was entirely blue. The company I worked at was associated with the color blue. I felt angry.

After going through the process of describing the work, talking about my associations with the color blue, and sharing my question with her, Louise invited me to listen to what the painting had to say. I heard: "You don't get to leave your very blue job yet because you haven't learned what you're meant to learn. If you change jobs now, it will only be worse at the next job."

As I was muttering my resentment, my Guide said, sweetly, "What if your current job was your dream job, Laurie? What conditions would have to be met?" I replied that her question made me want to throw up, but I eventually managed to say: "In order for this to be my dream job, all of me would get to come to work—not just my graphic designer self, but my healer self and my public artist self." Louise inquired about what that would look like. After considering this for a minute, I answered, "I can invite all parts of myself to show up each morning, ready to serve those around me." I felt skeptical about whether it would make a difference, but I committed to trying it.

Several months later, I was invited to redesign a stairwell in my company's main building so that employees could enhance their health and fitness by taking the stairs. I led a team that adorned our stairwell with poetry and murals, and the stairwell became such a popular place that employees in the other half of the building developed "stairwell envy," and lobbied to have theirs improved. We created one more beautiful stairwell.

I eventually joined the employee wellness committee, inviting life coach and psychologist friends to give talks on depression and self-care. After hearing about my private visioning workshops, an HR leadership coach asked me to lead a module for her classes. Even after I left the company—free from the resentment that once kept me stuck—she hired me to continue leading those modules.

## Evolution: From a Game to a Resource

The life-changing impact of my experience with the blue painting inspired me to share the process beyond the life-coaching community. In 2014, after reading about museums seeking interactive programs to engage younger audiences, I contacted staff at the Minneapolis Institute of Art (Mia). After receiving an experiential demonstration of Museum Sage, they offered me a chance to work with their visitors.

For Mia's upcoming exhibition on the diverse ways people experience and define what is sacred, the museum hosted events exploring personal interpretations of the sacred. I led an event involving seventeen trained Museum Sage Guides, each working with groups of four Sages. Among the powerful stories that emerged from that day were two high school students inspired by their Museum Sage experience to pursue college, with action steps of applying to at least one school.

A meeting with Elizabeth Merritt of the Center for the Future of Museums at the American Alliance of Museums (AAM) led to a workshop at the Phillips Collection and inclusion in AAM's *Trendswatch*.[1] Between 2015 and 2017, Museum Sage worked with institutions like the Peabody Essex Museum, the de Young Museum, and the Royal British Columbia Museum, while also gaining traction at major museum conferences at the High Museum and the St. Louis Art Museum.

In 2023, I developed a free app to address both the enthusiasm and the uncertainty among leaders about how to incorporate the practice into their museums. The app is called: *Museum Sage®* and is available at Apple and Android stores. It empowers users to experience Museum Sage independently, without requiring a trained guide. The instructions in the app are reproduced here:

> *START:* Play in groups of two to four people. Choose who will be the Guide and who will be the first player (the Sage). If you're the Guide, read this script. Other people in the group can follow along with you and the Sage. Everyone will get their turn, including you. Your role as Guide is to be a good listener and to be kind. Keep everything confidential. Follow museum visitor guidelines. Enjoy this unique experience of personal discovery while learning about art one piece at a time!
>
> *CHOOSE A QUESTION: You as the Guide will read everything in quotation marks to the person you're guiding. Start now:* "Choose a question about your life. It can be small, deep, playful, or serious. It can be about relationships, finances, health, spirituality—anything! However, it

should be meaningful to you. Don't share your question yet. If you can't think of the 'perfect' question, don't worry. Just pick a topic. Keep in mind that the artwork that 'chooses you' may answer another question entirely!" *Give them awhile to think of a question.*

*PICK A GALLERY AND AN OBJECT:* "Where in the museum would you like to start? Let's go there." *After you reach an exhibit area:* "I'll time you for one minute as you walk mindfully through the museum, looking at the floor about five feet ahead of you. When I say time's up, whatever piece you're closest to is 'yours.'" *Go ahead and time them.*

*GET INSIGHT:* "Choose the piece you're closest to and let's stand in front of it . . . Now close your eyes and take three very deep, slow breaths." *You too.*

1. "Open your eyes and look closely at the art for one minute. Then describe it to us in detail: size, shapes, colors, subject matter, what's in the middle, what's at the edges, atmosphere, anything." *Give them lots of time to answer.*
2. "What associations or memories does this piece call up?" *Give them lots of time to answer.*
3. "Can you share your personal question? If you don't want to, that's okay; the process will still work." *Let them respond.*
4. "What insights does this piece offer you about your question?" *Give them lots of time to answer.*
5. "Are you okay if I (and others) comment?" *Say what you notice, taking turns. Be kind and keep things positive. If the object depicts death, you can reframe it as, "What old beliefs may need to die?" Give everyone time to comment.*
6. "What's a small step you could take to act on these insights?"
7. "May I take a photo of you with your art, using your phone? I'll take a photo of the wall label too. Try researching the piece online—you might get more insight into your personal question." *Go ahead with the photos.* "There are journaling questions on museumsage.com if you want to reflect on your experience in a different way." Now trade places and let them guide you, or rotate if there are other people in your group.

## A Free Resource for Museums

I'm happy to offer Museum Sage® to museums free of charge as a flexible and versatile tool for visitor engagement. Museums can let visitors know about the free app, which they can use to guide each other, and/or provide a printed guide to the process (available as an illustrated PDF at MuseumSage.com). Co-branded posters—with the museum's logo alongside the Museum Sage mark—can promote the program.

Museum Sage could enhance special occasions, like Valentine's Day or a crowd-drawing annual museum event. It can be the focus of a corporate workshop that builds team dynamics, creativity, and communication, while fostering partnerships with the museum. Establishing regular weekly or monthly groups is another option. These are fresh ways to attract visitors and build donor relationships—and charging ticket fees, when appropriate, can help build revenue.

During these group sessions, staff or volunteers explain and model the process for the whole group of friends or family, who then do Museum Sage in pairs. Everyone reconvenes later to share their experiences (if they choose to) with the whole group.

This is a whole-brain activity that fosters mental health, intuition, and empathy. It strengthens connections among visitors and their loved ones. It bonds people to artworks, and to the museum where these artworks are on display. Sessions can be aimed to spotlight different parts of a collection, or to underline significant themes like career, relationships, equity, empathy, or DEAI work.

## A Family's Discoveries

When Jon and I first practiced Museum Sage, we focused on the questions, the answers, and the goals that the process brings forth. But over the years, I've been more impressed with the opportunities it offers people to learn about and feel for each other.

I worked with one extended family not long ago: Victoria, her husband Rick; their children, Noah (age 18), Noah's girlfriend Elise, and Truman (age 16); Victoria's sister Jenn, and Jenn's wife, Kelly.

Rick sought clarity on his professional path and sense of vocation. Eugène Delacroix's *View of Tangier from the Seashore* (Figure 17.1), with its challenging path leading to a shining city, resonated with him as a metaphor for overcoming obstacles. He valued the deep, uninterrupted engagement with the art, which fostered surprising personal connections. Victoria, reflecting on Leslie Hewitt's *A Series of Projections*, got tears in her eyes when a family member observed that its negative space formed a cross—a symbol deeply tied to her identity as a progressive pastor. Both emphasized the importance of family members' compassionate insights that enriched and deepened their experiences.

For Noah, the most impactful part of the Museum Sage experience was sharing it with a girlfriend and learning new things about each other. There were mutual discoveries that Kelly, her wife Jenn, and their nephew Truman made with the help of Museum Sage: Truman, a singer seeking clarity on his

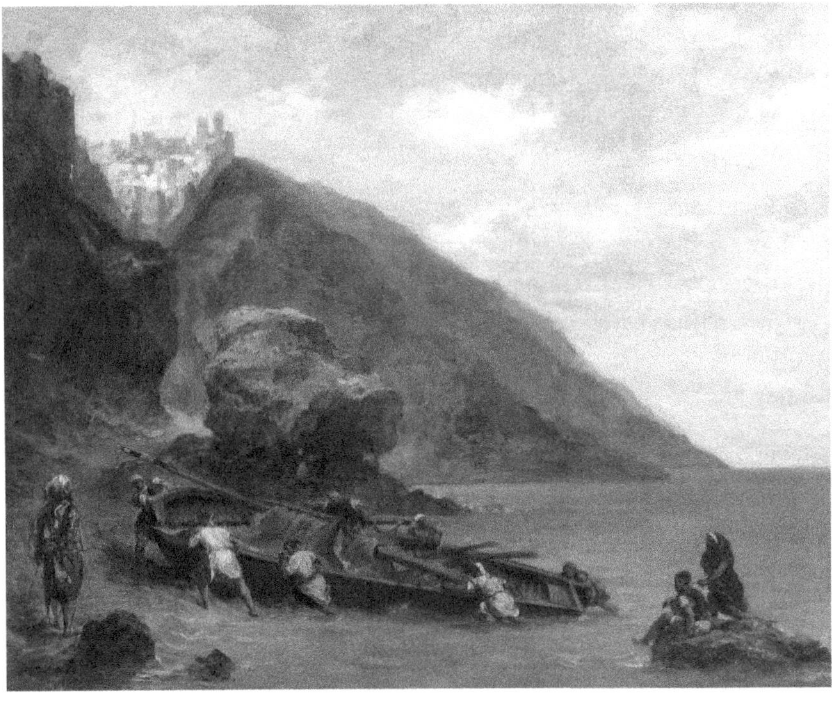

**Figure 17.1** Caption for the image: Eugène Delacroix, *View of Tangier from the Seashore*, 1856–1858, oil on canvas, 40 x 47x 4 in., Minneapolis Institute of Art. Credit: Minneapolis Institute of Art.

musical focus, reflected on a bust of General Guillaume Brune, interpreting its stoic demeanor as a reminder to seize musical opportunities and not remain indecisive.

Kelly, facing a prognosis of cirrhosis, asked if her best days were ahead. She ended up in front of Yoshitomo Nara's playful sculpture *Your Dog*, which symbolized living joyfully and in the moment. Jenn, pondering her relationship to work, was moved by a sculpture of a princess whose hands—one on her heart and one extended—prompted her to approach retirement decisions with balance and heart.

This shared museum experience deepened this family's connections and self-awareness, revealing new layers of vulnerability, reflection, and support among them. Inspired by insights from their artworks and their fellow Sages, each reported taking meaningful actions in the following weeks.

Museum Sage brings people closer to the museum where they discovered "their" artwork. Because the process includes a commitment to an action step, it can initiate major positive changes in people's lives. This can really endear their artwork to the Sage and create love and loyalty for the museum in which that work is located.

Museum Sage doesn't replace serious aesthetic and art-historical appreciation of museum art; in fact, Sages gain deepening insight from the wall didactics. On return visits to "their" work, Sages develop a real appreciation for what a museum does.

The main point is that Museum Sage can make the museum, my happy place, a happier place for many others. Instead of flying through the museum breathlessly as they try to see every piece, they're calm and in sync with each other. They're breathing deeply and are in the present moment. From that place, they can make discoveries that deepen their understanding of, and empathy for, themselves, friends, family, co-workers, and anyone else who is taking the Museum Sage journey with them. They learn about art one piece at a time while having a conversation about what matters most.

## Note

**1** Elizabeth Merritt, *TrendsWatch 2015* (American Alliance of Museums, 2015), 28.

# Part IV
# Practicing and Sharing Empathetic Organizational Policies and Methodologies

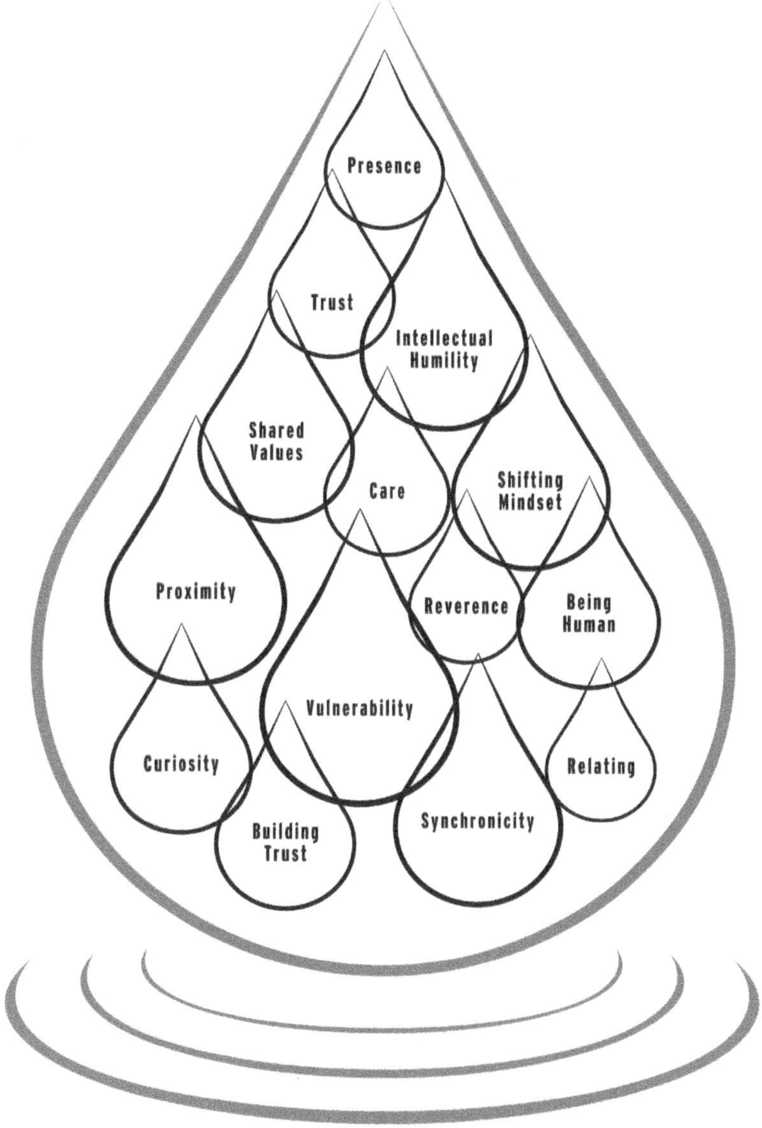

# 18 Radical Curiosity and Courageous Empathy

## Cultivating Compassion in Tumultuous Times

*Susie Wilkening*

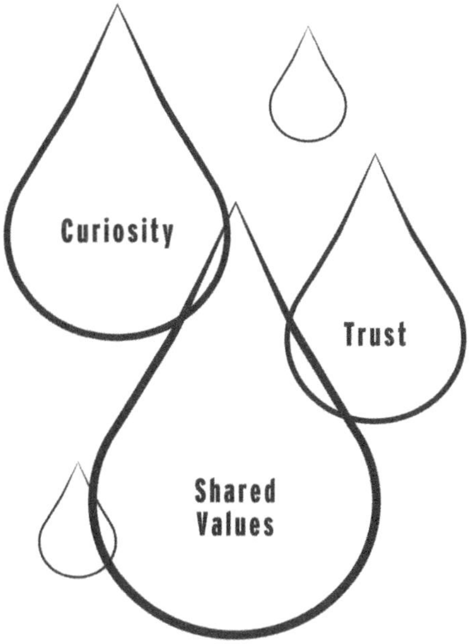


*My family and I took a trip to Washington D.C. when I was around 12 years old. One of the most impactful exhibits I've ever seen was the Human Origins exhibit in the Smithsonian. I remember looking at all of the skulls lined up carefully on the wall and realizing that each and every one was, at some distance, family. I am a product of them, we are related, and here I am standing in front of them, separated by time, evolution, and a plate of glass. In that moment I suddenly gained a deeper understanding of evolution and a deeper respect for the*

*people who came before us. I'd like to pay another visit someday, have another family reunion so to speak.*

*—Respondent, 2024 Annual Survey of Museum-Goers.*

Over 100 billion human beings have lived on this planet over the past 200,000 years. Over 8 billion human beings inhabit earth at this moment. Each one of those people shares many things in common: to inhabit a human body, to feel human emotions, to interact with other human beings. And yet each one has their own idiosyncratic blend of life experiences. While the vast majority of those life experiences are lost to time, a few are passed down to us as historical and cultural legacies. The responsibility of preserving and sharing the tangible legacies of human experiences, whether archaeological, artistic, historic, documentary, or scientific, often falls to museums.

Museum visitors, for the most part, are very much aware of this tangible legacy. Often seen as an inviolate truth, trust in museums is more resilient and durable than for many other institutions.[1] And yet museums are not divorced from the polarization and tension inherent in our society today. This tension pervades audience research, as some audience segments increasingly feel disillusionment and dismay about museum exhibitions and programs. Can we reconcile our purpose as places of shared humanity with the political reality that some audiences regard empathy and human connection as tools of their political enemies?

The complexity of these challenges cannot be solved simply through this chapter. But readers might come away with a better understanding of how disparate worldviews affect perceptions of empathy and connection to humanity so differently, as well as considering how these perspectives create landmines for museums. To do this, we will thoughtfully consider worldviews many readers may disagree with so we can better understand how they developed . . . and so that we can be more effective in our work.

Every year, in partnership with the American Alliance of Museums, Wilkening Consulting fields the Annual Survey of Museum-Goers. Over 200 museums field our survey to their communication lists: those who have agreed to receive emails and/or follow the museum on social media. Typically, around 100,000 frequent museum-goers respond to this survey. In past years, we asked museum-goers to share their thoughts on topics that have empathy and shared humanity at their heart. Some questions are what we call "direct questions," where the question explicitly asks about empathy, while other questions are "indirect questions," where an empathy response is one of many choices but isn't ostensibly the focus of the question. Both types of questions are important as they serve different purposes. Indirect questions help us identify those that likely care deeply about empathy, as they find and select responses related to empathy among a variety of different choices. Similarly, those who reject the idea of empathy or say empathy work doesn't matter in direct questions can be identified as more *resistant* to the idea of empathy in museums. By deploying both types of questions, we can begin to identify a spectrum of attitudes toward empathy content in museums.

Since 2020, we have asked about empathy indirectly, asking respondents, "What are the most important ways that museums should share and engage you with their content e.g., the history, art, science, animals, plants, etc. based on museum type?" This question provides nine different answer choices, and respondents can choose as many answers as they wish. One response says, "helping me gain more empathy or understanding for others." Results over the past several years have been a bit bumpy, ranging from a high of 32 percent choosing this answer in 2022 down to 26 percent in 2024.

When we ask museum-goers about empathy directly, however, we tend to receive a more enthusiastic response. In 2019, 81 percent of respondents said that informal learning in museums had either increased their empathy and compassion or that museums should actively work to increase empathy and compassion. Conversely, 16 percent of respondents said it was either not important for museums to cultivate empathy or that informal learning did not affect people in this way. As a direct question, this suggests that nearly one in five respondents responded negatively to the idea of empathy in museums.

Expressing a connection to humanity is also an indicator of cognitive empathy, as it suggests connection to and care for people we don't know. In 2023, we asked how museums should encourage visitors to consider and/or develop their connection to humanity. While the vast majority of museum-goers, 82 percent, responded positively, once again nearly one in five pushed back saying, "I don't think this is the role of museums." In this question, these respondents rejected answer choices that included: helping visitors consider who they are as individuals (and their place in greater humanity), encouraging visitors to consider and/or contribute to the well-being of others, motivating visitors to make the world a better place, encouraging visitors to participate in community affairs, sharing multiple viewpoints so visitors can consider perspectives other than their own, and cultivating a shared sense of humanity and care for others. For many of us who work in museums, these six possible answer choices embody the purpose of our work, and we may find it shocking or confusing that anyone would resist these ideals. Yet they fit into broader patterns we see among some museum-goers.

Overall, we estimate that, among museum-goers, one out of five are empathy cheerleaders that support empathy work wholeheartedly. Two out of five like the idea of empathy as an outcome of museum experiences, but it isn't a high priority. One out of five are ambivalent, and one out of five are actively *resisting* the notion of museums cultivating empathy. When we examine these results, especially through the lens of self-identified political values (a survey question as well), we know without a doubt that this is clearly tied to the polarization we are experiencing today. Those who resist the cultivation of empathy and connection to humanity in museums are also much more likely to resist other museum content areas that have been politicized, including climate change, belonging and DEAI, civics and our civil society, and the cultivation of hope. They also overwhelmingly cluster at the most conservative end of the political spectrum.

The "resistant" segment that resists these content areas, 20 percent of the overall sample, might seem relatively small. But in many ways, this segment has significant influence. That's because 20 percent seems to be the tipping point when like-minded people find each other more easily, validate one another's perspectives, and develop a shared language of resistance. Within this shared identity-based community, they can then promote their ideas more broadly, capturing even more attention, especially on social media and in the broader media. When they vote, especially in primaries, they also develop significant political leverage. This segment of the public has used that political leverage to roll back inclusive efforts, restrict how history is taught in the classroom, ban books, and more . . . even when most people disagree with them.

What will help? How might we face this seemingly formidable challenge? We know that finger pointing and demonizing those who resist the content we want to share is counterproductive, opening up the possibility that "resistant" individuals will dig in their heels (at best) or work publicly to threaten a museum and its staff (at worst). If we want to be effective, we have to understand the values and attitudes of individuals who are resisting these content areas and outcomes. Why do they resist empathetic experiences-- especially the experiences of people who look, think, or live differently than them? Doing this work to understand the *why* behind the resistance requires us to practice *Radical Curiosity and Courageous Empathy*.

"Resistant" people, that is, those who actively resist so many of the content areas and outcomes museums often explore, tend to view the world rather differently than those who embrace empathetic and more "open" experiences. A distinguishing difference is how "resistant" people might perceive allocation of resources in day-to-day life. Often, this means the distribution of financial resources such as jobs, or who is allowed or able to attend competitive colleges and universities (potentially determining future financial outcomes). But it can also mean resources of time, attention, and identity. "Resistant" people tend to view the world as one of scarce resources, and the allocation of those resources as a zero-sum game. Thus, *everything* is a trade-off. This is how climate change and inclusion can both be labeled as "Marxist" by resistant individuals: addressing climate change will require personal sacrifice, and inclusive content shifts resources of attention and identity from content areas "resistant" people want to privilege.

If everything is a trade-off, then at whose expense are resources, including financial, educational, attention, power, and identity, reallocated? More "resistant" people fear it will be at their expense. Which brings us to the heart of the issue: fear. The fears expressed by "resistant" people are strong, palpable, and defensive. They tend to fall into six categories, including: fears for the future, America, themselves, truth, society, and their values (including intergenerational transmission of values to children). These fears often prompt highly emotional responses in "resistant" people when they are presented in conjunction with content that they feel conflicts with their values or feels threatening.

When we consider the areas that get the most resistance in museums (e.g., climate change, belonging and DEAI, civics and civil society, cultivation of connection to humanity, cultivation of hope) through this lens of fear, how they developed resistance to these topics becomes more understandable. The fear-based responses of "resistant" people can range from skepticism to intense anger, as they feel this content is dangerous and does harm. The dangers they perceive then trigger defense mechanisms and tactics to shut down that content completely. Those attempts can also be highly publicized and politically motivated.

There are three main types of defense mechanisms we see:

- Coded language. This includes statements like "just give me the facts, and I'll make up my own mind," and adjectives like "important," "significant," or "real." These words and phrases are often used to privilege a white, heteronormative narrative that chooses what is important and excludes those with different life experiences.
- False choices. These include articulating perceived trade-offs (indicating that certain types of content come at the expense of preferred content) or the presentation of a both sides fallacy/fake debate. (This tends to elevate a contrary, typically pseudoscience/pseudohistory opinion as equal to scientific or historical evidence. Examples include creationism and Holocaust denial.)
- Diversionary tactics. These are logical fallacies, quote mining, or slothful induction to draw conclusions that are untrue, or simply stating that these content areas are "not the job" of museums.

Because "resistant" people resist these content areas and outcomes, this also means there is fundamental and significant underlying trust issue. Do they trust the content being shared? Do they trust the purpose of the museum? Do they trust the people working in the museum? And do they trust that their interests and well-being are valued? For many "resistant" people, the answer is simple: No.

What makes this especially challenging is museum practitioners are much more likely to be characterized as having an "open" viewpoint. "Open" viewpoints are typically rooted in ideas around shared humanity and curiosity, especially inclusive content or content that broadens perspectives about other humans. This viewpoint tends to be intrinsically empathetic, but especially empathetic for those who represent varying life experiences. That means that more "open" people also tend to find the trade-off mentality and more "resistant" viewpoints perplexing, confounding, and/or harmful. Additionally, because people who work in museums are human beings, this more "open" bias often comes through in the content being shared in museums, heightening the emotional response of more "resistant" people, as well as raising their defense mechanisms.

> *[Museum] experiences have challenged me to honor the complexity of experience, to acknowledge that context/perspective dramatically shapes*

*understanding, and that we are all more similar than different. I would love to see museums facilitate dialogue and experiences that foster empathy and related-ness with the 'other.' Social media echo chambers and political tribalism desperately needs a counterpoint, where seeking to understand the other is prioritized and celebrated.*

*—Respondent, 2024 Annual Survey of Museum-Goers*

People need the most compassion and understanding when experiencing moments of fear, and vulnerability. We are also more likely to feel vulnerable when we disagree. Only by understanding how fear drives more resistant values and worldviews can we consider how to calibrate our work so we can help more people broaden perspectives, learn about others, grow as human beings, and most crucially, overcome the fears that prevent those outcomes.

Building trust and credibility in these times is tricky, especially when motivations are suspect and facts don't change minds. Cultivating curiosity, however, can crack open worldviews by creating information gaps and developing new questions that museum-goers haven't considered and want to answer (thus avoiding a knee-jerk fear response). For newly discovered answers to those questions to be credible and trusted, however, they still must be grounded in supporting evidence. Tactically, there are things we can do to broaden empathy, especially since we can identify fears and defense mechanisms. Three of the most effective are to:

1. Consider how we can cultivate curiosity to build trust and credibility.
2. Build on shared values that we have in common as a foundation for content.
3. Be respectful of those we disagree with, showing them and modeling Radical Curiosity and Courageous Empathy.

These tactics allow us to build relationships based on shared values and mutual respect, from which we can then credibly share new ideas, perspectives, and evidence.

What are those shared values? As an area of ongoing work, we have found a few things that people do agree on, including:

- Museums are places of imagination. When we ask museumgoers how imagination can support learning and museums, only 1 percent resist that idea. One percent! Additionally, around three-quarters of museumgoers agreed that the following outcomes of imaginative learning are important: that museums should develop greater understanding of the experiences of people from the past through historical imagination, that museums should broaden our minds to imagine life experiences different than our own, that museums should recharge us mentally as we experience awe, wonder, or beauty, and that museums should inspire curiosity to wonder and learn on our own.

- Hope. While "resistant" people are highly skeptical of museums deliberately cultivating hope, nearly everyone does find hope in *something* (indeed, only 1 percent said they did not find hope in anything). What are the things that most people find that give them hope? Turns out, they are things that museums do really well, such as: sharing art and seeing beauty in the things humans have created, exploring nature and seeing beauty or wonder in plants, animals, and environments, and examining history and understanding how people in the past faced challenges and overcame them. But there is also something that's more human-to-human that gives hope: seeing people helping others.
- Being a good member of society. When we ask museum-goers what people should do to be a good member of society, only 1 percent gave a negative response. Five of our answer choices garnered agreement from three-quarters of respondents: that in our communities, people should be inclusive of others, conserving natural resources and making choices to reduce the effects of climate change, participating in community activities such as volunteering, attending community events or meetings, seeking out, listening and respecting the viewpoints of others, even when we disagree, and that we should learn more about our shared history, including the histories of those whose stories have been omitted in the past.

To be fair, while there is virtually universal agreement about these three broad categories of imagination, hope, and societal responsibility, we need to remain mindful that there is less consensus about *how* museums could go about that work, or even if museums *should*. After all, about a quarter of respondents did not select the specific tactics we provided as answer choices, and within that group are those who actively resist these ideas in museum settings specifically.

While "resistant" pushback is coming from a relatively small percentage of the public, that pushback is sometimes public, loud, and politically fraught. How should we deal with it? And how do we do this respectfully when, at times, the things being said are not always respectful (and can be offensive and harmful). Fortunately, tools and tactics have been developed to help with this work, including (Figure 18.1):

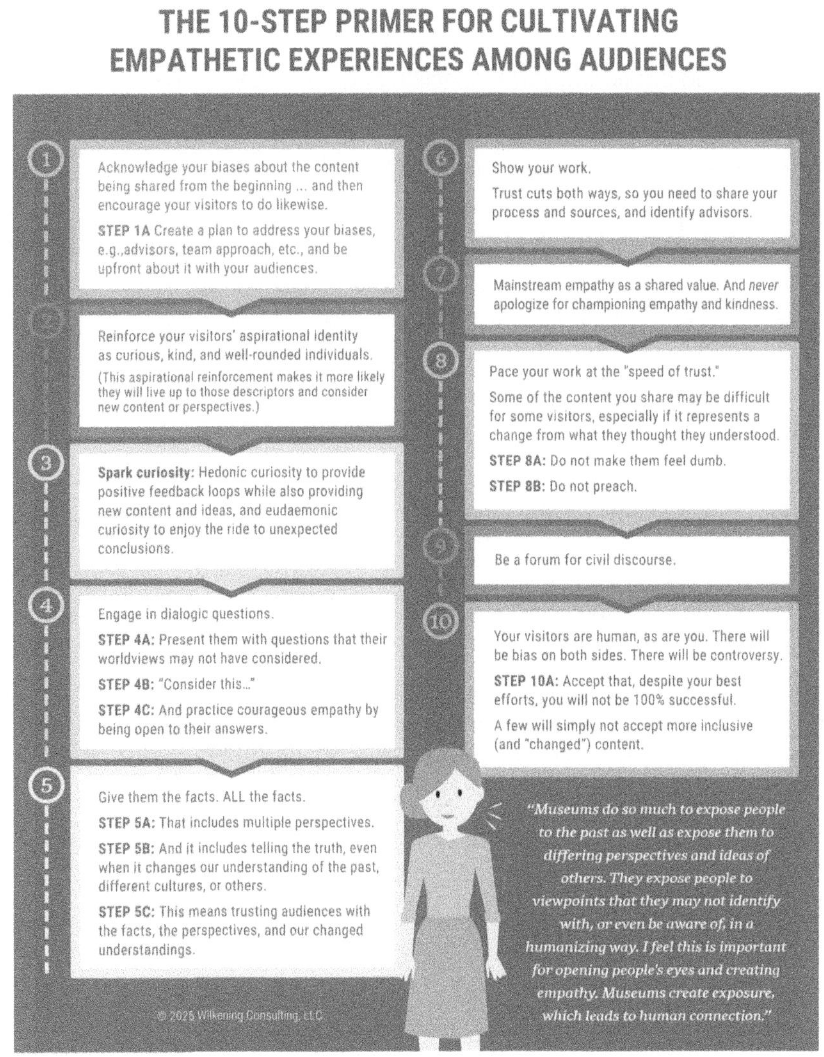


**Figure 18.1** The 10-step primer for cultivating empathetic experiences among audiences. Credit: Courtesy, Wilkening Consulting.

1. *Audiences and Inclusion. A Primer for Cultivating More Inclusive Attitudes Among the Public.* This publication (released by the American Alliance of Museums) specifically explores the role of curiosity in opening worldviews and gives a step-by-step guide for putting this work into practice.[2]
2. Developing and publicizing shared value statements, building off the values that many of us do share.
3. Practicing "disinformation inoculation" with staff, trustees, docents, donors, and the public. This process shows how evidence of broad public support for challenging topics can diminish (at least somewhat) negative responses from the public.[3]

No one expects this work to be easy. Indeed, this work is incredibly hard and can be emotionally draining for museum staff. Remembering and being mindful that the majority of people support empathy work is critical as we move forward into even more tumultuous times. Because the nature of these tumultuous times makes this work more important than ever.

## Notes


1 "Museums and Trusts 2021," American Alliance of Museums, 2021, https://www.aam-us.org/wp-content/uploads/2021/09/Museums-and-Trust-2021.pdf.

2 American Alliance of Museums, "Audiences and Inclusion: A Primer for Cultivating More Inclusive Attitudes among the Public," Wilkening Consulting, 2025, https://wilkeningconsulting.com/audiences-and-inclusion-a-primer-for-cultivating-more-inclusive-attitudes-among-the-public/.

3 American Alliance of Museums, "Beware! The False Consensus Effect," Wilkening Consulting, July 18, 2023, https://wilkeningconsulting.com/beware-the-false-consensus-effect/.

# 19 Building an Organizational Culture of Care

*Micah Parzen*

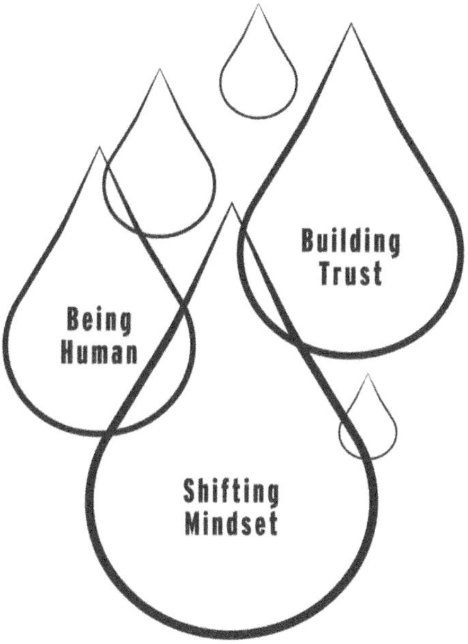


*Culture eats strategy for breakfast.*

—*Peter Drucker*

There is a clear correlation between the health of a museum's organizational culture and its overall success. Although we hold this truth to be self-evident, all too often, even the most well-intentioned among us neglect to put our people front and center in our decision-making processes. External pressures—whether from visitors, donors, trustees, or other constituents, can lead organizational culture-makers to prioritize the short-term bottom line over long-term well-being. After all, when "the buck stops with you," a leader's first instinct is frequently to cut human corners in the name of balancing the budget today, no matter the consequences down the road.

Unfortunately, this way of thinking typically results in management finding itself pitted against its own team members. This leads to decreased engagement, productivity, and retention. Addressing the consequences of this "death by a thousand cuts" requires significant, but often unnoticed, organizational bandwidth. That bandwidth could be devoted to many other projects needing attention in a museum.

This "us vs. them" mentality can even lead to the very legal claims that all museums seek to avoid. Most employment policies—typically drafted by attorneys with an eye toward worst-case scenarios—are not designed to cultivate healthy workplace cultures. Instead, they primarily seek to protect the employer in the event of litigation. This "CYA" approach often further strips team members—a museum's most valuable asset—of their agency, their individuality, and, ultimately, their sense of being part of something larger than themselves.

Evidence of the above abounds in our industry today. Museum workers are leaving (or intend to leave) the field in droves.[1] The Instagram account "Changethemuseum," whose self-proclaimed goal is to "pressur[e] US museums to move beyond lip service proclamations by amplifying tales of unchecked racism[,]" has more than 900 posts, mostly about workplace issues, with over 53,000 followers.[2]

Similarly, in an effort to communicate that enough is enough, "Museum Workers Speak," an organization that advocates for pay equity in the museum field, states: "It has become clear to us that when our institutions will not stand in solidarity with us, we must stand in solidarity with one another."[3] Toward that end, close to 13 percent of museums (i.e., well over 4,000) have already unionized, with many more undoubtedly on the way.[4] Indeed, organizational culture issues have become one of the most pressing challenges facing the museum field today.[5]

Thankfully, there is also good news. Many museums are already rethinking the role culture plays in creating healthier organizations, with necessity—as usual—serving as the mother of invention. While the Covid-19 pandemic forced many museums to find new ways of supporting their remaining team members during a time of unique challenge, the murder of George Floyd (upon so many others) helped expose the lived experience of Black, Indigenous, and other People of Color (BIPOC) museum professionals as utterly inconsistent with the inclusive values that so many of our institutions espouse. All this has pushed the field to do better, and many museums are committed to doing so.

Many forward-thinking organizational culture-makers in museums are taking an empathy-based approach focused on transforming their institutions from the inside out. They are asking: How might we better support our team members? What are their pain points? What steps can we take to productively address what we learn? What does it look like when we include team members in our data gathering, solution development, and decision-making processes? And, most important of all, how can we follow up with concrete actions that truly put our people first? Human-centered experiments that take these questions to heart can already be found in museums of all types and sizes throughout the field.

## Cultivating a Culture of Care

This is certainly true at the Museum of Us (formerly the San Diego Museum of Man), located on the unceded ancestral homelands of the Kumeyaay Nation in San Diego's Balboa Park, where I serve as CEO. Over ten years ago, we made the intentional decision to build a new kind of museum: one that is committed to doing anti-racist, decolonial, and otherwise human-centered work. Based on the realization that authentically serving the public meant we had to tend to our own team first, our goal has been to transform our museum from the inside out. We started by cultivating a culture of care. This included changes to existing policies and practices no longer consistent with our values as well as the creation of new policies and practices that were.

Some concrete examples may be helpful:

### *Investing in Forward-Facing Staff*

When the Museum of Us was allowed to reopen during Covid pursuant to public health guidelines, instead of returning to our pre-Covid staffing model, we decided to reimagine our forward-facing roles altogether. Specifically, we changed our Visitor Experience Associate position from part-time to full-time so that every team member would receive our generous benefits package, including a new retirement match of up to 6 percent. We raised the position's wage from $13.75 an hour to $20 an hour. We also committed to annual cost-of-living increases of 5 percent per year for our lowest-paid team members for a period of three years. In 2024, three years later, our entry-level wage is over $23 per hour.

We redesigned the Visitor Experience Associate role so that it is now a long-term career position. In addition to the pay increases identified above, we committed to a renewed focus on opportunities for professional development and growth within our organization. Finally, we adopted a compensation cap of 6:1 relative to what the highest-paid employee (currently, me) earns relative to what the lowest-paid employee (namely, our forward-facing staff) earns. This helps make our entire compensation structure far more equitable going forward and has enabled us to stay ahead of our pay equity goals, rather than losing ground each year.

## *Rethinking the Eurocentrism of Our Holiday Schedule*

The Museum of Us has long offered team members fourteen paid holidays every calendar year. Historically, these holidays were designated as mandated days off for employees who do not directly serve the public in a forward-facing manner. Thanks to the honest input of several of our BIPOC staff, however, we came to understand how many of those holidays are deeply rooted in a colonial paradigm: New Year's Day, Presidents' Day, Independence Day, Thanksgiving, Christmas, and so on. In response, we worked with the team to revise our holiday policy to allow team members to substitute (and even group together) holidays that are meaningful to them. Employees can still choose to take any or all museum-designated holidays off, if they wish, but the power to decide is now theirs. We call this policy "Holidays for All."

## *Offering Community-Centered Leave*

Like most employers, the Museum of Us offers various types of paid leave, including vacation and sick time. But when our Indigenous team members shared that they needed time off to participate in multi-day ceremonies in their home communities, they pointed out the obvious: Their absence from the office was neither "vacation" nor "sick" time. To the contrary, it was hard work, centered around cultivating community well-being. It was for the good of many, and for future generations, not for their personal enjoyment or convalescence.

We soon realized the ripple effect of good that could come from enabling all of our employees to take paid time off to build and support community. We considered classifying such leave as "professional development," but quickly saw the ways this would run afoul of applicable employment laws. So, we settled on a new paid leave category altogether. We call it "Community-Centered Leave," and it is specifically designed to encourage employees to support their communities in ways that are meaningful to them. Every team member at the Museum of Us may now take up to three days of paid Community-Centered Leave per year.

## *Experimenting with Interview Pay*

We recently set out to hire a new Director of Decolonizing Initiatives at the Museum of Us. Pleased to have received well over fifty applications, we held two rounds of interviews before limiting the pool to four semi-finalists. Three of these individuals were Indigenous, with the fourth having significant professional experience working with Indigenous communities. As the next step in our vetting process, we invited each semi-finalist to a one-hour interview with two separate review panels. Prior to the first panel, we sent each candidate our Decolonizing Initiatives Strategic Action Plan and asked them to review it in preparation for the interviews. Because we knew that each candidate's input would enhance our ability to advance our decolonial work, regardless of a job offer, we decided that, as with any Indigenous consultant, we would compensate them $200 apiece for their time and expertise. Each of the four candidates commented that our interview pay policy significantly reinforced their desire to accept the job if offered.

## *Reimbursing Trustees for Board-Related Participation*

Our efforts to cultivate a culture of care also extend to our trustees at the Museum of Us. Specifically, we have an extraordinarily diverse board, which includes Indigenous trustees, trustees who do not live in Southern California, and trustees with wide-ranging economic means. It is within this context that we recognize:

1) The history of harm done to Indigenous communities by the Museum,

2) The fact that some of our non-local trustees have to travel long distances to participate in board-related activities,

3) The reality that some of our trustees may need financial assistance to participate in board-related activities.

As a result, we developed a Trustee Reimbursement Policy that allows any trustee to request reimbursement for up to $2,000 on a per fiscal year basis so that they may participate in a wide variety of collective learning opportunities that are part and parcel of their board service. The specific reason for reimbursement need not be indicated in the reimbursement request, which is held in confidence by the Chair of the Board of Trustees, CEO, Executive Director, and team members of the finance department (on a need-to-know basis only). This policy not only serves us well in our trustee recruitment efforts, but also lets every trustee know that they are valued for much more than just their checkbooks.

## A Virtuous Cycle of Good

These (and other) changes at the Museum of Us have led to a virtuous cycle of good over the past several years. While this may sound like a bold claim, when an organization's culture becomes more caring, team members feel more seen, heard, valued, and appreciated, such that an almost magical spigot opens up and a wide variety of benefits begin to flow. When team members' insights directly inform organizational decision-making processes, organizations make better decisions, leading to better institutional outcomes. Team member engagement, productivity, and retention all increase, leading to projects with far fewer stops and starts. Teams begin to coalesce in powerful ways, firing on all pistons on a far more regular basis.

Sure enough, as teams grow stronger, the visitor experience improves, too. Indeed, just as happy nurses in hospitals make for loyal patients, happy forward-facing team members in museums make for loyal visitors.[6] Why? Because, just as nurses tend to, care for, and spend the most time with patients in hospitals, forward-facing staff greet, welcome, observe, engage, and bid farewell to droves of guests all day, every day in museums. So, if a museum wants happy visitors who join as members, leave wonderful social media reviews, and grow into generous donors, it would be well served by centering the needs of its forward-facing team. This approach pays off in the long run.

## Getting Started

The idea of transforming a museum's organizational culture into one of care can be a daunting—even overwhelming—prospect. While it won't happen overnight, of course, incremental changes build on one another to make a big difference in the long run. After all, how do you eat an elephant? One bite at a time. Here are some "how to" steps that a museum can take to begin that process.

### *Shifting Mindset*

Creating a culture of care starts with a commitment to a new way of thinking. Instead of presuming the false dichotomy between the interests of team members and those of the museum, start with the recognition that what is good for team members *is* good for the museum. They are one and the same. Rather than taking a "what have you done for me lately" approach, museums with healthy organizational cultures focus on playing the long game. While the benefits of a culture of care can be hard to see in the short term, they become crystal clear when we expand our horizons. Viewed in this way, investments in team members' well-being are not only the right thing to do, but they also make good business sense.

While it is absolutely critical that a museum's leadership team commits to this mindset shift, your organization's board of trustees must fully embrace it, too. You need a board of trustees that will be there for you when the going gets tough—because it will get tough. The path to transformational change is messy and periodically getting stuck in the mud of it all is a given. The journey is also often non-linear, taking unexpected twists, turns, and time. Your organization's trustees need to understand that these bumps in the road are, in fact, signs that positive change is afoot, provided you stay the course. Eventually, your annual budget becomes a moral document, which says a lot more about your organizational priorities that any values statement ever could. If you can get your board to play the long game with you in this way, you will be able to move mountains together.

## Building Trust

Creating a safe space for team members to share their perspectives in honest and respectful ways is the key to any culture of care. Unfortunately, most employees don't tell leaders the truth, even when explicitly asked to do so. Instead, they tell their employers what they think their leaders want to hear. Why? They aren't accustomed to having their perspectives valued in any meaningful way. To the contrary, they fear being labeled as "difficult" or, even worse, retaliated against if they speak their mind. As a result, leaders end up believing their organizational cultures are far healthier than, in fact, they are.

When leaders solicit direct input, deeply listen, and incorporate what they learn into the solution development and decision-making process, however, they can act, even in small ways, to authentically support team members' well-being. This builds trust over time. Eventually, team members will overcome their tendency to withhold information about problematic aspects of their lived experience as part of the museum. They will honestly share their pain points, offering up invaluable qualitative data that will help organizational leaders do better. Then, and only then, can a collaborative partnership and—in turn—a culture of care, emerge.

## Being Human

While museums are businesses, they do not exist without the people—team members, trustees, volunteers, visitors, partners, donors, etc., who comprise them. Museums with cultures of care strive to create conditions where these people can be as human as possible within the context of their organizations. This means that, rather than telling people what they can and cannot do, they find ways to afford them agency in making certain decisions for themselves.

Our "Holidays for All" and "Community-Centered Leave" policies are excellent examples of this. Rather than being told what holidays they must celebrate and take off, team members are able to tell us what holidays are important to them and then honor those days in whatever way they wish. Similarly, rather than dictating an organizational vision for what constitutes community, team members are able to determine what community means to them, along with how to best support it. No questions asked. While this might look like a community service project for one team member, it might be a yoga retreat, a family camping adventure, or even a trip to Disneyland for another.

### *Beta-Testing and Iteration*

Team member input is not only baked into our process of identifying pain points and developing solutions, but also into our implementation process. Specifically, every time we adopt a new policy or practice designed to help cultivate a culture of care at the Museum of Us, we explicitly announce it as something we are beta-testing for a specific period of time. Then, as lessons are learned during the implementation period, changes are made to the policy or practice, as appropriate. In other words, we always welcome our team members' input into our efforts to continually improve. If a new policy or practice just isn't working, we simply adjust or end that policy or practice, depending on what makes the most sense at the time. Then, we build on that learning as we continue to iterate in ways that better serve our team members' needs.

## Taking the All-Important Pause

Like a garden in constant need of cultivation, organizational cultures of care need regular tending, too. It's so easy to get caught up in day-to-day pressures that we often forget the importance of slowing down. Pausing to evaluate the impact of any given decision from team members' perspective, however, is critical. While bringing the lived experience of others into the mix may take time on the front end, it will pay off many times over in the long run. Moreover, it's only when we stop long enough to honestly reflect on if (and, if so, how) we are struggling that we can identify what levers we need to pull and in what direction. Bringing our team members into the pain point identification and solution development process is not only the right thing to do, but it also makes good business sense.

## Notes

1 Alarmingly, as many as half are considering leaving within the next three years alone. See, Rachael Cristine Woody, "Museum TrendsWatch 2023: The Future Workplace," *Lucidea*, May 31, 2023, https://lucidea.com/blog/museum-trendswatch-2023-the-future-workplace/; and "TrendsWatch 2025," American Alliance of Museums, 2025, https://www.aam-us.org/programs/center-for-the-future-of-museums/trendswatch/.

**2** https://www.instagram.com/changethemuseum/.

**3** "Museum Workers Relief Fund: A Museum Workers Speak Initiative," The Incluseum, May 16, 2020, https://incluseum.com/2020/05/16/museum-workers-relief-fund-a-museum-workers-speak-initiative/.

**4** Tom Seymour, "State of the Unions: Why US Museum Workers are Mobilising Against Their Employers," *The Art Newspaper*, February 2, 2022, https://www.theartnewspaper.com/2022/02/02/state-of-the-unions-a-new-renaissance-at-us-museums.

**5** *See, e.g.* "TrendsWatch 2025," American Alliance of Museums, 2025, https://www.aam-us.org/programs/center-for-the-future-of-museums/trendswatch/.

**6** P. M. Atkins, B. S. Marshall, and R. G. Javalgi, "Happy Employees Lead to Loyal Patients. Survey of Nurses and Patients Shows a Strong Link between Employee Satisfaction and Patient Loyalty," *Journal of Health Care Mark* 16, no. 4 (Winter 1996): 14–23, https://pubmed.ncbi.nlm.nih.gov/10169075/.

# 20 Centering Care while Measuring Impact

*Monique Davis*

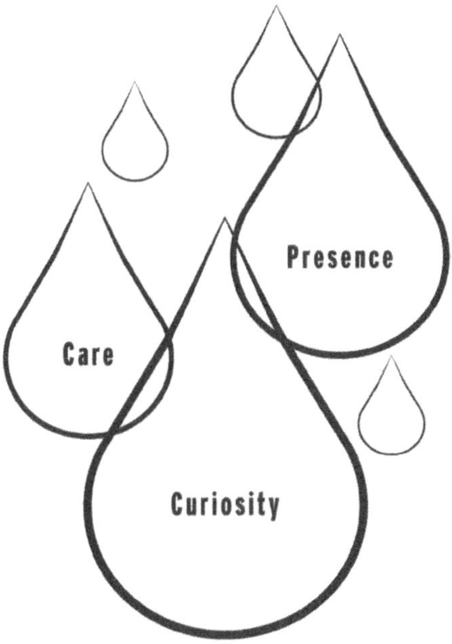


*Care is our greatest currency.*

—*Manolia Charlton*

## Current Political Moment

I am writing this after Donald Trump was elected president. His opponent was Kamala Harris, the current Vice President (at this writing), former senator, and district attorney of California. Donald Trump's victory has shaken me to my core; he used fear and division to tap into the worst part of us. While some may want to connect this victory to economic issues, something deeper and more concerning is at play. We have lost a belief in shared sacrifice for the common good. The First World War and the Second World War unified America, and the concept of democracy was worth defending. I also fully recognize that the Great American Experiment did not view Black and Brown people as equal participants (I am an African American woman whose family has suffered under the structures of racism and oppression). However, faulty execution does not detract from the values that support our democracy: Liberty and Justice for All. I mourn the loss of this shared understanding of the ability to disagree with civility. I also recognize that I need to create space and be curious about people with different perspectives. I may disagree with why a person voted for Trump, but I can commit to employing empathy and be curious about their why. To live with integrity, I must practice what I preach and commit to moving toward people I disagree with instead of away from.

In this chapter, you will discover practical tips on centering care as you develop methods to measure impact. More importantly, you will find inspiration to reignite your curiosity and act on what you discover, enhancing your community engagement strategies. Our institution experimented with two practices: *Front Porch Conversations* and *The Liz Lerman Critical Response Process*. Our experience with both will be shared in this chapter.

Before I delve into the methods, I want to share some of my background as my approach to this issue is informed by my experiences as a service provider (disaster relief) and advocate (homeless veteran program). Supporting people in their most vulnerable moments showed me the strength of the human spirit despite incredible trauma and hardship. It also highlighted that people know what they need, even during challenging times. That knowledge is priceless and should not be ignored. The people impacted by the issue have the wisdom to solve the issue. The missing ingredient is often resources. That is the lens I bring to audience connection and engagement as the Director of the Center of Art and Public Exchange (CAPE) at the Mississippi Museum of Art.

## Front Porch Conversations

In 2020, the Museum began planning the first exhibit of its kind for us. An exhibit about the Great Migration titled *A Movement in Every Direction: Legacies of The Great Migration*. The Great Migration was the most significant voluntary movement of black folks from the South to escape the terror of the Jim Crow South to create a better life in less oppressive communities. From

1916 to 1970, this movement saw over 6 million people leave the South, with Mississippi experiencing the most significant population loss. The exhibit was an exploration of the cultural legacy exported throughout the United States, born from the original sin of slavery and the terror that followed.

Twelve living artists were selected based on artistic merit and their familial connections to Mississippi. Many artists worked in abstraction, and we knew that meaning-making with this type of art can be challenging for many of our visitors. I should also note Jackson's demographics because they are pertinent to understanding our exhibit topic. Jackson, Mississippi, is a city of 200,000, with 82 percent Black, 15 percent White, and less than 3 percent a mix of Asian and American Indian.

Based on visitor feedback from earlier exhibits, we knew providing pathways to understanding abstract artworks was essential. Consequently, we prototyped "Front Porch Conversations," also known as front-end evaluations, to determine what tools our audience needed to engage with abstract work. These conversations were designed to be informal and open, allowing us to gather insights and feedback from the people impacted by the Great Migration. The Front Porch strategy was grounded in the philosophy of the disability activist James Charlton, who popularized the phrase "Nothing about us without us." This philosophy emphasizes the importance of mutual respect, transparency, and reciprocity.

Through these conversations, we discovered that our audience wanted to know about the artist's process, connection to Mississippi, and their sources of inspiration. Our interpretation team used this information to create engagement spaces and visitor guides.

We leveraged our Community Advisory Council (CAC), established in 2018, as credentialed messengers to help us build deeper relationships with the Black community in Jackson. We would not have been able to reach the numbers we did without this group of highly respected leaders. We are deeply grateful they were willing to use their social capital to support this groundbreaking exhibit.

I have developed a three-pronged evaluation system for thinking about community engagement. Conducting an honest assessment of the quality of your existing community relationships is needed. Use the questions below as a starting point.

## *Easy Questions*

1. How have you entered relationships with the community in the past? What worked and what did not work?
2. Has the institution caused harm, and if so, what efforts have been made to repair the harm?
3. Are your team members willing to use personal relationships to support relationship building for the institution?
4. Is your team ready to meet when it is convenient for your community?
5. Is Senior Leadership willing to actively engage with community members (This is important and signals authenticity.)
6. Are you willing to be transparent with how decisions are made?
7. Are you willing to feed people and provide childcare?

## *Harder Question*

What type of community engagement is the institution ready for? Use the three C's framework to guide you: Consultation, Collaboration, and Co-creation. This framework is a helpful tool that will provide a clear assessment roadmap for determining where you are now. You can't chart a path forward without understanding your starting point.

*Scenario: You have created an internal cross-functional team from the Visitor Services to the Development Team to develop an exhibition and are considering including community voices. How will you incorporate these perspectives?*

*Consultation:* The staff goes through the usual curatorial and interpretive practices. The community is invited in after the major decisions are made and the design is complete. The feedback does not influence the final design, and there isn't a demonstrated commitment to use the input in the future (transactional).

*Collaboration:* The staff leaves a component of the exhibition process open to community influence (e.g., labels, visitor guides, and program selection). This part of the decision-making process is visible and can be impacted by community feedback.

**Table 20.1 The Front Porch Assessment**

| | Relationship Qualities | Communication Style |
|---|---|---|
| **Consultation** | Surface level and transactional with room to grow. | Task-oriented, focused on meeting logistics and attendance. |
| **Collaboration** | Emerging mutual respect and reciprocity. | A feedback loop is created with multiple touchpoints beyond meeting logistics. For example, an invitation to an opening or program that aligns with members' interests. |
| **Co-creation** | Deep mutual respect and trust with acknowledged interdependence. | Continuous, frequent, and friendly. |

*Co-creation:* The staff leaves several components of the exhibition process open for influence and input, and community members are engaged early in the process. Attribution is given to the participating community members, and they are included as subject area experts for programs.

The categories also require different amounts of time and varying depths of relationships and trust (Table 20.1).

Empathy is activated by relationships that embody respect and care. Of course, I hope that all museums will be co-creators with their respective communities. And I also understand that each institution has a unique culture that brings challenges and opportunities. In full transparency, our museum is in the collaboration stage for most of our exhibitions.

## Critical Response Process (CRP)

The conversation between the Museum and its audience should be just that, an exchange, a dialogue. As we continued experimenting with measuring impact, we decided to use Critical Response Process (CRP) as a methodology to gather qualitative feedback from visitors about their experiences with programming and encounters with art in our galleries.

The CRP provides a framework for people to share feedback about an artist's creative work in progress and to push the artist's thinking forward. The CRP can be used for almost any kind of creative product: New works or interpretations of existing works in dance theater and other performing disciplines, not to mention writing, visual art, design, planning, public speaking, curriculum development, teaching processes, almost anything including a person makes even dessert.

I took the CRP 6-month intensive to better understand how to apply its principles to our evaluation practice. However, the course is not necessary to experiment with CRP, although I would highly recommend reading the book *Critique is Creative: The Critical Response Process* by Liz Lerman and John Borstel. It provides a detailed explanation of the practice and examples of different application scenarios.

## A Broad Overview of The CRP Steps

*Step 1. Statements of Meaning:* Responders state what was meaningful, evocative, engaging, exciting, or striking in the work they have just witnessed.

*Step 2. Artist as Questioner:* The artist asks questions about the work. In answering, responders stay on topic with the question and may express opinions in direct response to the artist's questions.

*Step 3. Neutral Questions:* Responders ask neutral questions about the work, and the artist responds. Questions are neutral when they do not contain an opinion. This step is one of the most fundamental, challenging, and misunderstood steps in the CRP.

Qualities of a neutral question:

- Invites honest reflection rather than defensiveness,
- Open-ended,
- Something the questioner does not know the answer to.

For example, a non-neutral question: Why do you travel so much on airplanes if you care about the environment? Rephrased neutral question: How does the environmental impact of airplanes influence your travel decisions?

*Step 4. Opinion Time:* Responders state opinions provided the artist consents to hearing them. For example, Responder: I have an opinion about the color palette you chose. Would you like to hear it?

CRP is anchored in observation and inquiry. It supports sharing multiple perspectives and the evolution of everyone's response to a work of art.

## *CRP and How We Get Over: We Grow, We Grow On*

Once a year, The Center for Art and Public Exchange invites artists to engage with communities in Jackson, Mississippi. These residencies explore legacies and issues that resonate both locally and nationally. They use art as a lens to inspire dialogue, empower personal experiences, and connect the city across geographic boundaries. The resulting art installations, performances, and programs will be the products of collaboration between artists, makers, participants, and organizational partners.

In 2023, we exhibited *We Grow On*, an outdoor installation that reminds us we don't get rid of grief; we grow through it. Through the incorporation of nature, we invite audiences into the Mississippi Museum of Art's garden to settle into the difficult and variegated experiences of grief and to find new experiences of softness, healing, and resilience. *We Grow On* used naturally occurring plants, flowers, and other organic materials to create a meditative place to consider grief and how we continue to grow in the wake of those experiences. The exhibition included a moss couch symbolizing a place of rest, respite, and recovery, a stained-glass installation, and signage with meditative quotes and works of art to aid contemplation and remembrance. *We Grow On* was a place to express grief and help in the healing experience through the installation, programming, and events.

This exhibit provided an opportunity for us to determine the impact of the artwork on the audience using CRP and determine if the effect aligned with the goals the artist wanted to achieve (invoking moments of respite and reflection). After visitors attended an artist talk and viewed the work, we took them through the Critical Response Process with the artists. The artists were surprised by the depth of comments and excited to return to the work and refine it. A small sample of "Statements of Meaning" is listed below to show how the audience connected to the work.

> Audience Member 1: "*When I first walked up to the couch, my first reaction was like instant tears. It wasn't sad tears. It felt like it was a release*

*because it felt like the couch was a place for me to just allow my grief to be absorbed. And I think it was because it was wet. You know, there was water there. It was very fresh."*

Audience Member 2: *"Just like the overall like human experience, the exhibit is showing you grow through it. It's just something that it's kind in your back pocket even though it can be uncomfortable, it isn't necessarily something that's like antithetical to your human experience."*

Audience Member 3: *"I think there is a level of emotional genius behind taking furniture that's usually used for interior and a window that's usually attached to and usually observed from the inside and putting it outdoors. And for me it kind of said that."*

## *Logistics*

Sometimes, when considering how to engage people in a productive discussion, I think what I am about to write is common sense. But I will listen to my father's wisdom, who often said: *"Common sense isn't so common,"* and share my helpful tips:

1. Practice the CRP process with a low-stakes activity before you try it with artists. We practice the method by pretending that one facilitator is a baker and asking the audience to provide feedback on a dessert. This warm-up activity injects a sense of fun into the experience and offers the opportunity to understand by doing.
2. Keep the group size below twenty and get a co-facilitator.
3. Read *Critique is Creative*, which is the foundational book for CRP.
4. Record the feedback on a phone or other device so you can focus on moving the conversation. Word can transcribe an audio file. (I just discovered this feature, and it is life-changing!)
5. Provide the artist with the transcription.
6. Pull out the most meaningful statements and send them to your Development Team for grant reporting.

## *Be Here With (A Moniqueism)*

Both methods are people-centered, analog, and take time. They call us to:

*Be—Acknowledge your full humanity.*

*Here—Be fully present.*

*With—Be deeply curious about the people you want to engage.*

## Closing

I have just returned from the Mississippi Hall of Fame induction ceremony, where five notable Mississippians (musicians, novelists, poets, and documentarians) were celebrated. I am renewed in my belief in the power of art to inspire and help us connect. We have dedicated our professional lives to sharing objects and experiences that display our complicated humanity, and fortunately, museums are still trusted to do that work. How we embed empathy, care, and curiosity in our work is THE WORK we have been entrusted with. Bring a sense of play and experimentation to the methods shared in this chapter, and share what you learn.

# 21 Considering Apprenticeship

## An Ancient Model for Relating, Learning, and Transformation

*Andrew Nemr*

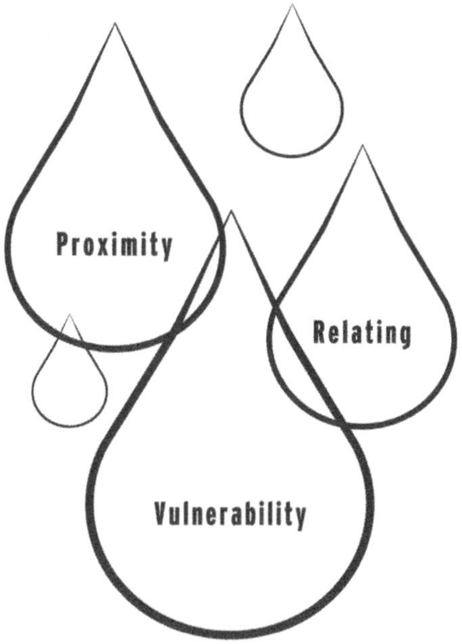


When we speak about empathy-building, or the cultivation of empathy, what we are really talking about is change. We are talking about changing the way we are as people—individuals, small groups, and large organizations. We are talking about changing the way we show up in relation to and interact with one another.

We can think about a specific change as moving from position A to position B, for example. However, there is another way to think about change. That is engaging with the ongoing process of formation that is occurring within us and in our organizations. We are always being formed. At any given moment, things are happening that shape the habits of our thoughts and actions; that cause us to reconsider and adjust our wants and desires; and over time, cause us to become different kinds of people. This is happening at a communal or organizational level, as well, when we are with one another.

The model that might be found implemented most consistently over time for the formation of a person (and by extension, a people) is that of apprenticeship. In my own journey as a performing artist, storyteller, and guide, I have borne witness, experienced, and utilized the apprenticeship model. I would not be the kind of tap dancer I am today without having been apprenticed the way I was, with the teachers I had. In considering empathy-building, it is important to note that the apprenticeship model goes much deeper than skills development because empathy is much more than just a skill. Empathy is a lens through which we may see the world, and ultimately, a character trait. So, the question becomes, "How might we cultivate the character of empathy in ourselves, in those around us, and in our institutions?"

I propose that the apprenticeship model, as a way of seeing interactive relationship for the sake of formation, is a powerful way to do this. Here, we will first explore specific elements of the apprenticeship model—knowledge as interactive relationship, trust and desire, and the role of the teacher, for example. Each element will introduce a key mechanism which is necessary for the apprenticeship model to function well. We will then explore how the apprenticeship may apply in the museum context at three scales—the individual, the team, and the programmatic, addressing the different considerations each scale needs when applying the model. Let us begin.

## Knowledge as Interactive Relationship

The apprenticeship model sits atop the idea that knowledge is interactive relationship. We may find ourselves in contexts in which knowledge has been relegated to the recitation of information. In reality, our knowledge of any given topic is directly related to our interaction with it. Our knowledge of chairs, for example, is directly related to the quantity and quality of interaction we've had with chairs over the course of our lives. We have likely taken this knowledge for granted, however it comes into play when we approach a chair, that by look, touching, or testing, seems untrustworthy for sitting.

We might also consider the learning we did to achieve this knowledge. No matter how many times someone may have told us about solid chairs, rickety chairs, or chairs that seemed suspect, or how many pictures, articles, or books we may have read about them, the more impactful learning has likely been our own interaction with a real-life chair —whether sitting in one, standing on one, or falling because of one. This is interactive relationship.

This works with you and your organization as well. Every time someone interacts with you or your organization, they are gaining knowledge. They are discovering the kind of character you and your organization have. Are you or your organization patient, kind, and gentle, or are you prone to anger, carry contempt, and willing to bulldoze to get what you want?

Knowledge, when thought of this way, is hard to get. It takes significant opportunity for interaction, a variety of opportunities, and time interacting. To gain knowledge of chairs, to go back to our earlier example, one needs to have a physical chair to interact with, would gain more knowledge by interacting with a number of different kinds of chairs, and requires the time to really experiment while interacting with each.

A trusted teacher, a key part of the apprenticeship model, which we will explore in greater detail later, may be helpful here. Teachers impart knowledge and can speed the formation of the student by pointing things out, guiding experimentation, and encouraging specific practices.

Knowledge as interactive relationship undermines the potential damage that rumor, gossip, and even false first impressions can cause. Rumor and gossip are only knowledge of the person doing the spreading of such things. For it is the person doing the spreading that you are interacting with. False first impressions do the same, except with ourselves. To pursue knowledge is to pursue the most intimate context for interaction—the closest possible relationship—and to create the space for such contexts and connections to be made. This, so that we can say that we really know. Naturally, this kind of pursuit can feel messy, vulnerable, and slow. It is also how we come to know one another in a fundamentally human way.

## Trust and Desire in the Learning Exchange

Trust and desire are also key supports of the apprenticeship model. Those pursuing knowledge will have a desire for that knowledge that empowers their pursuit. Their desire energizes them through the resistance that naturally arises when learning new ways. Teachers complement this desire by being trustworthy. Students can entrust their personal formation to a trustworthy teacher. If a teacher is found to be untrustworthy, the student's guard will naturally go up, doubt will enter the room, and the learning exchange will be interrupted.

## Considering the Whole Person

As you likely have sensed by now, the apprenticeship model is inherently human-centered. It considers the "who" in every role as much as the "what." To that end, it is not surprising that the unit of measurement in this model is the whole person. In many models of change, we consider the parts of the person to identify where we want change to occur. We might ask, "Is the change we want to see in our thinking, emotions, physical activity, or social relationships, for example?" There are many different models that come from the worlds of biology, psychology, and spirituality that describe the inner landscape of a person. For our purposes, the specific model is less important than understanding the unit of measurement. We want to be able to say that my friend is an empathetic *person*, for example. We would not want to say that their heart is empathetic, but their mind isn't.

The apprenticeship model addresses this complexity by its flexibility in teaching. Teacher's might use a variety of tools—thought experiments, physical practices, real world training, and mimicry, for example—to address a particular part of the person being taught. This, while always considering the whole person when assessing a student's progress.

Returning to our empathetic friend, the measurement of the character of empathy in them will be clear in their whole person. At fruition, their entire being will be seen to be aligned with the idea and expression of empathy in various situations. We will know that empathy is in them, because we will witness it come out of them—notably, even when they are not consciously thinking about it.

If we were to describe the goal of this kind of change—one at the level of character—it might be something like: "To become the kind of person (or organization) for whom empathy is the natural output of their being."

## The Role of the Teacher

The apprenticeship model gives high honor to the role of teachers. If knowledge is interactive relationship, then it follows that some people may have greater knowledge than others in certain areas of life on account of their interaction with those areas. There will be those among us who have cultivated the character of empathy more than others. Their knowledge of the journey of that cultivation is a key resource. What did they bump into along the way? What was the best way to contend for empathy in the midst of resistance? These are key questions that teachers are able to answer personally, with authority from tactile experience. The difference between a model and a teacher is that a model can only show you the goal, while the teacher can bring you on the way. Anyone who is empathetic can stand as a model of cultivated empathy. The teacher is there for their ability to bring students on the journey toward that end.

The honoring of someone else's knowledge is key in the apprenticeship model, but there is something deeper. Particularly when thinking about change at the level of character—things like empathy, generosity, or gratitude, for example. The character of the teacher is as important as their experience of the journey. Imagine a teacher bringing students on the journey toward greater empathy who cannot seem to express empathy toward their students. This will be addressed in greater detail later. Now it is enough to say that a teacher with knowledge of the journey *and* exhibiting the character trait themselves is necessary for a fruitful apprenticeship.

## How Does the Apprenticeship Model Work?

I began tap dancing as a little 3 ½ year-old in a local dance studio. The classes were engaging and focused on the skill of tap dance. I learned how to execute the moves required. I learned about my teacher's expectations of me. I progressed through the learning challenges and opportunities. I went from group classes to private lessons, eventually testing my skills in public performances and dance competitions. The training was scheduled and formal. There were goals to be met, a curriculum to get through, and everyone went through the same basic process. This was dance school.

Things changed when I found myself under the wings of professional improvizational tap dancers including Gregory Hines, Savion Glover, Mable Lee, and Jimmy Slyde. The teaching here was unscheduled and informal. We visited with each other as much as we practiced together, if not more. My teachers embodied their expectations of me. Instead of goals to be met, there were visions to be shared. Instead of a curriculum to get through, there was a path to discover. Rather than a standardized process, my journey (and that of my contemporaries) was expected to be unique. This was my apprenticeship.

While my personal experience apprenticing as a tap dancer was unique, the model of apprenticeship can be found in many other areas of practice. Consider the trades, traditional arts, and even some areas of practice in STEM fields. While apprenticeships may vary, there are a few attributes that seem to remain the same throughout.

Apprenticeships are usually one-to-one. Everything is personal. What, when, why, how, and even where the student is taught is crafted for the student's learning. The relationship between teacher and student is personal. Teachers often select their students, and students desire a particular teacher. They both come to know one another as people (not just in their role as teacher and student) and this informs the apprenticeship.

Apprenticeships deal with knowledge that is often undocumented or not easily accessible. The teacher has hands-on experience with whatever they are teaching and provides the student with insight they could not learn elsewhere. The method is hands-on as well. Teachers will often model. However, there is a push to provide the student with tactile experience. A teacher might say, "Watch me," and then, "Now, you try."

Apprenticeships lean into the transference of character that informs the expression of the skill. Said another way, the skill the student is learning—be it welding, painting, tap dancing, or the practice of empathy—is assumed to be tied to the character of the person. The teacher's honesty, compassion, tendency toward anger, or other expressions are assumed to affect their craftwork, and by extension, the student's. So much so, in fact, that in fields that use the apprenticeship model, a student's lineage (who they have been taught by), is often evident in the way they execute a particular skill *and* any surrounding activities. These surrounding activities may include learning how to deal with frustration in the work, communication with collaborators or clients, and navigating financial uncertainty (especially for freelancers), for example. All of this comes from watching and being informed by their teacher.

## Applying the Apprenticeship Model to Museums

The power of the apprenticeship model is in its idea that a whole person is learning from their teacher how to be a whole person who naturally executes a particular skill because of the character that is now formed in them. But how can a model that requires a lot of time and relational connection be applied to the museum context?

Here I will offer three ideas, each functioning at a different scale for the sake of cultivating empathy within an organization:

### *At the Individual Scale—Shrink the Time, Loosely Apply the Roles*

We have already seen the individual focus of the apprenticeship model. For a museum, anyone within the reach of the organization may be potential teachers or students. Teachers are the individuals interested in the journey of others and willing to share what knowledge they have. Students are individuals who desire knowledge and are willing to be taught. Moments of connection become opportunities for apprenticing. Instead of implementing a program, each individual seeks to be a possible agent of transformation, willing to teach or be taught, moment by moment.

Whether the connection is between staff and visitor, volunteer and board member, or leadership and vendor, any interaction can be a moment for the cultivation of empathy. The individual seeking the new way shows up curious, open to the possibility of something new, and seeking the opportunity to be part of the new pattern whether in the role of teacher or student. This idea may be difficult to implement. There is significant responsibility placed on the individual. However, this effort can be organic and may dodge organizational resistance. It is a practice of the small things that individuals do—an extra question in a conversation, a pause to acknowledge a colleague's or visitor's experience (be it good or challenging), or a small adjustment in response to a request—that can have a dramatic effect.

There are some individuals in your organization who are likely practicing this already. An acknowledgment or some encouragement, even privately, can do wonders to energize their efforts.

## At the Team Scale—Change the Ratio, Model the Vision

Organizations run on teams—small groups of individuals who have agreed on a common pursuit and shared methods to achieve that pursuit. Teams can be apprenticed in a one-to-many rather than a one-to-one ratio. The team leader—if not official, the person who is naturally looked upon for guidance—can propose small experiments designed to cultivate empathy within the group. Offering the experiment as an opt-in exercise will circumvent possible resistance. Perhaps it is starting team meetings with a personal check-in unrelated to work. Some possible prompts might be:

> *"What is one thing that made you go, 'hmmm'?"*
> *"What is one thing that you'd like to remember from the past week?"*
> *"What is something that you are carrying right now that you'd like to put down?"*

These are not meant to be conversation starters, but rather opportunities for sharing. The small and meaningful acknowledgment of the rest of their lives gives team members the permission to consider the totality of each other's experience while at work. When cultivated within the team, this practice of consideration can spill over into the way team members interact with other teams across the organization, catalyzing a possible cascade.

## On a Programmatic Scale—Museums Are Institutions and Institutions Run on Programs

Programs can work together to facilitate the apprenticeship model. The idea here is fishing. Not every visitor will want to take on the character of the institution. Some visitors just want to visit and leave. However, others may desire the deeper connection. We want to find those people.

Having a series of programs that allow a visitor (or staff member for that matter) to get closer and closer to the core of the museum gives an opportunity to those seeking it. Said another way, a well-designed series of programs can function as a progressive set of invitations into deeper relationship with the museum. The deeper the relationship, the more opportunity for individual apprenticeship.

The pyramid pictured is a tool to help see where current programs slot and what may be designed to invite people into a more intimate and committed relationship with your institution.

Programs in the bottom of the pyramid (Figure 21.1) reach the most people and require the least amount of commitment and interaction. These might include exhibitions or special events. The addition of a question posed to the viewer on an exhibition description or an intentional audience feedback activity following an event may be all that is possible to cultivate empathy here given the scale of these programs.

Programs in the middle of the pyramid reach less people and require greater commitment and interaction. These might be multi-session workshops or multi-day community events. These offer opportunity for the museum to

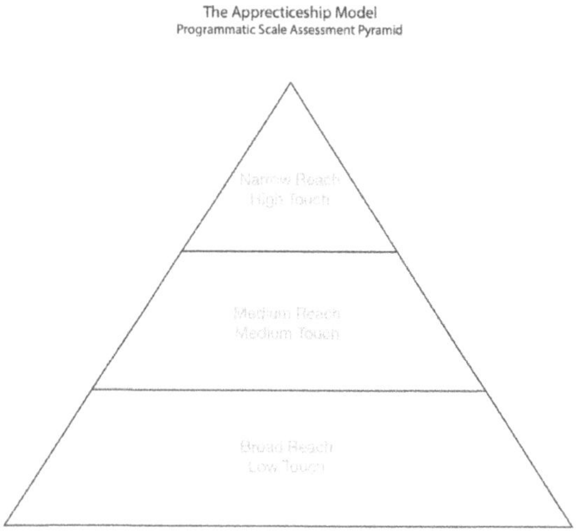


**Figure 21.1** The Apprenticeship Model, Programmatic Scale Assessment Pyramid. Credit: Illustration by Andrew Nemr.

establish deeper relationship with the participants and model empathy in the interactions.

Programs at the top of the pyramid reach the least amount of people and require the greatest commitment and interaction. A classic fellowship or internship might be listed here. These kinds of programs offer opportunity for participants to immerse themselves in the culture of the museum, including the cultivation of empathy. While the choice of people is important at all levels, it is especially so here. Because of the small scale, chosen teachers should be able to model and facilitate the kind of connection with participants that you would want the participants to ultimately embody.

As you consider your pyramid, here are a few questions you might ask:

- What is one thing we can do with this activity that would encourage the cultivation of empathy?
- What is something we are missing in this activity that might encourage the cultivation of empathy?

If a level is empty, you might ask:

- What is something we can try (small scale, low risk), that would fill the gap?

## Continuing the Journey

The apprenticeship model is old. It has stood the test of time. As our current context continues to shift, we might do good to consider a method that has stood the test of time as we seek new ways of relating, learning, and being. The challenge for us will be to apply the apprenticeship model to our current and individual contexts. This will take some imagination, experimentation, and effort. Please be encouraged. The seeds of the Apprenticeship Model can be planted with the smallest experiments, at the individual scale, even in the face of substantial resistance, and still have significant impact. If you feel drawn to this idea, start by starting. The benefits of deeper relationship, greater connection, and yes, empathy, are well worth it.

# 22 A Workplace Emotion Strategy

## Mindsets, Tools, and Practices to Manage Emotional Energy at Workplace

*Kürşat Özenç*

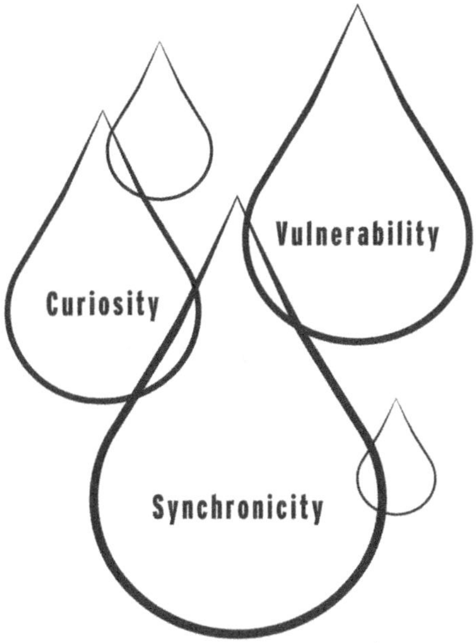

Kelly is back at work a week after she lost her father. The work is business as usual; however, she is not. Nadia is in the middle of an important meeting, but she was awake all night hearing devastating stories from her home country and is now trying hard to focus on the agenda. Matthew and Aaron are teammates working on a substantial project. Matthew is uneasy about how Aaron received all the recognition despite him doing most of the work. Brandon enters the office; the atmosphere is tense due to the layoffs announced earlier. As he makes his way to his desk, he wants to disappear. Wei works remotely for a company headquartered overseas. She struggles to read the emotional responses of her peers during meetings; she feels estranged. These hypothetical yet familiar situations share something central to our lives, but often organizations ignore them at work: emotions and emotional energy.

The tendency to ignore emotions at work is not new; this misconception dates back to the Industrial Revolution. Early industrialists thought work and personal lives were separate spheres, believing emotions should be left behind when entering the work environment.

A lot has changed since then. With the invention of the internet and the information revolution, the nature of work has evolved and become more flexible. Creativity and collaboration, which thrive with high emotional energy, have become differentiators. Companies that have embraced employees' emotional energy have developed paradigm-shifting products and technologies, such as Pixar. However, these companies are still a minority. The invisible core belief of ignoring emotions at work still haunts workplace culture from Tokyo to New York, Istanbul to Cape Town.

In today's fast-paced and interconnected world, emotions are at the forefront of interpersonal and organizational dynamics. They are deeply embedded in our cultural environments, shaping and shaped by our social interactions. However, the complexity of managing emotions—both our own and others'—has become a significant challenge, particularly in multicultural or high-stress settings.

How can we shift the workplace culture to acknowledge emotions? How can we nurture emotional energy to increase creativity, collaboration, and employee well-being? This chapter will explore these questions using a human-centered culture design lens and lay out several mindsets and strategies for creating a healthy, emotional workplace culture. In this chapter, as we investigate emotion strategies for the "workplace," we invite the reader to consider the content of this chapter to not only think of museums as workplaces that can utilize emotion strategies for their organizational well-being, but also gain an understanding of workplace needs in general, think of museums as potential community platforms where museums could become relevant spaces for developing emotional intelligence skills through museums' intentionally designed educational programs and empathy-building experiences.

## Human-Centered Culture Design Lens

Human-centered culture design is an approach that uses design thinking mindsets, tools, and methods to improve workplace culture.[1] It also uses systems thinking, experience design, and organizational behavior concepts. At Stanford d.school, we are testing and advancing this approach by experimenting with culture interventions.[2]

According to this approach, culture is a living system comprised of visible and invisible forces. Visible forces, such as behaviors, artifacts, and spaces, are easier to change. Invisible forces, such as beliefs, values, assumptions, and emotions, are harder to change. The interplay between these two forces defines culture.

Through discovery research, we unveil the forces in a given workplace culture. These give us insights into virtuous and vicious cycles inside an organization. For instance, a virtuous cycle could be between the company's customer-centricity value and a voice of the client ritual at the end of each town hall meeting where employees hear the stories of their customers. Then, we design culture interventions that facilitate the interplay between these visible and invisible forces. For instance, one of the teams discovered a vicious cycle of lack of communication between executives and individual contributors. Student teams designed a culture program that introduces new rituals, communication norms, and policies to flip that vicious cycle into a virtuous cycle.

During our design projects, we find three levers very effective in articulating the as-is state and designing new culture interventions: the visible and invisible forces of culture, drivers, and inhibitors of behavior, and emotional energy in the workplace. This article will focus on the emotional layer and discuss how we frame and leverage emotions to improve culture.

Let's articulate why emotions matter before entering the mindsets, strategies, and tools.

## Key Emotional Concepts

The study of emotions in the workplace has gained significant attention since the 1990s, marking a shift from when emotions were neglected mainly in organizational research. This shift, termed the "Affective Revolution," has led to a wealth of research exploring the role of emotions in various organizational processes.[3] Emotions are biological responses to environmental stimuli. These responses lead to physical and psychological changes influencing an individual's readiness for action.[4] Positive emotions contribute to well-being, while negative emotions signal challenges that people must address.

To better understand these challenges, we craft specific archetypical personas and characterize people's challenges in particular moments. This helps us anchor solutions in a much more concrete way. Similarly, we can return to the characters introduced at the beginning and unpack the key emotional concepts at play with each of them.

Kelly and Nadia are experiencing emotional labor.[5] This concept refers to employees' efforts to manage their emotions according to workplace expectations. It often involves displaying emotions that are not genuinely felt, particularly in service-oriented roles where employees are expected to maintain a positive and friendly demeanor regardless of their feelings.

Matthew and Aaron share similar organizational skills and levels. However, Aaron stands out more due to his soft skills and emotional intelligence.[6] This concept encompasses the ability to understand and manage one's own emotions and the emotions of others. Emotionally intelligent individuals can effectively perceive, use, understand, and manage emotions, contributing to their success in interpersonal interactions and workplace performance.

When Brandon enters a dead-silent office with a tense undercurrent, he experiences the effects of emotional contagion.[7] This phenomenon describes the spread of emotions from one person to another in a workplace setting. Emotional contagion can create a ripple effect, where one individual's emotions influence others' emotional state, impacting team dynamics and the overall workplace atmosphere.

One thread connecting these concepts is the cascading role of emotions: They start from an individual's internal states, open up to interpersonal situations and group dynamics, and finally shape the environment. Ashkanasy developed a model with a system lens that brings them all together (see endnote 4). A multilevel model of emotions in organizations provides a framework for understanding the interplay of emotions across various levels. This model highlights the influence of emotions on individual employees, interpersonal relationships, group dynamics, and the overall organizational climate.

For example, personality and emotional intelligence shape emotional experiences and responses at the individual level. Interpersonal communication, perception of emotions, and emotional labor influence interactions between employees and their colleagues, managers, and customers. At the group level, leadership styles and team dynamics shape the emotional climate within a group, affecting team performance and satisfaction (see endnote 4). At the organizational level, emotional culture and climate factors impact the organization's overall well-being and performance.

Another thread connecting all the layers is the power of workplace interactions and outside events to influence emotions. These workplace events trigger emotional reactions in employees, which subsequently influence their attitudes and behaviors. The Affective Events Theory (AET) articulates this.[8] For instance, positive events like receiving praise can lead to positive emotions and improved job performance. In contrast, adverse events like encountering a demanding customer may trigger negative emotions and decreased productivity (Figure 22.1).

## Introducing A Workplace Emotion Strategy

We've established that emotions significantly impact employee well-being and operate at various organizational levels. And leaders can shape events and practices to cultivate a positive workplace culture. Based on this understanding, we propose a workplace emotion strategy that combines mindsets, tools, and practices to enhance the workplace's emotional culture.

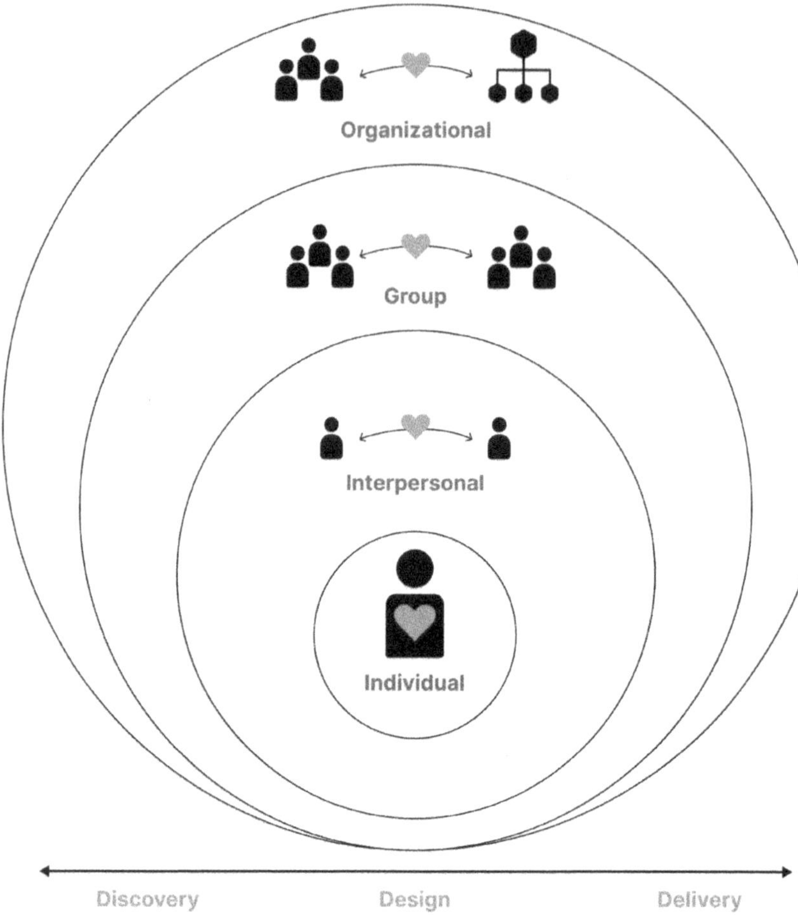


**Figure 22.1** Layers of emotions at work. Credit: Kürşat Özenç, PhD.

We will follow three key phases in designing this emotional culture: Discovery, Design, and Delivery. Our workplace emotion strategy toolkit overlays Neal Ashkanasy's four layers of emotions—individual, interpersonal, group, and organizational—onto these phases, recommending appropriate tools for each stage (see endnotes 1, 4). By integrating Neal Ashkanasy's multilevel model of emotions with these design phases, we ensure that our approach aligns emotional dynamics with structured processes, resulting in tools and interventions corresponding to strategic programming to sustain itself.

In managing workplace emotions effectively, a thoughtful and iterative approach combines discovery, design, and delivery to address individual and organizational needs. The journey begins with discovery—understanding the emotional dynamics at play. Organizations can map out employees' emotional journeys by combining qualitative focus groups with quantitative surveys, uncovering moments that matter most. These tools allow us to see beyond the surface and into the pulse of the workplace, revealing touchpoints where timely support can make a difference. For instance, emotional journey maps become living artifacts, capturing the highs and lows of an employee's experience and offering insight into how to respond with care and intention.

From there, the focus shifts to design. Here, interventions are crafted not as one-off solutions but as intentional programming with multiple touchpoints. Tailored rituals and thoughtfully designed practices meet the emotional needs uncovered during discovery. Mindfulness practices provide space for personal reflection, while structured connection rituals bridge the gap between employees (i.e., remote and on-site colleagues). These are not one-size-fits-all practices; they are anchored in employees' work cycles and designed to meet employees where they are, creating moments of resilience, fairness, and a sense of belonging.

Finally, the delivery phase ensures these practices are sustainable. Continuous feedback loops keep the program fresh, ensuring it evolves with the organization's needs. Pulse surveys and check-ins measure outcomes and signal an ongoing commitment to emotional well-being. The results—whether in improved collaboration, reduced turnover, or simply a sense of shared humanity—reinforce the value of this effort. In the long run, this strategy creates a workplace where emotions are not managed away but embraced as a vital part of how we connect, thrive, and move forward together (Table 22.1).

## An Example of How to Use the Workplace Emotion Strategy

Now that we have introduced the workplace emotion strategy let's see how we can apply it to a specific scenario. Imagine that the employees we introduced at the beginning work in the same company, and you are a people operations leader working with the executives overseeing the organization's culture. Employees like Kelly, Nadia, Matthew, Aaron, Brandon, and Wei highlight the emotional complexities of your workforce. You could approach their challenges using a discovery, design, and delivery model.

**Table 22.1 Emotion Strategy Methods and Practices**

| Phase/Level | *Discovery* | *Design and Deliver* |
|---|---|---|
| **Individual** | • Journey Maps: Map personal emotional experiences to identify patterns and triggers.<br>• Feedback Loops: Collect feedback to identify blind spots.<br>• Emotion Pulse-Checks: Integrate daily pulse checks using digital tools to monitor emotional states. | • Reflection Rituals: Establish journaling or mindfulness practices to deepen emotional understanding.<br>• Emotional Reset Practices: Use rituals like taking short walks or listening to calming music to maintain balance. |
| **Interpersonal** | • Active Listening Practices: Train individuals to understand emotional undertones. | • Empathy-Building Exercises: Role-playing to understand others' emotional perspectives.<br>• One-on-One Feedback Rituals: Normalize emotional feedback using structured frameworks.<br>• Connection Rituals: Informal check-ins to strengthen relationships.<br>• Celebration of Achievements: Acknowledge shared interpersonal successes. |
| **Group** | • Team Emotional Maps: Visualize team-wide emotional highs and lows.<br>• Observation Exercises: Train leaders to observe emotional cues during interactions. | • Conflict Resolution Practices: Co-create rituals for safe emotional expression.<br>• Feedback Circles: Establish structured rituals for constructive feedback.<br>• Inclusive Celebratory Practices: Design events catering to diverse preferences.<br>• Team Retrospectives: Reflect on emotional and project dynamics. |
| **Organizational** | • Cultural Emotional Audits: Assess how emotions are managed across the organization.<br>• Emotional Climate Mapping: Chart emotional climates using surveys and workshops.- Monitoring Emotional Impact: Use analytics to evaluate and adapt interventions. | • Onboarding Rituals: Design emotional transitions for new employees.<br>• Embedded Rituals for Growth: Gratitude practices to sustain alignment.<br>• Organizational Storytelling: Use storytelling to align teams with values and goals. |

## *Discovery: Understanding Emotional Dynamics*

To begin, you follow a mixed-research method to collect both qualitative and quantitative data:

- *Qualitative Data with Focus Groups:* Facilitate focus groups to explore employee experiences deeply, allowing stories like Kelly's grief or Nadia's stress to emerge. These sessions provide a rich context for uncovering pain points, identifying triggers, and capturing insights about how emotions manifest in the workplace. For example, leaders could proactively address Brandon's alienation after layoffs through focus group discussions that reveal underlying tensions and communication gaps.
- *Quantitative Data with Pulse-Check Surveys:* Use pulse-check surveys to gather real-time data on employees' emotional states across the organization. For instance, periodic surveys might highlight how employees like Wei, who work remotely, feel disconnected compared to in-office colleagues. Surveys also help track the emotional climate after significant events like layoffs or reorganizations.
- *Create and Maintain Emotional Journey Maps:* Combine the insights from focus groups and surveys to build *Emotion Journey Maps* that outline key emotional touchpoints for employees. For example, Kelly's emotional highs and lows throughout her return to work can inform where support is most needed. Treat these maps as *living documents*, updated regularly based on pulse-check results and evolving organizational needs. This approach ensures they remain actionable and reflective of the current emotional climate.

## *Design: Shaping Emotional Culture Programming*

Once you gather emotional insights, treat interventions as part of an *independent culture programming initiative*:

- *Design Ritual Practices:* Develop rituals tailored to address the specific emotional needs revealed during discovery. For instance:
  - For individual resilience: Introduce reflection rituals such as journaling or mindfulness sessions for employees like Kelly to process personal emotions constructively.

    - For interpersonal dynamics: Design connection rituals like structured coffee chats to help remote workers like Wei feel more engaged.
    - For teams: Create inclusive, celebratory practices that recognize all contributors equally and address fairness concerns like Matthew's.
- *Engage Managers Through Training and Workshops:* Managers play a pivotal role in shaping the emotional culture. Equip them with the skills to implement rituals and foster emotionally intelligent teams through hands-on workshops. For example:
    - Train managers to use tools like emotional mapping or feedback rituals to identify and resolve team tensions, such as those between Matthew and Aaron.
    - Include role-playing exercises to help managers practice empathy and active listening. This will enable them to support employees like Brandon in navigating emotional strain.

## *Delivery: Rolling Out and Sustaining the Program*

Finally, deliver and sustain the emotional culture programming by embedding continuous improvement mechanisms:

- *Feedback Loops to Keep Programming Fresh*: Regularly collect feedback through structured check-ins, surveys, and retrospectives to refine the program. For example:
    - Conduct quarterly reviews of emotional pulse-check data to identify gaps in existing interventions.
    - Hold retrospectives to understand the emotional impact of rituals and programming at team and organizational levels.
- *Measure and Adapt Emotional Culture Interventions*: Track the success of interventions through employee engagement metrics, qualitative feedback, and outcomes like reduced turnover or improved collaboration. For instance:
    - Use pulse surveys to gauge the effectiveness of storytelling sessions to foster unity post-layoffs.
    - Evaluate how gratitude practices embedded in meetings influence workplace positivity and emotional resilience.

## Conclusion

To make progress in this type of work, you can start small with pilot interventions, gather feedback, and scale what proves most effective. Over time, embedding emotional intelligence and supportive practices into every aspect of work life can transform individual experiences and the overall emotional culture. Future work needs to evaluate the efficacy of these interventions through longitudinal studies.

## Notes

**1** Kursat Ozenc, "Introducing Human-centered Culture Design," *Medium*, 2023, https://medium.com/ritual-design/human-centered-culture-design-building-better-organizations-70403398283d.

**2** Ozenc, "Introducing Ritual Design," *Medium*, 2016, https://medium.com/ritual-design/introducing-ritual-design-meaning-purpose-and-behavior-change-44d26d484edf.

**3** S. G. Barsade, A. P. Brief, and S. E. Spataro, "The Affective Revolution in Organizational Behavior: The Emergence of a Paradigm," in *Organizational Behavior: A Management Challenge*, ed. J Greenberg, (Mahwah, NJ: Lawrence Erlbaum Associates, 2003), 3–52.

**4** Neal M. Ashkanasy and Alana D. Dorris, "Emotions in the Workplace," *Annual Review of Organizational Psychology and Organizational Behavior* 4, no. 1 (2017), 67–90.

**5** A. R. Hochschild, *The Managed Heart: Commercialization of Human Feeling* (Berkeley, CA: University of California Press, 2019).

**6** P. Salovey and J. D. Mayer, *Emotional intelligence. Imagination, Cognition and Personality* 9 (1990): 185–211.

**7** S. G. Barsade, "The Ripple Effect: Emotional Contagion and Its Influence on Group Behavior," *Administrative Science Quarterly* 47 (2002): 644–75.

**8** H. M. Weiss and R. Cropanzano, "Affective Events Theory: A Theoretical Discussion of the Structure, Causes and Consequences of Affective Experiences at Work," in *Research in Organizational Behavior: An Annual Series of Analytical Essays and Critical Reviews*, vol. 18, ed. B. M. Staw and L. L. Cummings (JAI Press, 1996), 1–74.

# Part V
# Positioning Empathy-Building as a Shared Value in Multi-Sector Partnerships

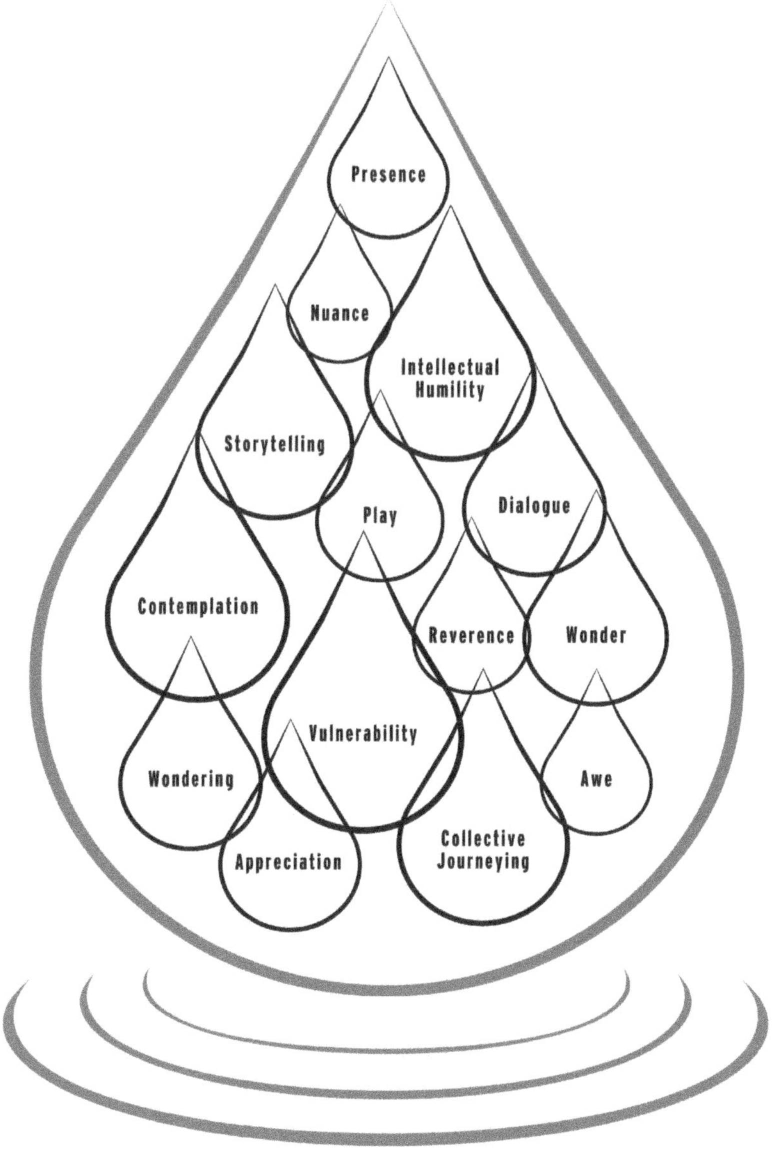

# 23 Beyond the Frame

## Centering Museums in Healthcare Spaces

*Lisa Abia-Smith*

*Elizabeth Lahti*

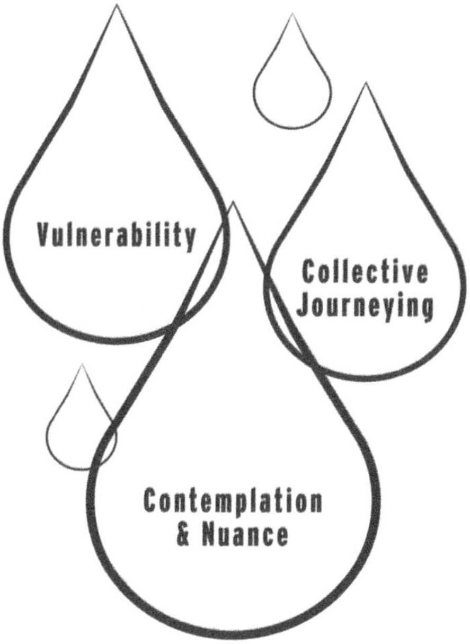


## Intersection of Art, Empathy, and Medical Practice

Integrating art and museum-based training into healthcare education equips professionals with essential tools for empathy, perspective-taking, and human connection. Arts and humanities in health professional education have seen a resurgence in the last decade. According to a National Academies of Science, Education, and Medicine report in 2018, arts and humanities teach an "understanding of different perspectives" and "an awareness of knowledge and emotions throughout the human experience."[1] In 2020, the Association of American Medical Colleges (AAMC) published the Fundamental Role of the Arts and Humanities in Medical Education report, recommending "increased collaboration among scholars of higher education, medical professionals, [and] arts organizations" to develop and teach medical students on their path to becoming physicians.[2] Burnout among physicians is widely recognized in the lay and professional press, however, burnout among medical students is also rising.[3] Arts and humanities embedded in education and healthcare settings are a way to teach critical skills and foster a sense of belonging and well-being.[4] According to the American Alliance of Museums, museums are "increasingly recognizing their role as agents of social change and community well-being. By collaborating with healthcare providers and embedding programs in nontraditional spaces, museums can serve as places of healing, reflection, and connection."[5]

The collaboration between the University of Oregon Jordan Schnitzer Museum of Art (JSMA) and Oregon Health and Science University (OHSU), separated by 100 miles, represents a groundbreaking partnership at the intersection of art, healthcare, and education. This collaboration highlights how museum education can move beyond gallery walls into a healthcare environment, meeting the goals of both institutions. The initial collaboration was to co-create a pilot curriculum emphasizing diverse artistic voices to address bias awareness and empathy among OHSU's clinical medical students. The curriculum is now in its fifth year and part of required coursework. The museum-health center collaboration built on its success and expanded to include optional art-based programming for OHSU faculty, staff, and trainees, with extensions to other institutions like Samaritan Health Services in Corvallis, Oregon, and New York University Grossman School of Medicine in New York City. In this chapter, we describe three programs, with workshop outlines and suggested materials specific to each experience:

- Workshop I—*Whole Personhood Exploration*. Theme: Pain.
- Workshop II—*Exploring Self: A Mixed-Media Creative Workshop*. Theme: Growth.
- Workshop III—*Hospital Art Walk*.

# Workshop I—Whole Personhood Exploration (Theme: Pain)

## *Workshop I—Background*

The *Whole Personhood* in Medical Education Curriculum was developed as a pilot program integrating arts and humanities, through close looking, close reading, and creative practice, into required medical school courses to foster empathy, perspective-taking, and bias awareness. Designed as an intervention study, the curriculum aligned with national competency goals set by the accrediting bodies for undergraduate medical education, AAMC and the Liaison Committee on Medical Education. The *Whole Personhood* curriculum offers medical students a unique opportunity to engage deeply with art and literature created by BIPOC, LGBTQ+, and artists living with a disability. Each session included *Visual Thinking Strategies* (VTS), close reading, and creative practice, using art as a lens to explore the topics of cancer, infection, cognitive impairment, and pain. Much like a museum exhibition theme, the course topics are designed to explore an idea or concept; in this case, the experience of a specific illness or symptom. Engaging with artwork and literature created by minoritized community members, students explored professional identity, patient experience, systemic inequities, cultural humility, and consideration of other perspectives.

Facilitators utilized VTS when examining art by Kerry James Marshall, Wendy Red Star, Belkis Ayon, Rick Bartow, and Hung Liu. VTS is an inquiry-based teaching method developed in the 1980s by cognitive psychologist Abigail Housen and museum educator Philip Yenawine.[6] Originally designed to help viewers engage with art more deeply, VTS has since evolved into a widely used teaching format in museums, classrooms, and health education settings. Grounded in Housen's research on aesthetic development, VTS fosters critical thinking, observation, and communication skills through guided discussions about art. By asking open-ended questions such as *"What's going on in this work of art?", "What do you see that makes you say that?", "What more can we find?",* and paraphrasing participants' answers, facilitators encourage participants to carefully observe, articulate their interpretations with evidence, and actively listen to others' perspectives.[7] VTS has extended beyond the museum field, finding applications in primary, secondary, and higher education where it supports language development, critical thinking, and social-emotional learning. VTS has also expanded into health education and clinical care where it has been shown to enhance medical personnel physical diagnosis and communication skills by training them to embrace ambiguity and remain open to multiple points of view. VTS' approach creates a nonhierarchical and inclusive environment where there are no "right" or "wrong" answers, empowering participants to share their voices and fostering empathy as they consider perspectives different from their own. Refer to (Table 23.1) for tips on how to lead a VTS discussion.

The *Whole Personhood* curriculum also utilized a Narrative Medicine based close reading technique examining poetry and prose from authors Audre Lorde, Victoria Chang, Jericho Brown, and Joy Harjo. Narrative Medicine, first described by Dr. Rita Charon, is any medicine practiced with narrative competence, "the ability to listen, absorb, metabolize, and be moved to action by the stories of illness."[8] One way to develop narrative competence is by closely reading texts in a small group. Through reading and discussion, practitioners learn to *think with* stories to bridge the gap between a patient's experience with illness and a clinician's experience with disease.[9]

After close looking at artwork and close reading of a text, students had dedicated time to write, draw, sketch, compose, or create in their own unique way. Magsamen and Ross write, "Creativity is the ability to imagine and come up with original ideas and solutions. It's a willingness to leave what is known, what exists, and open up to what is possible."[10] Medical students rarely have an opportunity within the formal curriculum to experiment, play, and create. Yet, responding to prompts like: "*Write about the color of pain*, or *You can't tell by looking*," one student composed music about red blood cells and their mother's chronic illness, and another wrote about finally unlocking a key feature of their patient's life. Delving into their imaginations allowed students to reconsider the experience of illness from multiple perspectives and think about the doctors they hoped to become.[11]

Our research showed that participants in the *Whole Personhood* curriculum reported greater openness to diverse viewpoints and enhanced ability to consider multiple perspectives in patient care.[12] Participants' empathy toward each other increased, and they recognized the potential for deeper connections to self, peers, and patients. The *Whole Personhood* curriculum offers a replicable framework for museums and healthcare institutions to design workshops centered on human connection and empathy-building. By collaborating with interdisciplinary teams, including museum educators,

**Table 23.1 Visual Thinking Strategy Technique and Tips**

| Tip | Description |
|---|---|
| Open | Always lead a VTS discussion with three questions<br>• What is going on in this painting?<br>• What do you see that makes you say that?<br>• What else can we find? |
| Echo back | When a participant responds, paraphrase and echo back what they say.<br>Fatima says, "It looks like they are sharing a meal, but that central figure looks kinda lonely."<br>Facilitator echoes back, "Fatima sees people sharing a meal but notices one figure looking lonely."<br>Michael says, "I see a shadowy figure in the back, walking away like he doesn't belong."<br>Facilitator echoes back, "Michael notices the darker shaded figure in the back who is walking away." |
| Solicit evidence | Ask for evidence that supports what a participant sees.<br>Facilitator asks, "Fatima, what specifically in the painting makes you say they are sharing a meal, and what about the figure makes you think they are lonely?"<br>Fatima says, "Well, there are plates covered with food on a table, and the wide eyes of the middle white figure appear to be looking for connection."<br>Facilitator asks, "Michael, what do you see that makes you say the figure in the back doesn't belong?"<br>Michael says, "Well he's turned to the side and is walking toward the outside of the frame, like he isn't part of the group."<br>While Fatima and Michael give evidence, Facilitator points out the plates on the table, white figure with wide eyes, the dark figure in profile toward the edge of the painting. This helps to clarify, reinforce, and validate what individuals see and describe. |
| Make connections | Provide scaffolding and make connections between what different participants say.<br>Facilitator says, "Fatima noticed that one figure in the group looks lonely. Michael noticed a shadowy figure in the back walking away from the group like he doesn't belong. Both of them see some kind of isolation even when you're in a group setting." |
| Ask content specific questions | • What is the relationship of the figures in the painting?<br>• What emotions does the black-and-white palette evoke?<br>• Do you identify with a figure in the painting?<br>• Is there any evidence of pain in the painting? |

healthcare professionals, and cultural organizations, museums can develop programs that introduce their collections into non-museum spaces. The following workshop outline can be used as is or may serve as a template for adapting the *Whole Personhood* curriculum to meet different institution and community needs.

### *Workshop I—Outline*

The workshop theme for this outline is Pain. Artwork and narrative elements are selected to explore the experience of pain from multiple perspectives. This activity will take ninety minutes and can be done in person or adapted as an online workshop. Images and prompts can be printed or put into a slide presentation. Ideal group size is 8–12 participants per facilitator. Introduce the session by letting participants know what you will do during the workshop: Introductions, Art Observation, Close Reading, Creative Activity, Discussion, and Closing (Table 23.2).

*Suggested Materials*: Pen, pencil, paper, watercolor paints and brushes, collage material, glue, colored pencils, markers, or fabric.

## Workshop II—Exploring Self: A Mixed-Media Creative Workshop (Theme: Growth)

### *Workshop II—Background*

Healthcare professionals, staff, and trainees face substantial challenges, including burnout, emotional stress, and isolation. Recognizing the transformative power of the arts to foster resilience and provide emotional decompression, JSMA and the OHSU Wellness Leadership Team collaborated to develop *Exploring Self* workshops. Unlike a required curriculum aimed at one group of students, these hands-on workshops are open to all employees and trainees at OHSU. The *Exploring Self* workshops integrate art-based approaches to decompress, build connection, and center well-being, addressing the growing need for support among everyone who works within a health center.

Held quarterly during the lunch hour, *Exploring Self* workshops are co-facilitated by museum educators and medical faculty and take place on-site at

## Table 23.2 Workshop I— Whole Personhood in Medical Education

**Introductions**
*10 minutes*

Ask participants to think of three words that describe their state of mind or how they feel right now. Invite them to introduce themselves by saying their name and sharing one or all of their three words.

Once everyone has introduced themselves, reflect as a group on the different words people shared.

Normalize positive and negative words and acknowledge that even though participants are starting the workshop from different places all perspectives are welcome.

**Art Observation**
*15 minutes*

Ask participants to look closely for 1–2 minutes. Remind participants they don't need to be artists or experts to view artwork.

Using VTS technique (see Box 23.1) examine *La Cena* by Belkis Ayón (1991; Museo Nacional de Bellas Artes, Havana, Cuba) and facilitate a discussion. Images may be printed or projected on a screen.

**Close Reading and Discussion**
*15 minutes*

Transition from art observation to close reading. Remind participants they don't need to be experts in poetry to read a poem.

- Read the poem *Once the World Was Perfect* by Joy Harjo, aloud. Ask participants to just listen.
- Ask a participant to read it aloud a second time; this time encourage participants to write down words or phrases that stand out to them.

Facilitate a discussion using the following prompts. The same VTS facilitator tips (Box 23.1) work for close reading.

- What word or phrase stood out to you, and why?
- Describe an emotion this poem evoked?
- What might this poem have to do with the topic of this course, *Pain*?
- Does the poem remind you of a patient or family member you have cared for?
- After hearing other participants' responses, what reflections do you have?

Reflect back what you hear, make connections, highlight differences, and validate responses.

(*Continued*)

**Table 23.2 (Continued)**

| |
|---|
| **Creative Practice**<br>*15 minutes*<br><br>Participants will have 15 minutes to create an original work: a poem, drawing, comic, paragraph, list, painting, collage, or combination of writing and art. What they create may depend on access to supplies. They may be inspired by the previous artwork, poem, and discussion, or their creation may stem from something else entirely. The only requirement is to spend 15 minutes creating *something*. Creative Prompts:<br><br>• The color of pain. . .<br>• First impressions. . .<br>• You can't tell by looking. . .<br>• Two worlds. . . or climbing into the next world<br>• *La Cena* by Belkis Ayón |
| **Discussion**<br>*15 minutes*<br><br>Invite participants to share what they created during the previous 15 minutes. If they are reluctant or hesitant to share, ask what the experience of creating was like for them. Remind them that sharing is not required.<br><br>Discussion Prompts:<br><br>• Tell us about what you created.<br>• Describe your experience or process of creating something unique.<br>• What was the spark that got you started?<br>• What is your favorite part of your creation? |
| **Closing Activity**<br>*10 minutes*<br><br>Close with the same opening activity of sharing three words that describe participants' state of mind or how they feel right now. Reflect as a group on how the words are the same or different as when you started.<br><br>Ask participants to consider the questions:<br><br>• What will you take away from our time together?<br>• Is there anything else you'd like to add to the conversation before we close?<br><br>Express gratitude for everyone's participation and dismiss. |

the medical school and a tertiary care academic medical center. Each creative workshop invites participants to explore their creativity while reflecting on their sense of self.

In evaluations immediately following *Exploring Self* workshops, participants report decreased stress levels and more connection to their professional community. Participants describe these sessions as a welcome reprieve from high-pressure and sometimes siloed environments, and a way to cultivate meaningful connections with colleagues. One participant wrote, "It seemed like a healthy way to dive into emotional expression and thought processes at work and allowed me to tap into deeper feelings about my sense of place here at OHSU and the differences I bring with me." Another described being surprised by the experience:

> *I didn't realize just how thought provoking something like this could be. I especially liked it when people shared their work with the class. I felt like it was a window into people. . . even though we all came from different departments. . . and different life experiences. In some ways our thoughts were beaded on the same string, but each was so personal and unique.*

This experiential and reflective approach encourages participants to explore their identities and fosters an appreciation for the diversity of "selves" within healthcare environments. The workshops align with the healthcare center's goal of fostering belonging, and support the museum's mission to promote well-being, connection, and creative engagement within a broader community.

## *Workshop II—Outline*

The workshop theme is Growth using the metaphor of a tree as a self-portrait. Artwork is selected to explore the components of a tree as a metaphor for self. This workshop will take 60 minutes and is best held in person due to the need for art supplies. It can be adapted to online if participants can gather their own supplies or the museum can send art kits ahead of time. We have led both ways. Ideal group size is 8–12 participants per facilitator.

Begin with a warm welcome and introduce the session by outlining what you will do in the hour: Introductions, Close Looking of two works of art, Hands-on Creative Activity, Discussion, and Closing Activity. Remind participants of the theme of the workshop: *Growth*. Emphasize the process of creation rather than the final product (Table 23.3).

# Workshop III—Hospital Art Walk

## *Workshop III—Background*

Art Walks at OHSU bring together staff from diverse roles, including, School of Nursing, School of Medicine, Library, Clinical and Translational Research, Clinical Care, Facilities, and Campus Planning. Many participants have never met, despite working for the same institution.

Using our VTS framework, which integrates Visual Thinking Strategies (VTS), participants closely examine artworks they may have overlooked, encouraging perspective-taking, bias recognition, and shared understanding.

Following discussions, participants engage in creative activities, such as writing, sketching, or sculpting. They might reimagine a portion of an artwork, write reflective responses, or create original pieces. There is no wrong way to participate, fostering an open and inclusive atmosphere.

Evaluations revealed that 95 percent of participants felt more connected to the OHSU community after the workshop. One participant noted, "It was so nice to see people from other departments, divisions, roles within OHSU! We rarely get to mingle." Another emphasized the "peacefulness of it" and the joy of "being present with curiosity." Additionally, 95 percent of respondents reported reduced stress, highlighting the workshop's role in promoting collaboration, reflection, and emotional well-being.

## *Workshop III—Outline*

The *Hospital Art Walk* is a 60-minute program. Ideal group size is 8–10 participants per facilitator. We recommend leading this experience with one Museum-based faculty and one Hospital-based faculty. Introduce the session by outlining what you will do during the hour: Introductions, Opening Activity, Close Looking of two works of art, Creative Activity, and Closing Activity. If there are more than ten participants, you will divide into smaller groups after the opening activity and remain in the smaller groups for the rest of the workshop (Table 23.4).

*Suggested Materials*: Small unlined notebook, pencil, optional air-drying clay like Model Magic by Crayola.

## Table 23.3 Workshop II— Exploring Self Mixed-Media Creative

| |
|---|
| **Icebreaker Activity**<br>*10 minutes*<br><br>Ask participants to share three words describing their current state of mind or what led them to come to the workshop today. Reflect as a group on the different words people share. Acknowledge the diverse perspectives participants bring to the session. |
| **Art Observation**<br>*10 minutes*<br><br>Using VTS technique (see Box 23.1) examine two works of art and facilitate a discussion. Images may be projected on a screen. View the paintings:<br><br>• *Gateway to September* by Charles Burchfield<br>• *Tree Series* by William Kentridge<br><br>Ask participants to look closely for 1–2 minutes. Remind participants they don't need to be artists or experts to view artwork.<br><br>Encourage participants to connect the artwork to their own identities and experiences of resilience. Spend only five minutes per painting, since the focus of this workshop is creating their own self-portraits. |
| **Hands on Creative Activity**<br>*30 minutes*<br><br>Following the discussion, participants engage in a hands-on creative activity—including drawing, painting, sketching, collage, or mixed media—emphasizing the process of creation rather than the final product. Our theme of *Growth* guides this self-portrait art-making process. Encourage participants to move around the room, gather supplies they need, and be open to the creative process. Remind participants they don't have to be trained artists to create art. Some participants may need prompts to get started. Offer the following prompts as sparks or ideas but remind participants they can follow their creative process wherever it takes them:<br><br>• Consider how the elements of a tree relate to your own self-portrait: *roots, trunk, bark, branches, leaves, fruit, flowers.*<br>• Show where texture, smell, sound, or sight show up.<br>• Explore growth or transformation as a part of your tree.<br>• Think about what words or symbols are part of your self-portrait. |

(*Continued*)

## Table 23.3 (Continued)

| |
|---|
| **Discussion and Closing Activity**<br>*10 minutes*<br><br>Invite participants to reflect, share, and discuss what they created. Ask questions to help discuss their creations.<br>• What images stand out to you in the artwork?<br>• What part of the tree did you most connect with?<br>• How does your identity show up in your tree?<br>• What surprised you about your own artwork?<br><br>Before the workshop ends, ask participants to share a one-word response to the question:<br>• What will you take away from this creative activity as you go back to work?"<br><br>Reflect back to the group what you hear, make connections, highlight differences and similarities, and validate responses. Express gratitude for everyone's participation and dismiss. |

## Table 23.4 Workshop III—Hospital Art Walk Workshop Outline

| |
|---|
| **Introductions**<br>*10 minutes*<br><br>Ask participants to write several words or sentences that describe why they chose to attend the ***Art Walk*** today. Invite participants to introduce themselves to the group by sharing:<br><br>• Name,<br>• Where within the healthcare system they walked from today,<br>• Words or sentences they wrote in the opening activity.<br><br>Once everyone has introduced themselves, echo back some of the words or sentences you heard and acknowledge that participants come from diverse locations, roles, and experiences.<br><br>Express gratitude for participants showing up during their busy workdays. |
| **Art Observation #1**<br>*10 minutes*<br><br>View the first work of art utilizing VTS technique (see Box 23.1). Ask participants to look closely for 1–2 minutes. Remind participants they don't need to be artists or experts to have an opinion when they look at art. |
| **Art Observation #2**<br>*10 minutes*<br><br>View the second work of art utilizing VTS technique (see Box 23.1) |

*(Continued)*

**Table 23.4 (Continued)**

| |
|---|
| **Creative Practice**<br>*15 minutes*<br><br>Describe to the group that after looking at two different works of art, they will now have a short time to create something of their own. They can write, sketch, or draw with the pencil and notebook, or sculpt with the clay. Offer prompts to get started, reminding participants to follow their creative processes wherever it takes them:<br><br>• Create an artistic response to the three words you shared at the start of the workshop,<br>• Consider what is missing from one of the artworks we looked at today,<br>• Write or draw the story of a figure or object in one of the paintings. |
| **Closing Activity**<br>*10 minutes*<br><br>Invite participants to share what they created during the previous 15 minutes. If they are reluctant or hesitant to read or show what they created, ask what the experience of creating was like for them. Remind them that sharing is not required.<br><br>Before the *Art Walk* ends, ask participants to share a one-word response to the question:<br>• What will you take away from this creative activity as you go back to work?<br><br>Reflect back to the group what you hear, make connections, highlight differences and similarities, and validate responses. Express gratitude for everyone's participation and dismiss. |

# Conclusion

Partnerships like the one between JSMA and OHSU demonstrate how arts and humanities can nurture a whole person, build resilient communities, and reimagine spaces of care as inclusive and interconnected. Our collaboration began with a pilot program and led to embedded medical school curricula, ongoing workshops, a permanent digital collection of resources in the OHSU library, and dissemination through publications and collaboration with other institutions to implement similar programming in their own unique environments.[13]

This framework aligns with the *Alchemy of Empathy* ingredients:

- Collective Journeying: Fostering shared experiences through art to deepen understanding and connection.
- Contemplation & Nuance: Encouraging reflection on emotions and perspectives.
- Vulnerability: Creating welcome and inclusive spaces for open, honest exploration and growth.

By integrating these elements, museums become instrumental partners for care and well-being. Partnerships like ours amplify the transformative potential of integrating art and science. Adapting this model will enable museums to partner with healthcare organizations, professionals, and students to nurture whole personhood, cultivate empathy, resilience, and human connection.

## Notes

**1** National Academies of Sciences, Engineering, and Medicine, *The Integration of the Humanities and Arts with Sciences, Engineering, and Medicine in Higher Education: Branches from the Same Tree* (National Academies Press, 2018), https://doi.org/10.17226/24988.

**2** L. Howley, E. Gaufberg, and B. King, *The Fundamental Role of the Arts and Humanities in Medical Education* (Association of American Medical Colleges, 2020).

**3** G. Morcos and O. A. Awan, "Burnout in Medical School: A Medical Student's Perspective," *Academy Radiol* 30, no. 6 (June 2023): 1223–5, https://doi.org/10.1016/j.acra.2022.11.023. Epub 2022 Dec 29. PMID: 36586757; PMCID: PMC9799176.

**4** Lisa Abia-Smith, "Cultivating Creativity: The Role of Art and Visual Thinking Strategies to Support Community and Resilience for Healthcare Professionals," *Tutor*, November 20, 2024, https://ojs.unito.it/index.php/tutor/article/view/11316.

**5** American Alliance of Museums, *Museums and Public Health: The Role of Cultural Spaces in Wellbeing* (American Alliance of Museums, 2019).

**6** Abigail Housen and Philip Yenawine, "Visual Thinking Strategies," Visual Thinking Strategies, June 2024, https://vtshome.org.

**7** Rita Charon, "Narrative Medicine: A Model for Empathy, Reflection, Profession, and Trust," *JAMA* 286, no. 15 (2001): 1897–902, https://doi.org/10.1001/jama.286.15.1897.

**8** Shannon Arntfield, "Narrative Medicine in Postgraduate Medical Education: Practices, Principals, Paradoxes," in *Health Humanities in Postgraduate Medical Education: A Handbook to the Heart of Medicine,* ed. A. D. Peterkin and A. Skorzewska (Oxford University Press, 2018), 45, https://doi.org/10.1093/med/9780190849900.001.0001.

**9** Susan Magsamen and Ivy Ross, *Your Brain on Art: How the Arts Transform Us* (Random House, 2023).

**10** Elizabeth Lahti and Natalie Lanocha, "Considering Bias Through the Mirror/Window of Art and Literature," *Survive & Thrive: A Journal for Medical Humanities and Narrative as Medicine* 7, no. 1 (2022): 62–74, https://repository.stcloudstate.edu/cgi/viewcontent.cgi?article=1309&context=survive_thrive.

**11** E. Lahti, N. Lanocha, C. Guzman, P. Pierce, C. Chan, A. Breidenbach, and L. Abia-Smith, "Whole Person in Medical Education: Visual Thinking Strategy, Close Reading, and Creative Practice with a Diversity and Equity Lens," *Social Science in Medicine,* December 17, 2024.

**12** Narrative Medicine Digital Collection, *Oregon Health & Science University and Northwest Narrative Medicine Collaborative*, https://digitalcollections.ohsu.edu/search?cc=Narrative%20Medicine&ln=en&p=&f=&rm=&sf=&so=d&rg=10&c=Narrative%20Medicine&c=&of=hb&fti=1&fti=1; Lahti and Natalie Lanocha, "Considering Bias Through the Mirror/Window of Art and Literature," *Survive & Thrive: A Journal for Medical Humanities and Narrative as Medicine* 7, no. 1 (2022): 62–74, https://repository.stcloudstate.edu/cgi/viewcontent.cgi?article=1309&context=survive_thrive; Lahti et al., "Whole Person in Medical Education."

**13** Elif M. Gökçiğdem, *Designing for Empathy: Perspectives on the Museum Experience* (American Alliance of Museums, 2019), xviii.

# 24 Empathy in the Healing Professions

## Curiosity, Communication, Caring

*Ray Williams*

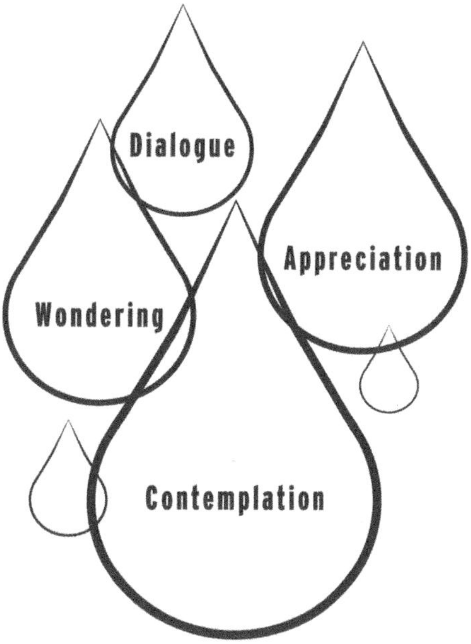


When we find ourselves facing a health crisis, whether our own or a loved one's, we all hope for genuine compassion and caring concern from our doctors and others on the care team. Of course, we rely on their medical expertise and scientific knowledge; we also need their kind, empathic communication. We need a sense that they are with us as we face the challenges ahead.

Is this too much to ask? Many of us have stories in which medical personnel have seemed robotic and uncaring in their delivery of bad news—or worse, became unavailable once the negative test results came back, leaving the uncomfortable conversation to somebody else on the team. Some physicians come across as condescending in their communication—impatient with questions, distracted, or eager to move along.

In the not-too-distant past, many physicians-in-training were taught not to get emotionally involved with patients, for fear they would become overwhelmed and unable to provide scientifically based medical care. While this concern is worth considering, recent research has linked physician burnout with an "erosion of empathy" that has been documented during medical training.[1] There is a cost to compartmentalization, to withdrawing from an authentic human connection with patients: Physicians may lose their sense of purpose and cut themselves off from a very real aspect of healing that their caring presence can offer patients in times of suffering and loss. Recent research by Dr. Helen Riess of Massachusetts General Hospital indicates that patients have better outcomes when they feel an empathic connection to their physicians; and "doctors benefit, too."[2]

Educators at Dell Medical School at The University of Texas at Austin have included three museum visits for all first-year medical students as part of a required course, "Developing Outstanding Clinical Skills (DOCS)." The two-hour workshops at the Blanton Museum of Art are designed to support skills in observation, empathic communication, and self-care/well-being. Each workshop is designed for a group of fifteen students with three faculty mentors. This chapter presents a detailed gallery lesson on "*Empathy and Compassionate Communication*" as a case study in hopes that it will be useful to museum educators preparing for similar partnerships with the health professions.

## Gallery Lesson for Medical Students: Empathy and Compassionate Communication

### *I. Welcome and Framing (15 minutes)*

*What is "empathy," and how does it operate in medical practice?* The introduction to this lesson plan takes the form of a mini lecture to frame the subsequent experiences with works of art. We begin with several quotations about empathy being read aloud by students, a move designed to generate a shared understanding of the meaning of the word "empathy" and how the medical definition is different from popular understandings of the word. Quotation sources include Meryl Streep, "Empathy is the engine that powers all the best in us!" and Barack Obama on our national "empathy deficit," as well as physicians Rachel Naomi Remen on the critical importance of listening and Dr. Helen Riess, whose research as a neurologist and psychologist is synthesized in *The Empathy Effect: 7 Neuroscience-based Keys for Transforming the Way We Live, Love, Work, and Connect Across Differences.*[3]

It is important for medical students and clinicians to understand that the museum experience is rooted in the medical literature and specifically designed to support their development as future physicians, so grounding this lesson in Dr. Riess' book is helpful. The last quote—one which has connections to the previous session on observation and the following one on avoiding burnout—we consider in this framing conversation is from Riess' introduction:

> *We know that when patients are treated with greater empathy and respect, they have a better experience and as a result are more likely to trust their doctor, stick to medical recommendations, and have better health outcomes. Doctors benefit too. Our research showed that increasing empathy in their interactions gave them greater job satisfaction and left them feeling less burned out. They reported that by learning to sit down and notice the whole person before them, and not just the illness or injured body part, they felt more connected to their patients and their profession.*[4]

This assertion that an empathic connection with patients mitigates burnout comes a surprise to some; historically, there has been an emphasis in medical training on compartmentalizing emotional responses and prioritizing "clinical objectivity." This session invites complicated reflection on the potential costs of repressing a human connection to patient suffering, along with concerns about being swept away by the amount of suffering a physician will bear witness to. The objective is not to prescribe a particular stance, but to complicate the thinking and suggest a spectrum of possibilities for empathic connection that may fluctuate depending on evolving circumstances for the clinicians.

Dr. Riess also offers a practical checklist to consider when working to communicate empathically that we introduce here: *E* is for Eye Contact; *M*, Muscles for facial expression; *P* is for posture; *A* is for affect; *T*one of voice; *H*earing the whole person; *Y*our response to the patient. With these elements of communication and these initial wonderings about the role of empathy in medicine, we are ready to look at a handful of carefully selected works of art together.[5]

## II. Interpretive Discussion: Claude Vignon's *David and Goliath*, 1621 (20 minutes)

We always begin by looking. I invite the group to take a portable stool and gather around this seventeenth-century painting featuring an intimate, life-sized view of a youthful, almost androgynous figure loosely holding a sword in one hand while the other cradles a heavily bearded, oversized severed head (see Figure 24.1). The group looks closely, and I ask them to note their first reactions to the imagery:

> *Remember that Dr. Riess suggests that clinicians develop the habit of naming the Affect they experience in the encounter with patients. What* **one word** *might you use to describe the affect or feeling you see in the main figure here? We'll start here on the front row and just go from left to right, hearing each person's reading of the emotion here....*

Typical responses include: Melancholy, exhausted, remorseful, disassociated, pensive . . .

After several minutes of close looking and a wide-ranging consideration of questions of gender, context, history, and meaning, I share the source story for the painting: The Biblical story of David's defeat of the Philistine giant, Goliath.[6] Next, the group considers the visual choices that the artist made to invite our thinking about David's psychological experience of killing an enemy soldier and being hailed as hero of the Israelites, honored by the king himself. It is a moment of transformation, coming of age, reflection—perhaps of moral injury. Is it possible for us to empathize with David's experience, despite our differences? I close the conversation by asserting my view that, although we can never fully understand another person's inner world—or perhaps even our own!—we need to try to lean in with humility, curiosity,

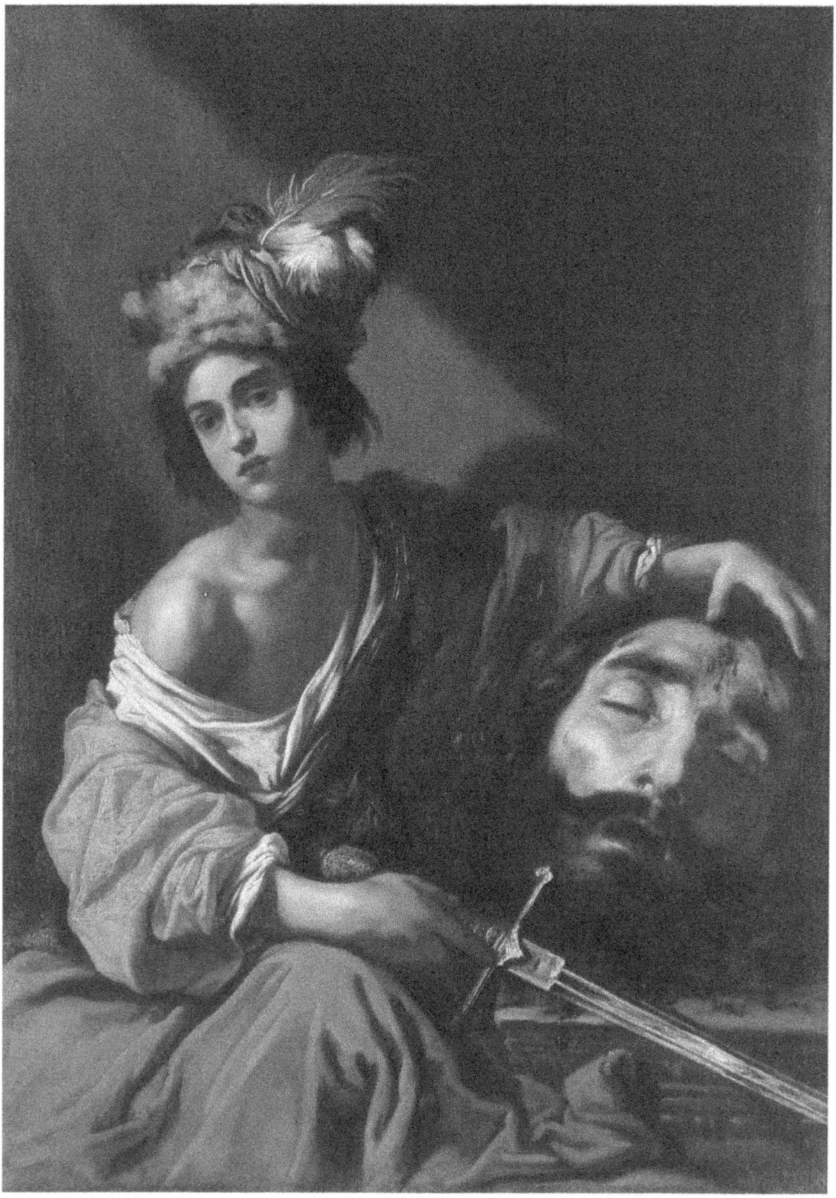

**Figure 24.1** Claude Vignon, *David with the Head of Goliath*, circa 1620–1623. Oil on canvas. Canvas: 52 5/8 x 38 9/16 in. (133.7 x 98 cm) Credit: Blanton Museum of Art, The University of Texas at Austin, The Suida-Manning Collection, 2017.1424.

and a warm concern for others. The next featured artwork offers practice in checking first reactions and inferences by generating strategic questions.

## *III. Interpretive Discussion: Luis Jimenez's Border Crossing, 1987 (20 minutes)*

Let's look closely at this larger-than-life painted fiberglass sculpture by Texas artist Luis Jimenez. Jimenez grew up in the border town of El Paso, so he had direct experience of seeing family groups like this one coming from Mexico. Indeed, an inscription in Spanish on the base dedicates the work to the artist's father, who crossed in 1922. We are confronted with layers of history around the ongoing (heated) issue of undocumented immigration to the United States.

What might we discern about these individuals and their situation? What choices did the artist make to engage our empathy? After a conversation about visual details and what we might infer about this family's experience, I remind the students about the important connection between curiosity and empathy:

> *Take three or four minutes to write a list of questions that come up for you, as you consider this situation. What do you* **wonder** *about?... Now put a star by the most important question, the one you care most about? As we encircle this sculpture intended to evoke an empathic connection to these undocumented people, let's hear one question from each of you. We'll go right around the circle, using the sentence stem "***I wonder...***" before posing the question that might deepen your understanding and thus, your ability to provide the care that is needed.*

We have moved from observations to making inferences to generating questions to test our first thoughts and deepen our empathic understanding of this complex human situation. I pose some closing questions for reflection, indicating that this work of art has put us in touch with a very real concern for future clinicians who will be working in Texas:

> *How might such a family's experience of crossing the border from Mexico without documentation affect their relationship to the health care system in the U.S.? What options might individual physicians have in meeting the needs of this family? Who deserves health care?*

## *IV. Small Group Discussions (30 minutes)*

This first hour has been focused and intense. It is time for a change of pace. As we move into the Modern and Contemporary galleries, I invite the group of twenty to divide into smaller groups of five. I have identified several works of art that feature a human protagonist in a complex situation. Each small group will spend about seven minutes with three of the works that interest them, rotating at my signal. The invitation is for individuals to write down:

- The emotion or affect they see in the individual.
- Something they could imagine the character saying to them.
- A strategic question that might lead to a better understanding of the character's needs or desires.

Secondly, the group compares notes and discusses the "case." The large group reconvenes after twenty minutes, and we look at each of the key works sharing highlights of the discussion.

## V. Clinical Anecdotes and Advice (15 minutes)

At this point, I invite the medical educators/faculty mentors to bring their expertise to the session. Earlier, comments from mentors tend to inhibit student participation—or they may generate awkward tangents to the key discussion points identified in the course goals. Faculty mentors have a wealth of clinical anecdotes to share that might relate to any of the several issues the works of art have raised. This is also a moment to revisit the earlier conversation about the relationship between empathic connection to patients, physician well-being, and clinical judgment. The intention is to maintain a sense of nuance and complexity, not to land on any one "correct" answer.

## VI. Reflective Writing (10 minutes)

Having passed out pencils and notepads, I ask participants to respond in writing to two of the following three prompts. They will not need to share their current thoughts with the group, rather this brief moment is offered to synthesize some of the wide-ranging ideas we have explored about empathy in the session—with an eye to considering practical implications for their future work. (Anonymous student responses to these prompts are provided in the end notes to this chapter.)

- How do I want empathy to manifest in my own work as a physician?
- How might I resist the "erosion of empathy" over time?

- What aspects of the museum experience (skills developed, themes explored, insights) were most relevant to my preparation for the world of medicine?

## *VII. Appreciative Portraits (10 minutes)*

To conclude the workshop, I ask participants to find a partner and situate their stools so that each pair is seated knee-to-knee. (They still have the pencil and note pad from the previous activity.)

> *You are going to make a 'blind contour' drawing based on close look at your partner's face. You will have just four minutes to draw, and I suggest you try to do this in silence, even if that feels a bit awkward. The rules are that once you put your pencil to paper, you* ***do not lift it****—you are making one continuous line that documents your looking. The second rule is that you* ***don't look down*** *at your paper!*

I assure them that these drawings have no chance of portrait-like resemblance, that they only document the visual exploration.

When the four minutes are up, there is a lot of laughter and connection as the drawings are shared.

> *There is one more step to our closing. Now I want you to think about your partner, your fellow student, and exchange some words of sincere appreciation based on what you have noticed about their personality or character. You have just moment to think, then about a minute each to share. And remember, when your partner is expressing appreciation for you, you are just to listen and take it in, without resistance.*

I allow a couple of minutes for each partner to share their appreciative observations, then close with an acknowledgment that this kind of interaction—this looking into another's face and expressing heartfelt appreciation—may feel socially awkward. "But what would happen in our work lives if we made an intentional choice to look for, and voice, positive characteristics and behaviors we notice in our colleagues . . . ?"

Thus concludes the lesson plan for this second workshop on *Empathy and Compassionate Communication*. Readers will note that the closing move (appreciations for colleagues) sets up the final workshop on *Wellbeing and*

*Self-Care*, and that other elements of the lesson resonate with the previous workshop on *Observation*. Each session includes several through-lines that make for an integrated experience despite the gaps of several weeks between museum visits.

A sampling of anonymous student responses to the reflective writing prompts mentioned below provides a glimpse of their thinking about the complicated issues of empathic connection and self-care for clinicians engaging in sometimes exhausting, vital work.

> *I want my patients to feel like I care. I want love to be involved in the healing process. I want to understand my patients' emotions and be equipped to deal with them properly. I want people around me to see as a compassionate physician.*

> *Caring, truly caring, is like drinking in a flood. There is much too much to feel and sometimes I drown in my sense of urgency to . . . to what? Feel less? Do more? I want my empathy to be a constructive flame, a fire that fuels something bigger. I fear that if I cannot contain it, I will simply burn.*

> *In order to prevent erosion of empathy as a future physician, I think that it will be important to allow myself the time to step back and process conversations that I am having and challenges that I face. I tend to turn inward and wall off my emotions when I feel overwhelmed. Doing this while caring for patients is not beneficial. . . . By opening up myself and showing vulnerability, I show my patients that it is okay and safe for them to do so as well.*

> *I will engage more on listening rather than waiting to talk next. I will check in with the patient often to see what they are most concerned with. I will pay attention to the questions they ask and ask explicitly what they want.*

> *I want to be able to connect with patients and understand their circumstances beyond the exam room. Imagine how the patients' socioeconomic elements impact their ability to take care of themselves . . . . I would imagine myself . . . as the patient and think about how I want the doctor to treat me or my family.*

These words give me hope for more healing connections within today's healthcare system, for a more sustainable career for these generous and hardworking young people, and for the potential of art museums to make a difference in our world.

# Notes

1 Mohammadreza Hojat et al., "The Devil Is in the Third Year: A Longitudinal Study of Erosion of Empathy in Medical School," *Academic Medicine* 84, no. 9 (September 2009): 1182–91, https://doi.org/10.1097/acm.0b013e3181b17e55.

2 Helen Riess, Liz Neporent, and Alan Alda, *The Empathy Effect: Seven Neuroscience-Based Keys for Transforming The Way We Live, Love, Work, and Connect across Differences* (Boulder, CO: Sounds True, 2018), 4.

3 "What Women Want Event (1999)," Simply Streep - The Meryl Streep Archives, January 22, 2025, https://www.simplystreep.com/videos/what-women-want-event-1999/; Michael E. Eidenmuller, "Barack Obama Ebenezer Baptist Church Address," American Rhetoric, January 6, 2022, https://www.americanrhetoric.com/speeches/barackobama/barackobamaebenezerbaptist.htm; Rachel N. Remen, "Rachel Naomi Remen – Generous Listening," YouTube, uploaded by @nicabm, July 20, 2012, 3:02, https://www.youtube.com/watch?v=UdhP6sR5uvk; Riess et al., *The Empathy Effect.*

4 Riess et al., *The Empathy Effect*, 4.

5 Riess et al., *The Empathy Effect*, 43–60.

6 1 Samuel 17 (NIV).

# 25 How Play and Making Can Be a Bridge to Practicing Empathy for Kids

*Anne Fullenkamp*

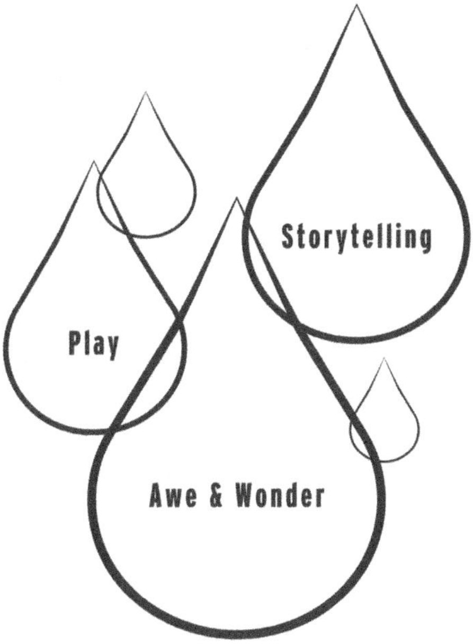


## Set Up

Adults often see teaching children abstract emotional concepts like empathy as a serious task, feeling pressure to help solve current behavioral problems or ensure long-term, prosocial outcomes. While adults should take this responsibility seriously, the methods they employ to do it don't have to be.

Open-ended play and making experiences intentionally focused on creativity and curiosity can be as effective for practicing empathy as more perspective approaches. Children approach the world with a natural sense of wonder and awe. Tapping into this outlook and their penchant for new experiences can make learning a complex social skill like empathy, joyful, playful, even fun.

## Intergenerational Communication

At the Children's Museum of Pittsburgh (CMP), we take this approach to develop exhibits and activities that support practicing empathy, focusing on family engagement, and making sure the grown-ups that bring children to the Museum can take part in these experiences too. This is a practice that we learned from Fred Rogers, a long-time friend of the Museum and role model for how we develop our museum experiences. Fred Rogers was groundbreaking in his approach to discussing important and challenging topics with children in a way that was forthright, yet age-appropriate. He respected children's ability to grasp sophisticated concepts when presented in ways that related to their everyday lives.[1] We keep his philosophy in mind to develop tangible ideas that can form a framework to convey the abstract emotional topic. In the case of empathy, we chose to build our experiences around the qualities of *communication*. Words, voices, and faces are common elements that can be used as tools for developing exhibits and activities that connect people of different ages, abilities, and interests. As design elements, they can be scaled to many formats and adapted for different audiences and contexts. Children and adults, from infants to senior citizens and everyone in between, have some ability to communicate. By concentrating on innate communication skills, we can create activities that support shared experiences and help people strengthen their "empathy muscles".

## Engaging the Body and the Mind

Related to developing tools to practice empathy, technology needs to be considered carefully. While smartphones were designed to facilitate communication by overcoming functional barriers like distance, ability, or culture, these and similar devices are also interfering with children's abilities to develop empathy-building skills and to foster healthy interpersonal relationships. Electronic and digital forms of communication are not as effective in conveying authentic human emotions as traditional and physical forms of communication that engage the mind and body in more natural and intuitive ways.[2] This is especially true for young children learning interpersonal social cues that support emotional intelligence and relationship building with friends and family for the first time.

## Productive Struggle

Similar to how exercise builds physical muscles, we can build our capacity for empathy by engaging in challenging activities that push us beyond our perceived limits. This practice is defined as *productive struggle*, the process of grappling with difficult tasks and persisting through obstacles to achieve mastery.[3] Often used to teach objective subjects like mathematics, this approach can also apply to subjective emotional skills and help develop character traits like perseverance and resilience. At CMP, we are employing this idea as an umbrella that can apply to various museum experiences for all ages and abilities. It addresses the idea of meeting people where they are and recognizing that people learn in diverse ways. For one person, a physical task is easy to master while a cognitive task is harder and vice versa. In the context of an interactive children's museum, the productive struggle focuses on the process and being present in the experience, not as much on the outcome or specific results. From this perspective, activities tend to be more memorable and meaningful because the participant overcame a challenge to learn something new, gaining confidence in their abilities and boosting self-esteem in the pursuit.

## Allowing Room for Mistakes

When that challenge is a shared experience or witnessed by others, people can learn from one another and build a common bond. Museums are appropriate spaces in which to engage in curated productive struggles that support the practice of empathy because the challenges are low-risk and allow room for mistakes. Safe, shared struggles can help people find a common interest, start a conversation, and form a connection. This can lead to deeper conversations about other struggles. This is especially impactful for adult-child relationships because the practice of empathy can become a habit, which can strengthen familial bonds and stay with a child into adulthood. Likewise, as we move into adulthood, there are fewer opportunities to practice empathy, so activities designed for children and families can be used with adults with equally impactful results.

## Audience as Co-Creator

A key strategy we employ when designing experiences to foster empathy is to make the audience a co-creator of their museum experience. By focusing on the design and presentation of the tools and devices, we help visitors step into the curator role and engage in the experience as a producer without having to worry about the outcome in advance. If the experience is successful, they will be pleasantly surprised by the result. Likewise, this approach encourages divergent outcomes, even if they are "failures," because the unexpected experience is more interesting and accessible to a broader range of participants. This approach also leads to more sustainable experiences over time by encouraging repeated use. Remember that people are experts in their own lived experiences and have a lot to contribute, especially when exploring the topic of empathy. By leaving room for them to participate as co-creators, it opens the door for surprises that can make your project better.

## The Scaffolding Approach

While adopting a collaborative mindset is how we approach Designing for Empathy, this requires a strong framework to scaffold experiences in a way that supports the creative integrity of the project. Using a scaffold analogy, an engineered structural system can take many forms and fit site-specific needs. It guarantees the safety of the user but also gives them autonomy and responsibility to assemble it correctly and get the job done. Like the structural counterpart, a strong, but simple framework supports the most important ideas, while also providing flexibility and customization to meet the immediate needs of the participants. The framework might include design elements like material and color palettes, vocabulary words, images or symbols, sensory and physical activities. What the experiences look like and what people will do are the elements you can control; how people respond to the aesthetics and interpret the activities you can not.

# Examples

## *Example I—Release The Negative*

Adults and children sometimes struggle with expressing their emotions, especially the ones like anger, sadness, fear, and others that are considered "negative". In *Release the Negative* (Figure 25.1), we created an activity that offers a tangible device through which people of all ages and abilities can express negative feelings in a way that is fun, social, and productive. To take part, people write or draw something that makes them angry, sad, or afraid on a piece of paper, and then use a crank-operated shredder to dispose of it. The destructive act of shredding the paper provides a cathartic release of negative emotions in a constructive and controlled way. This activity is impactful because it is a clear and powerful way to share a personal thought while also keeping it private. The physical act of turning the crank connects people in a shared challenge and can help build empathy among the

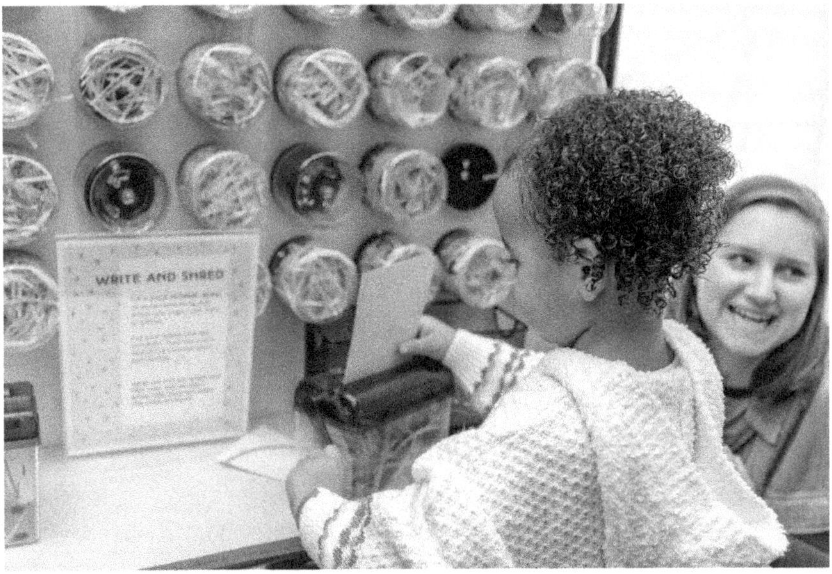


**Figure 25.1** In *Release the Negative* people of all ages and abilities can express negative feelings in a way that is fun, social, and productive. Credit: Children's Museum of Pittsburgh.

participants. Likewise, the activity provides a safe setting where adults can begin important conversations about emotional topics with children and to develop a deeper understanding of what their children are going through.

### *Release the Negative—How To:*

This activity has three steps: writing, shredding, and then disposing of the paper. While the goal is to share difficult emotions, the actual activity focuses on the physical tasks. The activity works for all ages because there is no expected outcome other than shredding the paper, regardless of your ability to articulate your feelings. For small children who are not ready to express complex feelings in words, they can crank the shredder and get a positive result; producing the paper shreds. Likewise, for adults who are reticent of talking about emotional topics with their children, the physical task of shredding is an accessible and safe way to engage. The only prompt directs people to:

> *On a piece of paper, write or draw something that made you angry, sad, hurt, or afraid. Put your paper into the shredder. Turn the crank and shred (release) your bad feeling.*

In this instruction we include simple, but key vocabulary words to frame the conversation. Since the intent is to offer an unfacilitated, user-guided experience, the instructions are meant to be guardrails to make sure our design intent is clear. To this end, we added this question following the instructions:

> *What do you do when you feel mad, sad or hurt?*

This language is meant to provide participants with a cue to start a conversation in the moment. It is intentionally open-ended and invites people to share their own lived experiences. This is also a chance to practice asking open-ended questions that can be repeated with their families and friends at home.

Since *Release the Negative* was designed to provide a way to transform negative feelings into something positive, it is important that next steps for using the shreds are included in the experience. In our exhibit, the shredded paper is stuffed into clear jars and arranged in a decorative wall display; this idea can also be adapted as a make-and-take activity. There are many other creative options, including using the spreads to make artworks, as environmental materials like garden mulch or bird nests, or simply as materials to be recycled. The type of paper used can add to the creative possibilities. Choosing what will happen to the paper after it is shredded is another opportunity to practice empathy by engaging in tangible activities that provide opportunities to start discussions about how our actions impact others. It is also a way to shift control of the experience to the participants by inviting them to bring their own content to the overall experience.

*Tools Needed*: Electric paper shredder, manual paper shredder, or scissors; paper (all kinds); containers to hold shredded paper; pens and/or pencils. This activity is very scalable and flexible. The same materials and tools can be used with various ages and abilities.

## Example II—Empathy Puzzles

Puzzles are effective tools for both independent and collaborative play because they are scalable and adaptable for different ages, abilities, and topics. To facilitate open-ended conversations about empathy, we used an infinity-style puzzle because it has no fixed shape, no starting point, no edges, and no wrong choices. The design consists of two shapes, both with curved lines that form shapes and patterns when assembled (Figure 25.2). In addition, each piece has a word, either a noun or an adjective, and a picture symbol that represents an emotional topic. The vocabulary was selected to help people tell stories about personal experiences and feelings, and practice empathy as they work on the puzzles together. We chose to include symbols as well as words to make the activity as accessible as possible, regardless of reading or language skills; having visual cues also helps people express feelings, even if they do not have the ability to verbalize them. The choice of the infinity puzzle was intentional to encourage adult—child interactions, offering a complex design balanced with a simple assembly method that people of different ages can contribute to at the same time. Adults and children can play together while also assembling different narratives. When adults can play alongside their children rather than watching them play from a distance, they are more likely to engage in meaningful conversations about their feelings and make more memorable connections.

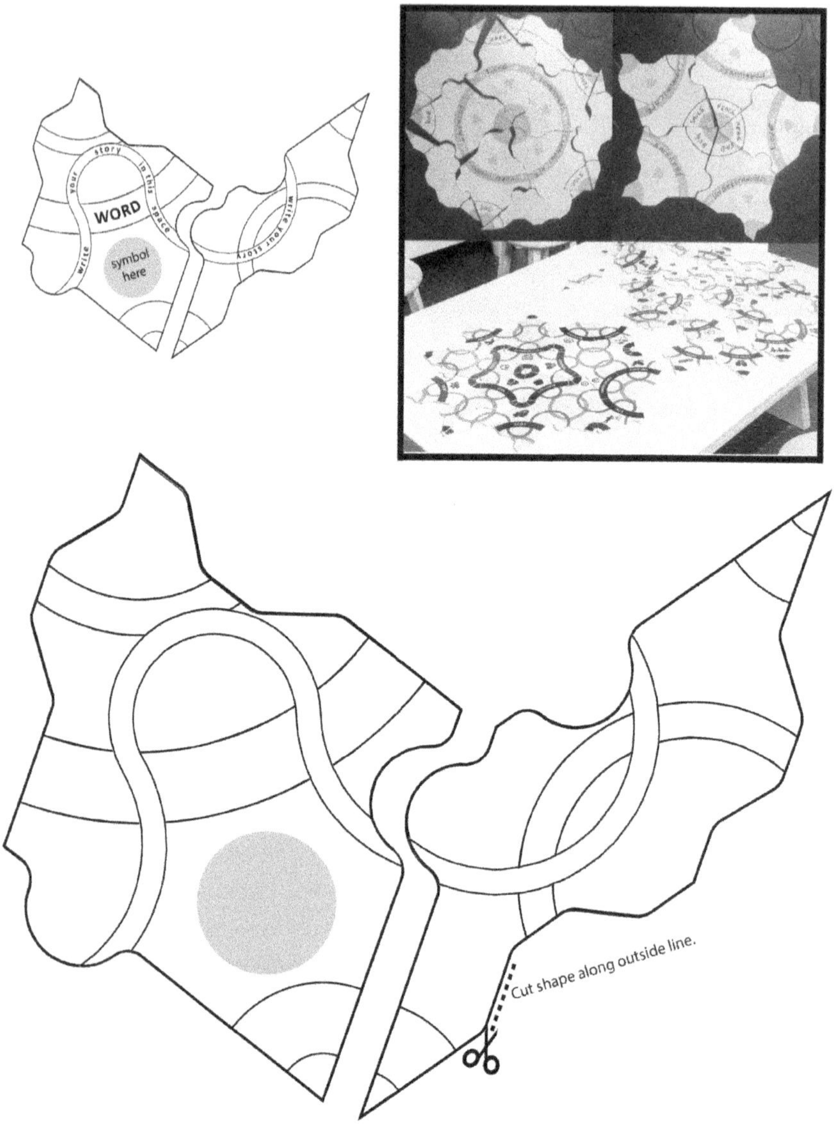


**Figure 25.2** *Empathy Puzzles* are scalable and adaptable for different ages, abilities, and topics. Credit: Children's Museum of Pittsburgh.

## *Empathy Puzzles—How To:*

The puzzle shape can be customized by changing the colors, symbols, and words to fit different contexts and audience. The pieces can be produced on different materials, like wood or plastic, for use repeated use, or printed on paper and cut out as a "make and take" activity. The design template can also be left blank, without words or pictures, and used as a guided workshop activity where participants can choose their own words and images to personalize the stories.

A key feature of the infinity puzzle is the ability to connect separate puzzles to make one collective story. When facilitating this activity, suggesting how one puzzle might connect with someone else's can be a way to help participants make connections with one another.

Other ways to encourage practicing empathy with the puzzle is to provide a larger collection of words and symbols that participants can choose from to customize their puzzle pieces. Do not be discouraged if people are creating patterns or shapes instead of selecting specific words and symbols. Even when assembling the puzzle decoratively, the activity can spark conversations about why story prompts are on the pieces and introduce basic vocabulary that can support deeper conversations later.

*Tools Needed*: Puzzle pieces, paper, scissors; paper (all kinds); containers to hold puzzle pieces and supplies; pens and/or pencils; table and chairs.

## *Tips and Tricks*

When presenting activities to encourage the practicing empathy, there are several key factors to keep in mind:

- *Kids are People Too*: Do not underestimate the ability of children. They are sophisticated, curious, and willing to try new things in ways that adults are not. They do not care about design trappings in the same way adults do and instead are singularly focused on the experience: how it works and what it does. They are tuned into their senses and thirsty for feedback, so an activity must catch their attention quickly and remain interesting after a few tries. In many ways, we are never smarter than we are before we go to school, so recognize their abilities rather than thinking of what they cannot do. Zero in on learning by doing; children are more capable than some give them credit for.
- *Invite Adults to Play Too*: Remember the adults when planning experiences for children. Since kids are very tuned into their emotions, they are capable of modeling behavior for adults when it comes to empathy. Provide seating for bigger bodies to make sure adults

feel comfortable participating. Likewise, recognize that signs can be a place to speak to adults directly, providing prompts for them to engage in conversations about emotions and empathy. We can acknowledge that most children eagerly try new activities if presented in a way that appeals to their sensibilities; adults are no different. Create space for them and they will participate. When adults actively take part in these activities, the benefits of the experiences amplify for not only the children in their care but for themselves as well. They will gain confidence in their abilities to be role models for their children, be better equipped to manage difficult situations when they arise, and benefit personally in their relationships with other adults.

- *Do Not Finish Every Thought*: When designing experiences for empathy, leave room for learning, surprise, and unexpected outcomes. While it is expected that museum exhibits and programs are thoroughly researched, designed, and prepared before they are presented to the public, this does not mean the outcomes need to be guaranteed or prescribed. If people are allowed to find their own way to the intended goal on their own terms, they will be more likely to internalize the intended goals of the exhibit or program.
- *Prototype, Play-test and Experiment*: When developing activities to practice empathy, it is important to test ideas and tools to make sure your work is hitting the mark. Taking the time to understand the exhibit thoroughly can be the key to long-term success. Prototyping is humbling, especially when designing experiences for children. What you observe may push you in a different direction, but that is okay. This is the time to get to know your audience, sit with the idea, and engage directly with the kids before your project is complete and it is too late to make changes. Embracing an iterative design process will produce more authentic experiences that have more impact and meaning. This design practice mirrors the practice of empathy because it acknowledges that you will not always get it right the first time, and there is always more to learn. You will be glad in the end.
- *Accept Failure as Part of the Creative Process*: We love the phrase *you can't fail museum*. Unlike what we experience in other parts of our world, children's museums are places where misfires and mistakes are not only tolerated but celebrated as part of the creative process that gets us to inspiration and innovation. Taking on risks with the

full understanding that results are not guaranteed is a key part of the experimental process. There will be a range of successes and challenges in both the process and the resulting work. Rather than expect every participant to walk away understanding empathy, accept that some won't and hope that they walk away being curious to learn more about how to foster empathy in their lives because they enjoyed the experience you presented.

## Conclusion

Expressing empathy is often triggered by a sad occurrence or tragic event. While being able to empathize with others in times of need may be a desired outcome, learning how to empathize does not need to be so serious. Instead, try reframing the practice of empathy as if mastering any other skill, like playing piano or learning to knit. People typically engage in these types of activities because they enjoy it on some level. Practicing empathy can be similar. Fun and enjoyment can be a part of serious, emotional learning, and if the experience can be enjoyed by adults and children together, it is more likely to be practiced regularly. Even if people are motivated by play to learn new skills, practice is rarely easy. When planning experiences about empathy, leaning into the hard work necessary to gain mastery can open the door for creative ideas that lead to great experiences that people want to try.

While there may be tragic events or heavy topics in your community that are accelerating the need for practicing empathy, you do not need to start the interactions on a heavy note. You only need to create the framework of a safe environment and an opportunity to talk about emotions. Let the adults make the decision about when and how they will talk about these bigger issues with their children. Your activities are the starting point.

> *Your empathy is a real gift to your child. It helps you become more attuned to your child's feelings, more patient and understanding, and better able to give what your child needs – reassurance as well as limits.*
>
> —*Fred Rogers*[4]

# Notes


**1** The Fred Rogers Institute St. Vincent's College, "Fundamentals of Learning And Growing: Inspired by Fred Rogers and Educator Practice," https://www.fredrogersinstitute.org/files/resources/97/sixfundementalsredesign_v5_compressed.pdf. Accessed January 30, 2025..

**2** Alon Schwartz, "Our Kids Are Losing Their Empathy & Technology Has A Lot to Do With It," *Medium*, September 20, 2017, https://medium.com/p/7f18f2654a7f. Accessed January 30, 2025.

**3** Matthew Roberts, "Embracing Productive Struggle the Key to Success for College Students," *University Times* 56, no. 14 (2017), University Center for Teaching and Learning, University of Pittsburgh, https://teaching.pitt.edu/resources/embracing-productive-struggle-the-key-to-success-for-college-students/. Accessed January 30, 2025.

**4** The Fred Rogers Institute, "Empathy," St. Vincent's College, https://www.fredrogersinstitute.org/files/resources/126/empathy.pdf. Accessed January 30, 2025.

# Index

Note: Page numbers in *italics* refer to figures, tables and boxes.

# About the Editor

**Elif M. Gökçiğdem, PhD** is an art historian and an international thought leader in positioning museums as empathy-building incubators. She is a contemplative designer of empathy-building experiences and spaces that enrich the possibility for humans to deeply connect with their innermost selves and unlock the hidden potential within interconnectedness. After coining the term *empathy-building through museums* in 2006, Elif created the Designing for Empathy® Framework, The Annual Designing for Empathy Summit and Workshops, and founded ONE – Organization of Networks for Empathy: www.oneempathynetwork.com. Her books include: *Fostering Empathy Through Museums* (2016), *Designing for Empathy: Perspectives on the Museum Experience* (2019), and *An Empathy-Building Toolkit for Museums* (2026).

# About the Contributors

**Lisa Abia-Smith, MA,** is Director of Education at the Jordan Schnitzer Museum of Art and Senior Instructor II at the University of Oregon. She specializes in arts in healthcare, museum education, and interdisciplinary teaching. Her research and museum programs enhance empathy, observation, and well-being among healthcare professionals and diverse communities.

**Sarah Brenkert** (she/hers) is the Principal Evaluator at the Seattle Aquarium and a faculty member in the Master of Arts in Museology program at the University of Washington. Sarah holds a degree in English from Carleton College and a Master of Science in early childhood and elementary education from Bank Street College of Education.

**Claire Bown** is a museum educator, facilitator, and creator of the Thinking Museum® Approach. She develops professional learning opportunities worldwide and is the author of *The Art Engager: Reimagining Guided Experiences in Museums*.

**Julie A. Carmean** serves as Senior Educator and Manager of National Teacher Programs at the National Gallery of Art. She creates and leads professional development programs for educators nationally and internationally, onsite and online, advocating for the importance of art in learning and society. She and her team recently produced the online course *Teaching Complex Thinking through Art*.

**Brenda Cowan** is a Professor of Graduate Exhibition & Experience Design at the SUNY/Fashion Institute of Technology, where she teaches exhibition development and evaluation, and object, audience and museum studies. She is a Fulbright Specialist in the disciplines of museums, objects, and mental health. Her publications include *Museum Objects, Health and Healing* and *Flourishing in Museums* and she is the co-host of *Matters of Experience*, a podcast about design and museum experiences.

**Monique Davis** is the Director of the Center for Art and Public Exchange (CAPE) and the Chief Equity and Inclusion Officer at the Mississippi Museum of Art (MMA). Monique is dedicated to creating human-centered spaces that inspire meaningful dialogue and foster understanding such as the CAPE, where the transformative power of art is used to spark conversations about race and equity, challenging perspectives while celebrating shared humanity.

**Elizabeth Diament** is a Senior Educator at the National Gallery of Art where she manages and designs tours for school and public groups, overseeing 130 docents who facilitate visitor-centered, conversation-based tours and experiences. She conducts professional development for teachers and recently co-created the online course *Teaching Complex Thinking through Art*.

**Hakan Elbir** is a social entrepreneur with more than fifteen years of experience, and the Founder of transformative ventures like the Istanbul Dialogue Museum, Dialogue Cafe UK and Turkey, and Dialogue Hub in London, fostering inclusion by employing disabled individuals and hosting immersive experiences that bridge social divides.

**Bengü Ergüner-Tekinalp, PhD,** is Professor of Counseling at Drake University, Des Moines, Iowa. Her research interests in contemplative practices, positive psychology, multicultural counseling, and Adlerian and humanistic theories have produced many journal articles and book chapters, along with four books written in her native language, Turkish. She is the Past President of the North American Society of Adlerian Psychology (2022–2024).

**Anne Fullenkamp** is an Associate AIA, LEED AP, and Senior Director of Creative Experiences at the Children's Museum of Pittsburgh. Anne oversees creative experiences and exhibits at the Children's Museum of Pittsburgh. In 2014, she was the lead designer for "XOXO: An Exhibit About Love and Forgiveness," a traveling exhibition designed to further the principles of love and forgiveness.

**Amy Glenn** is the Director of Education and Tours at Glencairn Museum. Her background is in early childhood education and education in informal learning environments.

**Philippa Pham Hughes** is a social sculptor and educator, who creates transformative spaces for cross-cultural dialogue through art. As a Kennedy Center Social Practice Resident and University of Michigan Museum of Art Visiting Artist, she designs creative experiences that strengthen democracy and human connection.

**Donna Jonte** is the Head of Experiential Learning at The Phillips Collection, where she develops and implements programs linking art and wellness.

Named DC Art Educator of the Year in 2019 by the local affiliate of the National Art Education Association, Donna has a master's in teaching from George Mason University.

**Dr. Elizabeth Lahti** is Associate Professor of Medicine and Director of Narrative Medicine at Oregon Health Science University in Portland, Oregon. She co-founded the Northwest Narrative Medicine Collaborative, a nonprofit that brings health professionals, patients, caregivers, artists, and scholars together to explore the experience of illness through narratives of all kinds.

**Jamie Lawyer** is the Deputy Executive Director at The Rubin Museum of Himalayan Art, and an educator with extensive experience in developing strategic, audience-centered experiences. She has held leadership roles in experience design, interpretation, digital strategy, and audience engagement, shaping inclusive, innovative cultural experiences that prioritize visitor connection and staff empowerment.

**Andrew Nemr,** Founder of the Nemr Institute for Spiritual Formation and Creativity. Andrew is an international artist, teacher, and speaker. His work as a tap dancer has spanned the worlds of music, dance, theater, and visual arts, exploring art as a vehicle for individual and communal formation.

**Lidewij Niezink, PhD,** is co-founder of Empathic Intervision, a researcher, author, and an Applied Psychology teacher. Lidewij develops empathy interventions and education and writes and speaks on empathy for scientific, professional, and lay publics.

**Kürşat Özenç, PhD,** is a lecturer of organizational culture at Stanford d.school and a design executive in enterprise software innovation. Kürşat received his PhD from Carnegie Mellon University. His research interests lie at the intersection of design, AI, and organizational behavior, bringing a human-centered lens to shaping the cultures of organizations through cultural practices such as rituals.

**Micah Parzen, PhD, JD,** is a nonprofit leader, anthropologist, and attorney. He has served as CEO of the Museum of Us (formerly the San Diego Museum of Man) since 2010, where he and his team are focused on developing better and better practices in what an anti-racist and decolonial museum can look like.

**Laurie Phillips** is the Co-Founder and Executive Director of Museum Sage®. She is an award-winning artist/designer, life coach, and leadership trainer.

She's led workshops for top museums coast-to-coast, Target Corporation, Medtronic, Adler School of Coaching, New England Museum Association, and the American Alliance of Museums.

**Zorana Ivcevic Pringle, PhD,** is a Senior Research Scientist at the Yale Center for Emotional Intelligence and the author of *The Creativity Choice*. She studies the role of emotions and self-regulation in creativity, as well as how to use the arts (and art-related institutions) to promote emotion and creativity skills.

**Rebekah Rodriguez-Boerwinkle, PhD,** is a researcher at the Yale Center for Emotional Intelligence. Her work examines psychological processes underpinning creative behavior and art engagement, especially in applied and virtual settings. Her work is committed to promoting open science practices and tackling methodological challenges facing research in the arts.

**Edwin Rutsch** is the creator of Empathy Circles and founding director of The Empathy Center. After a BA in Economics and years in the computer industry, he now dedicates himself full-time to developing an international Empathy Movement.

**Aparna Sadananda, PhD,** is a yoga teacher based in Washington, DC. Formerly a cellular neuroscience researcher, she leads empathy-building, art-based meditation programs for The Phillips Collection and the Smithsonian's National Museum of Asian Art. Visit her at https://www.innerstillnesswithaparna.com/

**Leah Smith** is the former Visitor Experience Manager at Glencairn Museum. She has over twenty years of experience in museum education and tours, and continues to work as a guide and educator.

**Mary Hall Surface** is a playwright, theater director, and museum educator. She has presented her art-inspired writing workshops at the National Gallery of Art, Smithsonian American Art Museum, Chautauqua Institution, and at Harvard's Project Zero Classroom. A Helen Hayes award-winning director, her plays have been produced worldwide, including seventeen productions at the Kennedy Center.

**Pablo P. L. Tinio, PhD,** is a Professor and Head of the Creativity and Aesthetics Lab at Montclair State University. His work focuses on the psychology of aesthetics, creativity, and the arts; arts and aesthetics in education; learning and engagement in cultural institutions; and gifted and talented education.

**Katherine Train, PhD,** is co-founder of Empathic Intervision. She develops learning materials, presents training, and facilitates group processes for the application of empathy in organizations. Applications include design thinking, human-centered design and research, peer support and learning, and service design.

**Jim Wharton, PhD** (he/him/his) is the Chief Executive Officer at Connecticut's Beardsley Zoo. Jim spent twelve years at the Seattle Aquarium working with a team that was instrumental in elevating empathy as a conservation and communication strategy among zoos and aquariums.

**Susie Wilkening** is the principal and founder of Wilkening Consulting, an audience research firm focusing on the role of museums in society. She holds an MA in Early American Culture from the University of Delaware and is based in Seattle, WA.

**Ray Williams, MA, EdM,** has worked extensively with students and clinicians in the health professions through his work as director of education at both the Harvard Art Museums and the Blanton Museum of Art in Austin, Texas. He is a co-author of *Activating the Art Museum: Designing Experiences for the Health Professions* (American Alliance of Museums, 2023).

**Rosalma Zubizarreta-Ada, PhD,** is a researcher in the area of facilitating democracy. With a doctorate in Organization Development and Change from Fielding Graduate University, she was a Democracy Visiting Fellow at the Kennedy School's Ash Center for AY 23–24.